ESSENTIAL GUIDE TO

# ORGANIC VEGETABLE GARDENING

Techniques and Know-How for Planning, Planting, and Tending a Home Vegetable Garden Organically

**Quarto.com**

© 2025 Quarto Publishing Group USA Inc.

First Published in 2025 by Cool Springs Press, an imprint of The Quarto Group,
100 Cummings Center, Suite 265-D, Beverly, MA 01915, USA.
T (978) 282-9590 F (978) 283-2742

All rights reserved. No part of this book may be reproduced in any form without written permission of the copyright owners. All images in this book have been reproduced with the knowledge and prior consent of the artists concerned, and no responsibility is accepted by producer, publisher, or printer for any infringement of copyright or otherwise, arising from the contents of this publication. Every effort has been made to ensure that credits accurately comply with the information supplied. We apologize for any inaccuracies that may have occurred and will resolve inaccurate or missing information in a subsequent reprinting of the book.

Cool Springs Press titles are also available at discount for retail, wholesale, promotional, and bulk purchase. For details, contact the Special Sales Manager by email at specialsales@quarto.com or by mail at The Quarto Group, Attn: Special Sales Manager, 100 Cummings Center, Suite 265-D, Beverly, MA 01915, USA.

29  28  27  26  25          1  2  3  4  5

ISBN: 978-0-7603-9281-2

Digital edition published in 2025
eISBN: 978-0-7603-9282-9

Library of Congress Cataloging-in-Publication Data available

Design and Page Layout: Samantha J. Bednarek, samanthabednarek.com
Cover Images: Tracy Walsh Photography (front background), JLY Gardens (front insets),
Niki Jabbour (back top), and Susan Mulvihill (back bottom),
Illustration: Greta Moore on pages 43, 46, 47, 52, 79, 100, 118, and 120

Printed in China

# MEET *the* AMERICAN HORTICULTURAL SOCIETY

**FOUNDED IN 1922,** the nonprofit American Horticultural Society (AHS) is one of the most respected and longstanding member-based national gardening organizations in North America. The Society's membership includes more than 22,000 aspiring, new, and experienced gardeners, plant enthusiasts, and horticultural professionals, as well as numerous regional and national partner organizations. Through its educational programs, awards, and publications, the AHS inspires a culture of gardening and horticultural practices that creates and sustains healthy, beautiful communities and a livable planet. AHS is headquartered at River Farm, a 25-acre site overlooking the Potomac River that is part of George Washington's original farmlands in Alexandria, Virginia. www.ahsgardening.org

Twenty-five-acre River Farm is the home of the American Horticultural Society. It's located on part of George Washington's original farmlands overlooking the Potomac River.

# CONTENTS

**INTRODUCTION**
Your Organic Garden
6

**SECTION 1**
## INSPIRATION

**CHAPTER 1**
History of Vegetable Gardening in America
11

**CHAPTER 2**
Gallery of Gardens
19

**SECTION 2**
## GETTING STARTED

**CHAPTER 3**
Planning with Purpose
29

**CHAPTER 4**
Deciding What to Grow
51

**CHAPTER 5**
Exploring Planting Styles
75

**SECTION 3**
## TECHNIQUES AND MAINTENANCE

**CHAPTER 6**
Soil and Site Prep
95

**CHAPTER 7**
The Act of Planting
131

**CHAPTER 8**
Garden and Plant Care
153

**CHAPTER 9**
Plant Protection
189

**SECTION 4**
## THE FRUITS OF YOUR LABOR

**CHAPTER 10**
Harvesting
217

**CHAPTER 11**
Edible Plant Profiles
232

Join the AHS  266

Acknowledgments  266

Photo Credits  267

Index  268

# INTRODUCTION:
# YOUR *Organic* GARDEN

**GROWING YOUR OWN FOOD** is among the most basic ways to unplug from devices and plug in to all that the natural world has to offer. As you create a plan for your organic vegetable garden—big or small, city or country—you are creating a foundation for this larger connection.

Look outside the closest window at all the living things around you. Even from the tallest high-rise, you can see a tree in the distance, an insect crawling on the window, or a potted plant on a terrace below. Nature is all around us, regardless of how far we may feel from it.

Gardens were once ubiquitous among households, and gardening was a regular daily chore. Rather than checking social media to see how many likes a post has, our great-great grandparents were checking their gardens to see how many carrot seeds had germinated. Social credibility had more to do with the size of your cabbage than the size of your following. Today, we have the option of balancing both an online and in-ground presence.

## NOW'S *the* TIME TO GARDEN

**THE REASONS TO START** an organic vegetable garden are many. You may have your own personal reasons in addition to those generally talked about and accepted, among them:

**Homegrown food tastes better.** Food that's grown under ideal conditions, picked ripe, and consumed soon after harvest has a different flavor than food that's grown in depleted soils, picked on a schedule that's convenient for transportation, and consumed after traveling hundreds or thousands of miles. When growing your own vegetables and herbs, you can choose the varieties whose taste you like best, as opposed to the varieties the grocery store has on offer.

Vegetable gardens come in all shapes and sizes. Finding the right fit for you is essential to success.

**Fresh vegetables are more nutritious.** The nutrients in fresh vegetables degrade over time. Eating kale that came from a garden outside your door this morning means you are getting more nutrition for your calories than eating kale that was harvested a week ago in a place far away.

**Gardening has mental health benefits.** Anecdotally, you may recognize that you're in a better mood and feel better overall after spending some time outdoors. Now this feeling is being backed by science. Lower stress and anxiety levels is one gardening benefit outlined in a study published in the January 2023 issue of the *Lancet Planetary Health*, and additional studies and books—such as *Your Brain on Nature* by Eva Selhub and Alan Logan—share similar findings.

**Gardening has physical health benefits.** The activities associated with gardening—bending, lifting, pulling, etc.—offer the opportunity for moderate exercise. Surveys show gardeners do about 40 more minutes of moderate-to-vigorous exercise per week than nongardeners. Also, time spent in the sunshine aids your body's production of vitamin D.

**Gardeners tend to eat more vegetables.** Eating a diversity of vegetables provides your body with a diversity of nutrients. It stands to reason that if you have easy access to fresh foods, you're more likely to consume fresh foods. Gardeners are more likely to eat vegetables than people who don't grow their own. According to the *Lancet Planetary Health* study, gardeners eat about 7 percent more fiber than nongardeners each day.

**Food security is important in our changing climate.** The more links there are between your food and your plate, the more likely that the chain can be disrupted. If you have vegetables—even a small amount—growing in your backyard, you have some assurance that when floods, extreme drought, or a late freeze affect a whole growing region, you have some buffer from skyrocketing food prices and reduced availability.

**Homegrown food has a lower carbon footprint.** Eating food that's grown closer to home also reduces the food's planetary impact. It's the difference between shipping a bushel of broccoli 1,000 miles in a refrigerated truck and simply harvesting a few heads from outside your door. You're also doing away with all that cardboard, foam, and plastic packaging that comes with shipping, displaying, and selling fresh produce.

**You have more control over inputs.** In a small home garden—and particularly an organic garden— you have less need to use chemical controls and synthetic fertilizers. You're able to monitor and get ahead of any issues before the need for harsh inputs arises.

**Gardening connects us to our past and our future.** Some gardeners look to regional, heirloom, and ancestral seeds as a means of honoring where they've come from and carrying on a lineage of growing vegetables and herbs. Seed saving and sharing ensures we'll have these foods for generations to come.

**Gardens are beautiful.** Food crops and vegetable gardens are attractive and can be a productive enhancement to a landscape. When included in a garden, fruit and nut trees also provide the same benefits as other small trees, such as providing shade, adding a windbreak, and providing habitat for birds, with the added bonus of a fresh and tasty yield.

Studies show that gardeners tend to eat more vegetables and a greater diversity of fresh foods than nongardeners. Plus, homegrown produce is fresher and has a higher nutrient content than produce shipped over a great distance.

# ABOUT *Organic* GARDENING

**THE TENETS OF ORGANIC GARDENING** are the tenets of caring for the Earth and its inhabitants. In talking about gardening and farming, the words *organic* and *conventional* are often used to differentiate between growing food using more sustainable practices that work alongside nature, and growing food using synthetic inputs in a more extractive manner.

Some people will say it's not fair to associate the word *conventional* with this human-first model, because conventionally—in our great-great grandparents' time— everyone grew food using organic methods. Our great-great grandparents didn't have access to chemical nitrogen fertilizers or synthetic pesticides and herbicides. They had to work with nature. Resources were scarce and precious, demanding ingenuity to repurpose and reuse.

In a commercial sense, the word *organic* is regulated by the United States Department of Agriculture (USDA). Nothing can be labeled "organic" unless it meets the National Organic Program (NOP) standards and is inspected and labeled as such. In the context of a backyard garden, *organic* means different things to different people. You may be a by-the-book kind of person, and in this case, you'll want to get to know the details of the USDA NOP standards. (Find them at www.ams.usda.gov/rules-regulations/organic.) In the less technical sense, organic gardening follows ecological principles, and the decisions you make in the garden are made because they are what's best for the world around you. Organic gardening avoids synthetic chemical use, including pesticides to control insects, fungicides to control fungal diseases, and herbicides to control weeds. Naturally derived pesticides and herbicides can be used, but sparingly, and only as a last resort. Organic gardeners look for ways to work with beneficial insects, to increase plant diversity, and to be creative in their planting and planning to disrupt the cycle of pests. Soil is viewed as a living system, and care is taken to build soil health with the understanding that healthy soils grow healthy plants.

Unless you're planning to certify your garden as USDA organic—which is an important distinction for commercial producers but may have less benefit to home gardeners— it's up to you to develop your personal definition of organic and decide how to best manage your garden under that definition.

# IN *This* BOOK

There's no one right way to garden. Over time, you'll find the style, techniques, and varieties best suited to your site, your lifestyle, and your taste.

**EVERY GARDEN IS DIFFERENT.** This concept cannot be stressed enough, and it's one that this book revisits time and time again. Gardening is a pursuit that can be adapted to your space, climate, vegetable preferences, and aesthetic.

This book gives a short history of vegetable gardening in America, from Indigenous lifeways before the land's European colonization to the 2020 pandemic-era gardening boom and where we are now.

Throughout the book, you'll find examples of different types of gardens and gardening styles. You will learn that you don't have to have a one-acre plot in the country to grow a great garden. Working with the land and resources you have is essential.

In chapter 3, the plan for your organic vegetable garden begins taking shape, and each chapter builds on the one before it. Your reading progresses through garden placement and design, getting to know your climate and weather patterns—and how these are changing—and making decisions about what to plant and how to plant it. Soon you're breaking ground for your new garden, learning all about soil and its care—and filling out a soil progress report card to track your soil health over time—and getting excited about compost and more compost. You get a primer on maintaining the garden, a seasonal garden to-do list that distills main points into easy-to-digest tasks, all you need to know about vertical growing, and a rundown of organic pest control that especially focuses on prevention. The book wraps up with best practices for harvesting and storing your produce and profiles of how to grow common—as well as less common—garden crops.

Throughout, the text focuses on working with what you have, adapting to climate change and weather worries, and making gardening a sustainable practice for yourself and the planet. Many chapters end with a spread of useful tools related to that chapter's subject.

Even with all of the information you're about to receive, the greatest lessons will be found in your own experience. Start small, whether you are new to gardening in general or are a more advanced gardener starting out in a new place or with a new gardening style.

Learn all you can from this book, bring it into the garden with you, and let each bit of knowledge build on the last. In no time, you'll have a beautiful garden that's producing not only food but also joy. A whole world of vegetables awaits.

CHAPTER 1

# History of VEGETABLE GARDENING in America

**THE STORY OF VEGETABLE GARDENING** in America twists and turns. What started as a necessity for many people has—over the years, decades, and centuries—become a tool for self-reliance, an act of patriotism, a way to protect nature, a connection to ancestors, and a balm for stress and anxiety. Today, as it has always done—but perhaps more than ever—organic vegetable gardening gives us hope, and it brings us confidence and a sense of empowerment over our individual capacity to provide for ourselves and others. Our hope lies in our care for the soil, and for some, in reflecting on the past as a way to build a better future.

## CELEBRATING THE FIRST AMERICAN GARDENERS

Many gardeners are looking back to the ways of preindustrial Americans, including methods of the first people to grow here: the Indigenous gardeners. Native Americans were cultivating crops in what is now the United States at least 2,500 years before Europeans landed ashore, perhaps much longer. While hunting and foraging continued, the rise of agriculture led people to be less nomadic, settle in place, establish communities, build structures, and innovate with advances in construction and production, including advances in irrigation. As long as 1,000 years ago, Indigenous peoples across the United States were growing corn, beans, sunflowers, gourds, squash, and tobacco.

Shown here is an illustrated example of a Hohokam agricultural system. The Hohokam are thought to be the first North American Indigenous culture to develop a sophisticated irrigation system of canals and ditches to water their crops in the desert Southwest.

Without modern industrial tools or fertilizers, and more interested in efficacy than order, Indigenous gardeners embraced mixed plantings, combining crops for mutual benefit. The archetypal example is the Three Sisters garden of corn, beans, and squash, primarily used by the Iroquois people, and specifically the Seneca Nation. Tall, sturdy corn serves as a trellis for climbing pole beans, while full-leaved squash shades the soil as a living mulch, reducing moisture loss and preventing weeds.

11

This circa 1927 image shows a dry-farming method called Latdekwi:we, also known as a waffle garden. These gardens were created by the Zuni, Indigenous Pueblo people native to the Zuni River valley in western New Mexico. According to the New Mexico Department of Cultural Affairs, the Indigenous Zuni peoples created a wafflelike structure out of dirt and mud to concentrate water around plant roots.

This image from circa 1906 shows Navaho corn patches between canyon walls, exhibiting the ingenuity required to grow food in challenging conditions.

Seed saving was vital, and choosing the best seeds to save in different regions developed heirloom varieties attuned to different soil and climate conditions. Women traditionally held the esteemed role of the tribal seed savers. Many Indigenous heirloom plants are available today thanks to the matriarchal seed-saving lineage of various tribes. The value of these seeds was also recognized by non-native seed collectors and institutions such as museums in the late 1800s and 1900s, even as populations of Indigenous people were being forcibly moved onto reservations by the U.S. government. (Some of these valuable seed collections are now being returned to the original tribes to reestablish food traditions.)

## PUTTING DOWN ROOTS

When the first English and Dutch colonists came to America in the early 1600s and established settlements such as Jamestown in Virginia, Manhattan in New York, and Plymouth in Massachusetts, they brought their own seeds for their gardens and farms. But they quickly learned the value of growing Indigenous crops like corn, beans, pumpkins, and squash that were already well adapted to local conditions. Adopting these native crops was vital to their survival in the new land.

At the same time, enslaved Africans brought to America carried seeds of survival with them, introducing new crops like okra, field peas, and watermelon. Enslaved people who worked plantations often cultivated their own small gardens, and these foods became fundamental to African American and Southern cuisine.

The trade of plants between the Americas and other parts of the world was big business. The Spanish brought many plants to the Americas and also took back crops never before introduced to Europeans, including the tomatoes and potatoes that are now beloved all over the world. Corn quickly became a significant crop in China. Capsicum peppers and peanuts became important in China and India. Philadelphia botanist John Bartram is believed to have introduced 150 plants from America to Europe, but it is founding father and third U.S. president Thomas Jefferson who's best known for his interest in agricultural crops. In the gardens at Monticello, his estate in Virginia, Jefferson, his staff, and enslaved people tested and cultivated 250 varieties of vegetables, as well as fruits and flowers.

Jefferson kept meticulous records. We know he loved salads and succession-sowed (every 2 weeks) lettuce and radishes to keep them in harvest as long as possible. He adored English peas (trialing fifteen types), introduced "new" plants like tomatoes and eggplant to the home garden, and swore by manure compost to keep plants healthy and able to defend themselves from insects and disease. (Open to the public today, Monticello takes great pride in the vegetable garden, which was re-created to show how it existed when Jefferson lived there.)

The Louisiana Purchase in 1803 opened up the central United States to European settlers, who brought their seeds and gardening styles west of the Mississippi River. In 1850, California came into statehood, and the United States rapidly established a coast-to-coast citizenry that, by 1870, was linked by transcontinental railways. Pioneer and, increasingly, urban families planted kitchen gardens influenced both by their ancestral homes and by the Indigenous techniques they observed in America. As with Indigenous peoples, keeping the garden and saving seed was typically the role of women settlers, who planted a mix of vegetables, medicinal herbs, and flowers.

## SPREADING THE MESSAGE OF GARDENING

While many seeds were what we would call heirloom seeds today, settlers in the 1800s started having access to a new commodity: retail seeds. The first seed stores opened in the late 1700s and early 1800s in urban areas such as Philadelphia and New York City, giving rise to the seed industry. The D. Landreth Seed Company in Philadelphia was the first to issue the mail-order seed catalog, and many pioneers making their way west could order seeds from the catalog or find them in general stores in larger towns. Landreth introduced new Americans to now-beloved garden plants including zinnias, tomatoes, and white potatoes.

Other brands we still know today, like Burpee and Ferry-Morse, began marketing their seeds in the mid- to late 1800s with beautifully illustrated advertising, seed packets, and catalogs. Burpee truly changed the game in 1901 by introducing photography to their catalogs. Ball Seed Co. was established in 1905 and mailed their first one-page seed catalog to growers in 1918. Seed companies also bred and marketed their own competing varieties. "New and improved" became the calling card for vegetable and flower varieties bred to be bigger and better. With an exploding American population, plant breeding became so fiercely competitive that Burpee reportedly had their Pennsylvania trial gardens—where 'Iceberg' lettuce and 'Big Boy' tomato were created—protected by armed guards.

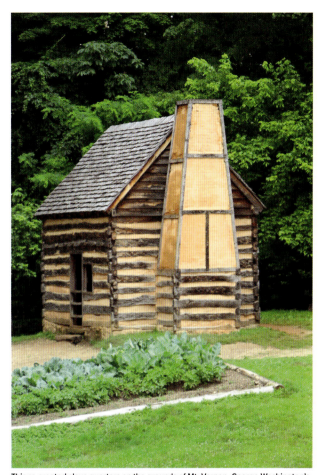

This re-created slave quarters on the grounds of Mt. Vernon, George Washington's former farm on the banks of the Potomac River in Virginia, shows how some of the enslaved people at Mt. Vernon tended a plot of vegetables just outside their door.

The current garden at Thomas Jefferson's home, Monticello, was re-created to show how it looked when Jefferson lived there. Tended primarily by enslaved people, Jefferson's garden grew over 250 varieties of vegetables, fruits, and flowers.

Left: The D. Landreth Seed Company of Philadelphia was the first company to produce a mail-order seed catalog. Right: Burpee, another Philadelphia-based seed company, was the first to introduce photography to their seed catalog in 1901. Their colorful catalogs continue to charm and entice gardeners to this day.

Seed companies advertised at country stores and in newspapers, but they also found a niche in women's magazines, marketed to farmers' wives and housewives of the new middle class. *Better Homes & Gardens,* for example, launched in 1922, sold door-to-door to women of the household and is still thriving today. (The American Horticultural Society coincidentally launched the same year.) Magazines became a primary source of gardening information and inspiration.

## THE RISE OF URBAN AND SCHOOL GARDENS

American cities typically depended on surrounding rural areas for fresh produce, but with an economic downturn in the late 1800s, many cities, including Detroit, San Francisco, and Boston, started converting vacant city lots into urban gardens so urbanites could grow their own produce. Urban gardens allowed immigrant factory workers, many of them unemployed at the time, to cultivate food for their families in the city, using knowledge—and mostly intensive gardening techniques—they had from growing up in homelands as diverse as Poland and China.

The original school gardens were also established at the turn of the century, with the first in 1902 on the west side of Manhattan. Fannie Griscom Parsons, who pioneered school gardens in the United States, led the creation of hundreds of small plots where metropolitan children, mostly immigrants, could learn about gardening and the natural world. Each child was responsible for a 4- x 8-foot plot where they grew corn, onions, carrots, and peas, among other vegetables, and learned "civic virtues" like industriousness and self-respect. In just a few years, thousands of school farms had been created throughout the country based on Parsons's model.

The early part of the twentieth century saw the large-scale movement, now called the Great Migration, of African Americans in the mostly rural South to cities in the North and Midwest such as Chicago, Detroit, New York, and Pittsburgh. Though they left rural life behind, these new northerners brought with them knowledge and passion for growing food, planting gardens wherever they landed. African American neighborhoods in metro areas became known for their vegetable gardens as well as their sense of community.

## COOPERATIVE GOVERNMENT AND VICTORY GARDENING

Agricultural and gardening societies popped up in cities and in counties throughout the country. Many held annual fairs and exhibitions as well as regular meetings for sharing the latest crops, techniques, products, and innovations. This knowledge-sharing led to farmers' institutes, and then to publicly funded land-grant colleges and universities aimed at agricultural education, including many historically Black colleges and universities. In 1862 the U.S. Congress passed a series of bills constituting the Morrill Land-Grant College Act, which were signed by President Abraham Lincoln. At this same time, the United States Department of Agriculture was created, having been established earlier as a division of the Patent Office, with the head of the division, Isaac Newton, continuing as commissioner. These events set the stage for the first State Agricultural Experiment Stations in California and Connecticut in 1875. Eventually, the federal government established the Cooperative Extension Service, which was formalized by the Smith–Lever Act in 1914. (The program did not include tribal colleges until 1994, when the Tribal College Extension program was created.) Cooperative Extension still works through land-grant universities today to educate communities about gardening, including the popular Master Gardener program.

Gardens again became a symbol of community during the world wars as the U.S. government promoted planting food gardens as an expression of national pride and support. During WWI, they were called war gardens, but a rebranding during WWII had more appeal, and these patriotic gardens are still known today as victory gardens. The gardens furthered several goals, including freeing up the means of production for the war effort; offsetting the loss of agricultural workers to the military; and promoting the health, fitness, and nutrition of the American population along with a sense of self-reliance and community.

Victory gardens, like this one on a school property on First Avenue in New York City in 1944, became an expression of national pride during WWII.

Victory gardens were grown wherever there was open space: farms, backyards, schoolyards, rooftops, vacant lots, and public lands. Victory gardens were even grown, surprisingly, at internment camps in the West, where many Japanese Americans were forced to live by the U.S. government during the war but still, somehow, wanted to do their part and grow food. Many of the American gardeners who broke ground on a victory garden were gardening for the first time, and the government and other organizations rallied to provide gardening education to newcomers. These groups also educated citizens about food preservation. By the end of the war in 1945, victory gardens had grown between 8 and 10 million pounds of food.

Partly in response to the sudden shortage of nitrogen fertilizer during WWII, organic movement pioneer J.I. Rodale established Rodale Press and began publishing *Organic Farming and Gardening* magazine in 1942. Rodale wanted to share his experience and research from his own farm on the outskirts of Emmaus, Pennsylvania, which was a model for organic methods. In 1947 he founded what would become the Rodale Institute to study and demonstrate the value of organic agriculture. The institute continues to research and promote organic methods to this day.

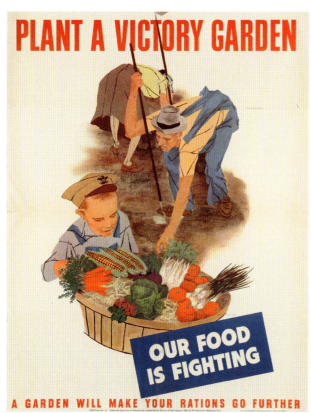

Posters promoting victory gardens were used to encourage the practice throughout the war years. By the end of the war in 1945, these gardens had produced 8 to 10 million pounds of food.

Boston PBS affiliate, WBGH-TV, launched *Crockett's Victory Garden* in 1975. The show, eventually called *The Victory Garden*, aired for 40 years with various hosts, including Jim Crockett, Bob Thomson, Roger Swain, chef Marian Morash, and others. This archive photo from the collections of the Henry Ford Museum shows the show hosts in 1993. Shown second from right is current AHS board member, Holly Shimizu.

# FROM SUBURBAN LAWNS TO ENVIRONMENTAL LAWS

Post-war, the rise of the suburbs saw more attention put on lawns, and vegetable gardens in particular were relegated to the backyard. Considered unsightly or too utilitarian for curb appeal, the backyard garden provided some convenience, as the popularity of outdoor living grew on patios and decks and around grills. Homeowners also became familiar with commercial products for lawn and garden, as synthetic fertilizers became widely available and heavily advertised post-war.

In the 1960s, interest in environmental health and wariness around pesticides and herbicides, further sparked by Rachel Carson's groundbreaking book, *Silent Spring*, led some home vegetable gardeners to take a hard look at inputs in their gardens. The contemporary organic gardening and organic agriculture movements were born alongside the larger environmental movement that saw the establishment of Earth Day (1970), the Clean Air Act (1970), the Clean Water Act (1972), and the Endangered Species Act (1973). But the Organic Foods Production Act, which established standards for organic labeling of foods as well as other products like soils and fertilizers, was not enacted until two decades later in 1990.

From the late 1970s to early 1990s, devoted fans of the PBS show *The Victory Garden* learned valuable skills for vegetable gardening, cooking, and preserving, through their TV screens. Many of them needed the education, as there was a new generation of suburbanites who knew little about where their food came from and how it was grown. With food made more conveniently available than ever before—in supermarkets and fast-food chains, in both rural areas and urban ones—the desire to grow food at home started coming less from necessity and more from curiosity.

Modern growing techniques, such as permaculture, treat the garden as a functioning ecosystem, rather than simply as a human-centric system of production.

## GROWING FOR HEALTH OF PEOPLE AND THE PLANET

The transition to the new millennium in the early 2000s saw another resurgence in community-based gardening programs, primarily in urban areas to address rising health crises such as childhood obesity. This was inspired in part by the chef Alice Waters and her Edible Schoolyard Project in Berkeley, California. School gardens popped up in cities across America, and a new generation of children was able to learn how to grow a cabbage or carrot.

In 2009, when the Obamas moved into the White House, First Lady Michelle Obama oversaw the installation of a kitchen garden on the South Lawn—it was the first vegetable garden at the White House since WWII, during the victory garden heyday. The garden was expressly meant to encourage national conversations around health and well-being in the United States. The vegetable garden once again became a symbol of vitality and self-reliance for the country.

More recently, gardeners have broken new ground regarding increasing concern about climate change and the impact of food choices in a global economy. From farmers' markets to homesteading to growing a small garden at home, the local food movement aims to address these issues from the ground up. And organic gardening has become a requirement for many gardeners, with newer versions of organic gardening going even further than the basic standards of zero synthetic chemical inputs. Contemporary methods such as regenerative gardening and permaculture (see page 25) aim not just to do no harm, but to actually improve the soil and the ecosystem, providing habitat for pollinators and other creatures while also absorbing carbon from the atmosphere, one garden at a time.

During the global COVID-19 pandemic in 2020, Americans turned to gardening in droves. Many cited food security and a sense of control as the reasons they first turned to food gardening during this uncertain time, but as the crisis stretched on into 2021, their reasons for gardening shifted more toward overall well-being, stress relief, connection to nature, and delight in experiences of beauty and joy. Gardeners shared their trials and tribulations—and their harvests—on social media, but more than that, they shared in an activity that has uplifted Americans for generations.

## SOWING THE SEEDS OF OUR FUTURE

Today, the popularity of heirloom seeds has never been greater. These seeds hold the stories of the past, and perhaps also the keys to our future. Heirloom seed collections, including those of Indigenous Americans, contain a wealth of genetic diversity that evolved and was preserved before the influence of industrial agriculture. They could prove valuable for the entire country as we consider ways to ensure food security in the face of climate change. But it's not just about the seeds. Our vegetable gardening heritage has deep roots. From the first gardens of abundance, filled with corn and sunflowers, to the victory gardens that helped us win two world wars, to climate-resilient gardens of today, America is a country of gardeners. Let's grow forward together.

CHAPTER 2

# GALLERY *of* GARDENS

*Which One Is Right for You?*

**ONE OF THE MOST EXCITING PARTS** of growing your own vegetable garden is that you can give it whatever aesthetic you'd like. There are as many styles of gardens as there are plants that you can grow in them. As seasons change, so may your garden style. You'll learn more each year, try new experiments, and borrow from others. The good news is that rarely will you make changes in a garden that cannot be reversed. Let your creativity flow!

This chapter will provide you with inspiration for what your garden could become. The photos throughout have been taken from backyard, patio, rooftop, and indoor gardens all over the country. Big and small, each is packed with vegetables and herbs—not to mention with ideas that the rest of us can learn from.

As you look at these photos, think long-term. Gardens cannot be rushed. Do not be discouraged when setting out to build your garden and have empty patches of soil at the start. These plants will grow—give them time. Also realize that a photo may having been taken in a different season or a different growing climate than your own. Comparisons have no place in gardening! Each garden is beautiful in its own right, and yours will blossom over time.

Take notes about the gardens you love in this chapter. In chapters 3 and 5, you'll learn more about garden placement and styles, pulling together the information you need to turn your garden dreams into reality.

# RAISED BED GARDENS

🌿 This productive suburban homestead uses raised beds that are simply built with 2x4s and 2x6s. These wood boards used to build the beds may have been repurposed, adding to the sustainability of this gardening effort. Within the beds, crops are tightly planted in easily distinguishable blocks. You can see the gardener has a plan for what they're growing by the thoughtfulness of this planting pattern. The width of the raised beds requires a bit of a reach to get to the center. You wouldn't want to build beds any wider than this.

🌿 Not all raised beds have frames. These mound beds are raised: The soil has been dug out from either side of the bed and piled on top of the bed so the growing area is higher than the walking path. Beets, greens, chives, marigolds, and other vegetables and herbs appreciate the drainage that having a mounded raised bed offers. In a row garden like this, the mounds make obvious where the aisle begins and the planting area ends, which helps alleviate soil compaction caused by walking on the growing spaces.

🌿 Compare this photo to the one above it: Both of these gardens use raised beds, but this urban garden is more formal than the suburban homestead. The gardeners have cleverly combined flowers, herbs, and vegetables in a stylish and manicured way. What a tranquil space to pass through as you enter and exit your townhome in a busy city! The boards used to build the raised beds may be black locust, which is an expensive but durable choice. The finials show off a bit of the gardeners' formal style.

🌿 In another example of unframed raised beds, the mound beds in this garden have aisleways smartly mulched with straw. Garden-aisle maintenance is a chore, and the mulch will keep down weeds—not to mention it makes an attractive visual frame for the garden beds. As the mulch breaks down, its nutrients feed the soil around the beds, keeping alive the web of soil microbes. Alternatively, the gardener can remove and compost the mulch at the end of the season or pull it into the bed to use as mulch around next season's plants.

**20** American Horticultural Society | *Essential Guide to Organic Vegetable Gardening*

🥸 If you are looking for a garden with a formal style, this is a lovely space to use as inspiration. The Corten steel raised beds contain ornamental plants and edible plants in beautiful combination. The gardener has created depth and height with several types of plant cages and a water feature. The gravel walkways tie together the whole space and do away with the need for weeding around the raised beds. This style of garden can be installed in a large or a small format and can even be placed on a rooftop or patio.

🥸 In case you aren't sold by now, this garden is further proof that gardens can be situated anywhere and in any configuration. If you don't have space at ground level, maybe you have space on the roof, like this gardener! Raised beds constructed of wood and steel frames hold a spread of vegetables and flowers. The trellises mounted to the beds allow for vertical growing. And, being on a roof, these plants receive full sun, which most vegetables prefer.

🥸 This delightful garden features mounded beds with straw-mulched aisles. The whole garden is set apart by a colorful living frame: Chives, lupine, irises, and more attract pollinators and draw you in to all that is happening within. The garden beds are wide enough to plant two rows of many types of crops but not so wide that the gardener can't reach across. This design is a smart way to incorporate both order and whimsy into an outdoor space. All that's missing is a café table and chairs for a place to sit and enjoy!

🥸 If you were to try to plant right into a hillside, erosion would carry your garden soil down the hill. Cutting into the hill and creating flat beds, like these quirky terraced beds, allows you to work with the landscape in front of you. Humans have been building terraces to grow food for as long as they've been growing food. Attractive terraced beds like these should give hope to every gardener who has a sloped yard. Use it to your advantage!

Gallery of Gardens  **21**

# IN-GROUND BEDS

If order is what you want in your vegetable garden, a classic in-ground row garden is an option. No raised beds required, this gardener shows us that a simple straight-row design can still be attractive. You'll notice the crops are planted alongside their relatives. The taller plants needing stakes and cages are set along the edges so as to not block the sunlight from the shorter plants. This is a no-frills garden that anyone with a bit of outdoor space can bring to fruition.

If the plants in this garden were ornamentals, you might pass by the home and think, "What a lovely garden." But here, the gardeners have used edible plants for their landscaping choice, and it is a delightful surprise! Plants of all types, heights, colors, and textures are tucked in among one another to create a busy but beautiful outdoor space. The garden sprite and sitting area nearby show the gardeners intend to spend time in and enjoy their outdoor space.

This fun arrangement of crops is hemmed in by a natural-log frame to separate the growing space from the walking space. The log frame also contains the soil as it's built up with compost each season. Notice that the crops are growing in straight lines and also geometric patterns, giving the garden an organized but informal feel. The appealing mulched space between the rows gives the gardener a place to move around the crops and keeps down weeds.

# THE POTAGER GARDEN

Once held on high as the best way to design a formal garden, the centuries-old potager style is still around, still beautiful, and still practical. The word comes from the French *jardin potager*, which means kitchen garden. Traditionally, the potager provided all of the vegetables, herbs, and cut flowers, plus various smaller fruit trees and berries, a household would need. Potagers are generally placed close to the house and always arranged in a geometric layout. The formal potager pictured exemplifies a mix of ornamental, herb, and vegetable plants within a triangular, straight-line design.

Less formal potagers are also possible, keeping the geometric and straight-line design while incorporating fanciful fencing, various containers, and other personal touches. This potager has more of a focus on edible plants, with an oversize Swiss chard, oregano that takes over the center planting bed, and additional greens and herbs throughout. While the more formal potager in the previous photo used in-ground beds framed by brick, this one features wood-sided raised beds to corral its plants. Comparing these two gardens is a great way to see the flexibility of the potager style.

Gallery of Gardens 23

# CONTAINER GARDENS

Gardening in small spaces is now popular enough that you can find containers to match every style, size, and need. These versatile containers can be stacked and unstacked, with more containers added for even more vertical growing space. This container garden includes both fast-growing, cool-weather greens and a tomato and a pepper that can take over the space as the weather warms and the greens finish producing. It's a good demonstration of how to get multiple harvests from a small space.

The gardeners who planted these grow towers must love salads! Kale, lettuce, arugula, and herbs are thriving in this vertical planter. Grow towers are a great option for growing these plants and more. You could plant a different type of plant in each pot of the grow tower, making for a diverse garden on your deck. You can use vertical grow towers indoors, too. While the grow towers pictured are meant for soil-grown plants, aeroponic and hydroponic grow-tower setups are also popular.

Here's further proof that container gardening can match all manner of styles and aesthetics. A wood-built container gives a growing space a more natural feel than plastic and ceramic containers. The tiered container provides depth to the planting and takes advantage of a gardener's potentially limited horizontal growing space. Add a couple of flowering plants for a pop of color, and you can have a vibrant and productive vertical container garden. Line up planters like this to turn the railing of your deck into a green wall.

Look at the size of these containers! Large plants, like tomatoes and squash, have no problem growing the root systems they need to thrive in containers like this. Look closely and you'll see drip irrigation tubes running to the pots, as well. Set on a timer or run manually, drip irrigation saves time and water while getting plants the moisture they need. A container garden may be right for you if you are unable to plant directly in-ground because of lease restrictions, contaminated soil, or any other reason.

Similar to the photo at left, these extra-large pots can accommodate any vegetables—and even small trees. These pots are large enough, in fact, that some are planted with more than one crop, such as the tomato and basil toward the right of the image. The containers are also large enough to handle stakes and cages for these large plants. Unlike the other large-container garden, the garden here features containers of the same kind, giving it a more formal, uniform appeal.

24　American Horticultural Society　|　*Essential Guide to Organic Vegetable Gardening*

# INDOOR GROWING

A few small plants in pots on a windowsill can brighten your home and your plate. Gardeners and aspiring gardeners put a lot of pressure on growing outdoors and in the ground, but there's a lot to be said about having plants indoors. The dwarf tomatoes pictured here will provide snacks and salad toppings. Your windowsill garden could feature herbs, greens, or another favorite vegetable. A big bonus to the windowsill garden is that you can keep it growing year-round, regardless of what the weather is like outside.

This gardener has chosen to grow their greens indoors using grow lights. In living spaces with poor natural light, when windowsill space is at a premium, or when you have a basement, closet, or spare room just begging for some life, keeping a container—or containers—of vegetables under grow lights is doable. Like a windowsill garden, it makes no difference what the weather is like, because you're controlling the light, temperature, and moisture for your plants. Grow greens, like this gardener, or other crops of your choosing.

# PERMACULTURE

Permaculture plantings mimic natural systems to benefit nature, people, and communities. This garden illustrates permaculture principles with its intensive planting, its mix of annuals and perennials, and its use of groundcover, mid-level, and vining growth. On a larger scale, permaculture looks at spaces in terms of zones: zone 1 being the home and zone 10 being farthest from the home. The zones closest to the home are those most often used—a kitchen garden—while those farthest are least often used—such as unmanaged spaces. Whole properties and communities can be designed using this permaculture zone theory.

Just as a natural forest has multiple layers, so does this food forest. The columnar apple tree is a space-saving fruit provider, while the trellis allows beans to climb—just as vines would climb trees in nature. At ground level, various ornamentals are providing groundcover. Just beyond the beans, asparagus fronds provide three-season interest as well as habitat for insects and birds. This wild-looking mix of annuals and perennials is a beautiful use of garden space.

Gallery of Gardens  25

# INTENSIVE PLANTING

In an intensively planted bed, you get the most vegetables out of your space while also shading out many weeds. If you require structure and order in your life, this may not be the style for you; but if you can go with the flow, intensive plantings are fun and productive. One caution for a garden like this: It's difficult to access the middle of the bed for weeding, harvesting, trellising, and other maintenance tasks. Either design your bed narrow enough that you can reach into the middle or give yourself space to step in between plants.

# HÜGELKULTUR

A hügelkultur mound packed with nasturtium, sunflowers, and strawberries is a pollinator's dream! Hügelkultur is a traditional German gardening method of planting in a raised bed filled with topsoil, wood, and organic materials. It's a great garden option if you have an abundance of downed wood and grass clippings to bury. As the wood or other organic matter decays, it feeds the soil microbes—like a self-fertilizing garden bed. After some time, the bed will need to be rebuilt as its organic materials break down.

# STRAW-BALE GARDEN

Yes, these really are vegetable plants growing out of straw bales. This is straw-bale gardening! Gardeners who use a wheelchair or prefer to not squat and gardeners who can't break ground to grow their plants are great candidates for straw-bale gardening. This gardener has peppers, beans, cabbage, and more growing in their large garden. Anything you can grow in the ground, you can grow in a straw bale. Just add sunshine, water, fertilizer, and a little bit of potting soil to create the perfect gardening conditions.

# SQUARE-FOOT GARDEN

In a square-foot garden, you can intensively grow a lot of food in a little space. Here, you see the wooden grid that marks square-foot sections of the raised bed. In each section, this gardener has planted the number of plants prescribed by the Square Foot Gardening Method to get the most yield out of the least space. In a 16-square-foot bed like this one, you can even install a trellis to grow vining plants—like tomatoes—or a "top hat" to increase the depth of the planting bed to grow root crops—like carrots.

26 American Horticultural Society | *Essential Guide to Organic Vegetable Gardening*

## LASAGNA GARDEN

🌱 While there are no lasagna noodles growing here, this garden is layered like any good lasagna, hence its name. Also called sheet mulching, this is a way to build a garden in-ground without tilling. Layering up cardboard, compost, newspaper, and mulch, the sod dies back while the soil is fed. After a few months, it's ready for planting, and the result is a rich, mulched planting bed like this one. This gardener's mix of basil, lettuce, and tomatoes shows all range of plants can be grown in a lasagna garden.

## A LITTLE BIT OF EVERYTHING

🌱 It's encouraging to see how much vibrant life can be packed into a small stretch of yard. In this intensively planted garden, raised beds, in-ground plantings, and an arbor hold more than a dozen edible and ornamental species. Simplicity can have an impact: Look closely and you'll see that the arbor is a piece of cattle panel fence bent into an arch to support the climbing cucurbit. While you can find stunning, sculpted pieces to add to your garden—and they do have their place—you can also do a lot with inexpensive, everyday materials.

🌱 This simple brick patio space is populated with growing containers of all kinds and flanked by raised beds to take advantage of as much vegetable-growing space as possible. The gardener has done a beautiful job of blending plant textures and colors with some purple basils and red lettuces, flowering herbs and ornamentals, and both large and small plants. The trellis holding tomatoes and the archways supporting several types of vines provide a wall, creating an outdoor room full of flowering and edible delight.

As you move through this book, you'll learn about types of vegetables and their growing habits, techniques for watering and weeding, what to do come time for your long-awaited harvest, and much more. Know that these ideas apply regardless of what your garden looks like.

In the next chapter, you'll take the inspiration and ideas you found here and start to form the plan for your garden based on your climate, your available space, and your personal preferences.

Gallery of Gardens   27

CHAPTER 3

# PLANNING *with* PURPOSE

**THINK OF YOUR GARDEN** as an extension of your home. Just as you need a plan to construct a house, a plan will do wonders for the structure and organization of your garden. In suggesting a plan, it doesn't mean a multipage architectural drawing on a large-scale roll-out sheet of paper. You just need a basic drawing or sketch that includes a few essential elements.

Your garden will likely be different from your neighbor's garden in every sense: size, layout, aesthetic, and plant choice. In this chapter, you'll learn about the growing season and climate for your region, the microclimate of your specific yard, the ideal location and orientation of your garden, and how to start the planning process to create the vegetable garden you've always wanted.

# GET TO *Know Your* SEASONS

**FROM NORTH TO SOUTH** and east to west, this continent is a tapestry of climates and microclimates. These features dictate the vegetables, herbs, and flowers that can grow and thrive in your garden. Before you can pick out your seeds and plants, you must first understand the conditions you're asking them to grow in.

## STEP OUTSIDE

We'll look at resources and scientific data in a bit. For now, consider the power of observation. If you've lived for some time in the place where you plan to garden, you may already have a sense of when the seasons change, how much winter and summer temperatures can fluctuate, and from which direction the wind comes through your yard. If you're a new gardener, you're likely eager to get your garden started, and any advice to start small and go slow particularly pertains to you.

While decades of scientific measure and recordkeeping can tell you which United States Department of Agriculture Plant Hardiness Zone you live in (see page 31), predict your first fall frost and your last spring frost (see page 32), and offer an average annual rainfall for your region, these measurements mean less than what is actually happening in your garden. As our climate conditions become less predictable, your own observations will become more essential. Give yourself time to get to know your space, weather, climate, and microclimate before investing significant time, energy, and expense in a garden space. Patience will pay off.

Weather records have been kept continuously worldwide since the 1880s, and while climate change is scrambling these records, there is something to be said for long-term scientific observation. For this, the USDA and National Oceanic and Atmospheric Administration have information to aid your garden planning.

## USDA PLANT HARDINESS ZONES

Specific to planning for perennial edible plants and herbs (those that live for many seasons, see page 33), your USDA Plant Hardiness Zone dictates which will thrive in your garden. Each zone is based on the average annual extreme minimum winter temperature. Being an average, you could experience a cold snap with temperatures lower or higher than this number. The coldest temperatures could last a few hours or a few days. The worst of the weather could come alongside humidity and precipitation or not. Each of these factors play into a plant's ability to survive a weather event. Each USDA zone is meant to be a general guide rather than a strict rule.

### *How to Use USDA Plant Hardiness Zones*

Plant tags and seed-packet descriptions for perennial plants list the USDA Plant Hardiness Zone for that variety. This tells you whether a plant can be expected to survive and thrive in your garden year-to-year.

Find a searchable version of the USDA Plant Hardiness Zone map at planthardiness.ars.usda.gov. Enter your zip code, then zoom in on the map to find your exact location. You may find the zone on your property differs from the zone just one mile away, particularly if you live in a mountainous or coastal area. Do not despair if you live in a zone your favorite perennials don't favor. Many perennials can be grown as annuals. Others can be grown in containers and moved indoors for the winter. If you're eyeing a plant rated for a half-zone or even a full zone above yours, you may still be able to add it to your garden. This is where the usefulness of your garden's microclimates shines. Read about microclimates on page 36.

**30** American Horticultural Society | *Essential Guide to Organic Vegetable Gardening*

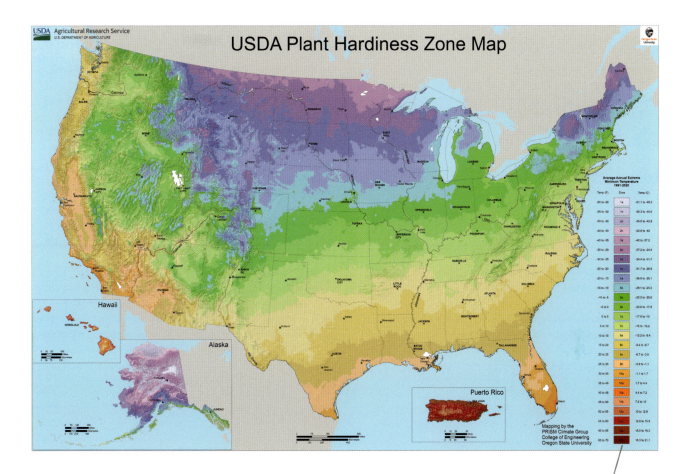

To create the map, the United States—including Alaska, Hawaii, and Puerto Rico—is represented in 5°F increments: Zone 1a in the extreme Arctic areas of Alaska to Zone 13b in coastal Puerto Rico. If you live in the capital city of Kentucky (Frankfort) or Kansas (Topeka), you're in USDA Zone 6b, and the average extreme minimum temperature you'll see is −5°F to 0°F. In Sacramento, California, you're in 9b, with an average extreme minimum temperature of 25°F to 30°F. In Concord, New Hampshire, your USDA Zone 5b garden has an average extreme low of −15°F to −10°F.

The last update to the Plant Hardiness Zone map was in 2023, and in 2012 before that. The 2023 edition uses the average of extreme low temperatures from 1991 to 2020, a time frame experts believe smooths out the fluctuations of year-to-year weather variation.

There is no zone map for the upper end of plants' temperature survivability. For this, you'll need to use your observation and accounts from other gardeners, university and Cooperative Extension sources, and commercial seed and plant producers.

**Average Annual Extreme Minimum Temperature 1991-2020**

| Temp (F) | Zone | Temp (C) | Temp (F) | Zone | Temp (C) |
|---|---|---|---|---|---|
| -60 to -55 | 1a | -51.1 to -48.3 | 0 to 5 | 7a | -17.8 to -15 |
| -55 to -50 | 1b | -48.3 to -45.6 | 5 to 10 | 7b | -15 to -12.2 |
| -50 to -45 | 2a | -45.6 to -42.8 | 10 to 15 | 8a | -12.2 to -9.4 |
| -45 to -40 | 2b | -42.8 to -40 | 15 to 20 | 8b | -9.4 to -6.7 |
| -40 to -35 | 3a | -40 to -37.2 | 20 to 25 | 9a | -6.7 to -3.9 |
| -35 to -30 | 3b | -37.2 to -34.4 | 25 to 30 | 9b | -3.9 to -1.1 |
| -30 to -25 | 4a | -34.4 to -31.7 | 30 to 35 | 10a | -1.1 to 1.7 |
| -25 to -20 | 4b | -31.7 to -28.9 | 35 to 40 | 10b | 1.7 to 4.4 |
| -20 to -15 | 5a | -28.9 to -26.1 | 40 to 45 | 11a | 4.4 to 7.2 |
| -15 to -10 | 5b | -26.1 to -23.3 | 45 to 50 | 11b | 7.2 to 10 |
| -10 to -5 | 6a | -23.3 to -20.6 | 50 to 55 | 12a | 10 to 12.8 |
| -5 to 0 | 6b | -20.6 to -17.8 | 55 to 60 | 12b | 12.8 to 15.6 |
| | | | 60 to 65 | 13a | 15.6 to 18.3 |
| | | | 65 to 70 | 13b | 18.3 to 21.1 |

Planning with Purpose 31

## SUNSET CLIMATE ZONE MAPS

While the USDA Plant Hardiness Zone map shows the lowest temperature gardeners should expect, the Sunset Climate Zone maps take into account a range of climatic conditions: length of growing season, timing and amount of rainfall, temperature lows and highs, wind, and humidity. The catch is the maps only cover certain parts of the United States.

Looking up Sacramento, you'll find you're in Sunset Climate Zone 14: Northern California's inland areas with some ocean influence. The website below offers a summary of the area's climate and a list of Sunset Plant Collection's ornamentals that would do well there. You can take the information provided and compare that to the needs of the varieties of vegetables and herbs you're considering growing to find the right match for your garden.

If your garden is in Arizona, California, Colorado, Idaho, New Mexico, Nevada, Oklahoma, Oregon, Texas, Utah, Washington, or Wyoming, you can find your Sunset Climate Zone at sunsetplantcollection.com/climate-zones.

## FROST AND FREEZE DATES

When growing a vegetable garden that focuses more on annual plants (those that are grown only for a single season, see page 35), it's more critical to know your average frost and freeze dates. The success of frost- and freeze-sensitive plants in your garden depends on your ability to protect them from the elements. This starts with knowing the last date to expect these cold bursts in the spring and the first date to expect them in the fall.

A freeze is the more severe of the weather events. This happens when ambient temperatures drop to 32°F. At this point, water in plant cells freezes and expands. In plants not adapted to withstand this condition, the cell walls are damaged, and plants can die.

A frost can occur at a warmer temperature than a freeze: most likely between 33°F and 36°F, but patchy frost can even happen at 42°F under the right conditions. Frost is a layer of ice that forms on surfaces at or below 32°F. While the weather station hanging on your fence might read warmer than 32°F, the air temperature at ground level—

Knowing your last and first frost dates is the best place for new gardeners to start. This critical information lets you know the length of your growing season.

particularly in low-lying areas on clear, calm nights—can go lower, because cold air sinks. The ice crystals on the surface of plants can damage leaves and blossoms, and they can kill frost-sensitive plants.

To determine your average first and last frost dates, *The Old Farmer's Almanac* has a resource that compiles National Oceanic and Atmospheric Administration (NOAA) climate data by zip code. Visit www.almanac.com/gardening/frostdates. From there, you can assume your first and last freeze will be within a few weeks of the date listed.

Your Cooperative Extension office is also a good resource for freeze and frost dates and information (see sidebar at right).

## GROWING SEASONS

This emphasis on knowing your first and last frost dates is important because you want to get plants in and out of the ground in the ideal time frame for them. The period between your last frost in the spring and your first frost in the fall is considered your garden's growing season.

The number of days in a growing season dictates the annual plants and varieties you can grow. Seed packets and catalogs outline the days to maturity for each crop and variety, and this information can help you determine what vegetables you can grow and what varieties are best for your growing zone. For example, there are tomato varieties that mature in just 55 days of warm weather, as well as varieties that mature in 100 or more days.

In Concord, New Hampshire, the average last spring frost is May 15, and the average first fall frost is September 29. The 136 days in between constitute Concord's growing season. To grow tomatoes in Concord, gardeners may want to plant varieties that ripen sooner—within 70 days—so they can enjoy a couple of months of this summer favorite. A late-ripening tomato may never ripen on the vine if a particular summer features a stretch of cool weather. Meanwhile, in Sacramento, the 281-day growing season means gardeners can plant and harvest any variety of tomato through most of the year.

## *Using Your Cooperative Extension*

Gardeners in the United States have a free, underutilized resource within reach. For more than 100 years, local Cooperative Extension agents have provided advice and training to farmers, gardeners, land stewards, home cooks and preservationists, artists, and others in every county.

The Cooperative Extension is a division of land-grant institutions—an *extension* of these centers of knowledge—paid for partly with your tax dollars. It's your Cooperative Extension office that offers 4-H and Master Gardener programming, as well as the SARE (Sustainable Agriculture and Research Education) training and grant program, workshops, short courses, field days, seed swaps, and more. Within the Extension system are professionals located at the universities themselves, as well as in each county. Cooperative Extension agents can offer garden advice tailored to your location and interests and identify pest and disease issues. Some offices offer low-cost soil testing for gardeners. In addition to in-person offerings like these, Cooperative Extension's online publications are invaluable.

All of this technical support hinges on proven, research-based models, techniques, and advice from researchers at their associated universities. While Cooperative Extension is based at universities, each of its county offices is locally responsive, with programs and resources tailored for their county's needs.

Find your state Cooperative Extension at www.landgrantimpacts.org/extension. From there, you can locate your county office.

Planning with Purpose  **33**

While some crops, such as this kale, are tolerant of frosts, others are not. Knowing which crops fit into which category is key to a successful gardening season.

Annual plants that prefer cooler growing weather (see Cool-Season Crops, page 56) and those that are frost tolerant can continue growing through frosts. Some of these plants may be able to continue growing through freezing temperatures, as well. Peppers and cosmos will be done at the first sign of frost, but beets and snapdragons will do just fine in a frost, and hardier crops like kale and spinach can even survive freezing temperatures.

Season-extension techniques can extend your growing season by a few weeks or longer, protecting sensitive plants from the cold and the heat. In your season-extension toolbox are cold frames, greenhouses, row covers, shade cloth, cloches, and more. You'll read more about season-extension options and how to use them in chapter 9.

Season-extension techniques, such as using cold frames and row covers, allow you to lengthen your growing season by a few weeks.

## *Determining Your Growing Season*

Use this space to record your growing season details:

Average last frost:

_____

Average first frost:

_____

# days in growing season:

_____

## *Regions with No Frost*

Weather is a defining factor, and diverse regions experience seasons differently across the United States. Much of the country sees some degree of wintertime cold that kills annual plants and puts a pause on your outdoor gardening efforts. However, a sliver of the country experiences "reverse-season climates" wherein summer temperatures become the hurdle. To avoid extreme heat, gardeners in these regions grow many of their crops during the winter months that rarely, if ever, dip below freezing.

Southern gardeners can seed much sooner in the spring than their northern neighbors, who may have to wait until summer to sow any plants at all. And those in the Southern Plains, with hot and dry summer months, may pause and wait for a cooler, wetter fall to plant and grow.

It's important to know your average precipitation amounts during each part of the season. This can determine which crops are suitable for growing in your climate.

## AVERAGE PRECIPITATION

Just as average and extreme temperatures are changing, so are precipitation amounts. Droughts and flooding are now almost expected. Outside of these extremes, it's helpful for you to know how much precipitation your garden could receive and in what months. Average precipitation numbers help you decide whether to plant drought-tolerant or water-loving vegetables, fruits, herbs, and flowers. Having this information up front allows you to set up systems to support your plants in overly wet or overly dry times of year, as well.

NOAA's U.S. Climate Normals website compiles average temperature and precipitation data from thousands of observation stations across the country. Search by state and city at https://www.ncei.noaa.gov/access/us-climate-normals/.

# THE CHANGING SEASONS

While it's reassuring to look at data and make garden plans based on what we think we can expect from the weather, climate change is upending much of what even the most seasoned gardeners thought they could count on.

The average temperature over land from 2006 to 2015 was 2.75°F higher than it was from 1850 to 1900. These few degrees may not seem like much, but coupled with changing precipitation patterns, they've changed the start and end of growing seasons, reduced regional crop yields, reduced freshwater availability, and further threatened biodiversity. Ongoing climate change has resulted in more dry climates and less polar climates, with heatwaves projected to increase in most parts of the world. Therefore, flexibility and adaptability are more important than ever in the home garden. Throughout this book, you'll read about climate-smart gardening practices, which include planting drought-tolerant, heat-tolerant, and regionally adapted varieties; conserving water; mulching; and more.

NOAA State Climate Summaries offer insight into what you might expect to see regarding long-term climate trends and extreme weather events in your area. Look up yours at statesummaries.ncics.org.

## *Microclimates*

A microclimate is a pocket of your garden or neighborhood that may be more protected or exposed and thus differs from the larger climate around it. Within a small geographic area, microclimates cause differences in rainfall, temperature, wind speed, and other weather events.

Cities are a good microclimate example, as they tend to hold more heat due to their large areas of concrete and blacktop. This heat-island effect can bring cities into a higher USDA Plant Hardiness Zone than the suburbs and rural areas just outside of city limits.

Other large-scale microclimates include:

- The marine layer is a major microclimate in the Pacific Northwest of the United States. The marine layer is a moist air mass over a large body of water that becomes trapped by a temperature inversion—warmer, drier air is lighter, so it keeps cooler, wetter air below it. At ground level, you see moderate temperatures, high humidity, and fog.
- In deep mountain valleys, the cold-sink effect can keep gardens in a pocket of static cold air. The cold air from higher elevations sinks into the valley, and as warmer air lifts over the mountains, the cold air remains trapped.
- Adiabatic cooling and the rain shadow are other coastal phenomena. Moist air blows uphill, cools, and creates precipitation on the ocean side of mountains through adiabatic cooling. On the inland side of the mountain, air warms and dries, creating a rain shadow, or lack of precipitation.

- The Great Lakes are so large that changes in their water circulation, temperature, and ice cover create a regional microclimate. The water gains heat in summer and releases it in cooler months, giving downwind areas cool springs, warm falls, delayed frosts, and lake-effect snow.
- High-altitude areas have colder temperatures: 3.5°F to 5°F colder for every 1,000 feet of elevation.

Zoom in closer to your area, and you discover that your yard and garden—and in fact, small pockets of your yard and garden—have their own microclimates. Create your own microclimates as part of your garden design. Use these to extend your perennial-plant options beyond your typical USDA zone and raise vegetables and herbs outside their peak growing periods.

Some microclimates you may find in your yard include:

- Each side of a building has its own microclimate: The south side is warmest, even in winter. The north side is shady, cooler, and moister. The west side gets direct sun in the afternoon, gets more wind, and becomes drier. The east side sees morning sun, gets less wind, and typically stays moister.
- Buildings, solid fences, decks or patios, and large rock features in direct sun act as thermal sinks and reflect warmth even after the sun sets. These may also act as wind breaks.
- Shady areas of the yard are typically cooler and may provide a break from constant direct sun for crops that prefer cooler temperatures in the summer.
- Persistent winter snow cover acts as insulation for roots against extreme cold.
- Gardens on a south-facing slope get the most sun.

This beautiful garden sits in the warm microclimate created by two brick and stone walls that absorb heat during the day and release it at night.

- Gardens on north and east slopes stay cooler all year long.
- The base of a slope generally has wetter soil than the tops of hills.
- Cool air drains to low spots, especially at night, making low spots in the garden more likely to see frost.

As you get to know your yard and garden area, you can experiment with its microclimates and the plants that grow best in each.

Planning with Purpose

# WORKING *with* WATER

If rainwater harvesting is allowed in your region, don't be afraid to collect rainwater from your roof in rain barrels or cisterns for use in the garden.

**ADAPTABILITY IS THE SUCCESSFUL** gardener's word of the century. Dealing with water in the garden may be the best illustration of this idea. Hard as you may try, you can't control the weather, and especially not the rain—or the lack of rain, as the case may be. Both heavy rains and more frequent dry periods are expected into the future, meaning gardeners should be prepared for anything. From a garden-planning perspective, you should understand how water moves on your property and how to best access water for your outdoor space.

Productive crops can be water-intensive, and as more communities face water shortages, paying attention to efficient water use in the garden is important—even more so in drought-prone places. If you're frequently under water restrictions, you can still have a vibrant garden. Follow water-restriction guidelines, including which days and times of day you're permitted to irrigate. Prioritize—and when possible, group together—the plants that need water most, and deliver water directly to their root zones, where they can use it most efficiently. Before you even begin planting, choose varieties adapted to your climate.

Rain barrels and cisterns allow you to collect rainwater from your roof for garden use. Some cities restrict their use, so know your ordinances. In areas that do allow rainwater collection, pay attention to what you irrigate with that water. The cleanliness and safety of water collected from surfaces is debated.

As you deliver water to your plants, you want to keep it there. Mulch is an easy way to cool the soil and prevent water evaporation. Watering in the early morning and late evening helps too. You'll find more advice on smart watering on page 169.

# GARDEN PLACEMENT *and* DESIGN

Start by selecting the best location for your garden. The ideal site receives ample sun, is easily accessible, and does not retain standing water after a rainstorm.

**CREATING A BEAUTIFUL,** sustainable garden is a benefit to your life as well as to your ecosystem. Part of what makes a garden sustainable is how all of its parts work together and how the garden integrates with your landscape and lifestyle.

## GARDEN PLACEMENT

The design of your garden begins with the right placement. While you're excited to start designing and planting, the proper placement means the difference between a successful season and a labor of love, heavy on the labor. The way the sun moves across your yard, the way the water pools after a rain, how easy it is to water the plants that need it, and more factor into the ideal garden location.

**Direct sunlight.** The most important factor in determining a garden spot is the amount of sunlight it receives—particularly for a vegetable garden. You may be able to get by with 4 hours of direct sunlight for crops that do not produce fruits, like leafy greens and cilantro, but fruit-producing crops, such as tomatoes, peppers, and cucumbers, require 6 to 8 hours or more. Notice how the shade moves across your property throughout the day and throughout the year and choose your garden spot accordingly. It's easier to add elements to create shade in a garden than it is to remove elements to create sunny spots.

Planning with Purpose 39

Trees and shrubs can add beauty to the garden, but their roots can also create competition, and their foliage can block sunlight. Raised beds are useful for overcoming invading roots, and planting upright, narrow trees can help reduce shading.

A garden that's right outside the back door is easy to tend, harvest, and visit on a daily basis.

**Water movement.** Whether your region receives a lot of precipitation or hardly any, get to know how rainwater moves across your yard. A garden placed where water travels or settles will leave you with soggy soil and unhappy plants—unless you're planting a rain garden, which is the subject of a whole other book.

Go outside in a rainstorm or just after, and watch how the water flows. Even if you think your yard is level, the water will find the low spots. Do your best to avoid those areas for garden placement. You'll find more about the importance of drainage on page 112 in chapter 6.

**Water access.** Just as too much water is not good, a lack of water access is also not good. Beyond a climate standpoint, you need to be able to hook up a hose for irrigation or hand watering. An outdoor water supply near your garden spot will save you from hauling buckets or running endless hoses to water your plants.

**Trees and shrubs.** Trees and shrubs provide beauty and ecosystem services in yards, but they're not typically friends of the vegetable garden. While well-placed trees and shrubs can give a garden shade from harsh mid-day summer sun in hot growing regions and offer a windbreak, these plants' negatives outweigh their positives. Trees' and shrubs' continual growth may shade out a garden entirely in just a few seasons, and their roots can run into garden spaces to soak up the water and nutrients meant for your vegetables.

**Microclimates.** You read about these pockets of alternative climate areas on page 36. Try to place your garden to take advantage of the best of your yard's microclimates and to avoid the worst of them. Small pocket gardens may even work in yards with significant microclimates at play.

**40** American Horticultural Society | *Essential Guide to Organic Vegetable Gardening*

## The Less-than-Ideal Garden Spot

After reading through the ideal location qualities, you may realize it's hard to find the perfect placement for your vegetables. The good news is plants want to grow. The ideal conditions listed here allow them to grow to their fullest potential, but even without checking all of the boxes, a good-enough location sometimes has to do.

Here are some common scenarios that require creative thinking for vegetable-garden placement:

- An ornamental garden already exists in the ideal vegetable-garden spot. If some members of your household are dedicated to keeping the ornamental garden, look for the compromise. Can you relocate the ornamental garden? Reduce its size? Interplant it with vegetables? Could you put the vegetable garden in the next-best location?
- The yard is too shady. Trees and shrubs can be altered or removed to make way for more direct sunlight in the yard. Can you relocate smaller trees or shrubs? If you have multiple trees and shrubs, can you remove some? Can you prune them?
- The part of the yard that makes the most sense for planting is also the wettest. In chapter 6, you'll learn about soil, including how to build soil, add drainage, and use raised beds to work around soggy soil conditions.
- Perhaps the best place for your new garden is at a nearby community garden plot, rather than at your home. Sometimes a viable location doesn't exist on your property. In that case, conduct an internet search for local community gardens in your region and explore the options.

**Proximity.** All of the garden-placement considerations listed here need to be balanced with the convenience of your garden location. Proximity of your garden to your daily habits will influence how much attention is paid to this space on a daily basis. A small herb garden easily accessible from the kitchen means more fresh herbs will make their way into your meals. A garden spot that can be worked while you watch for your kids' bus to arrive is one that will be well weeded. If your garden is close to your home and enjoyable to be around, you are more likely to spend time there.

## GARDEN DESIGN

The layout of your garden affects what you can grow and how much you'll enjoy spending time there. Designing a vegetable garden is not so different from designing an ornamental garden. Your design tastes and basic design principles still apply, whether we're talking about switchgrass or Swiss chard.

**The aesthetic.** Edible gardens can be just as beautiful and add to a yard's aesthetic just as much as gardens dedicated to ornamental plants. Each plant has its own texture, size, shape, and color. Many vegetables and herbs have beautiful and interesting flowers and foliage that come and go throughout the seasons. Even left standing in winter, the dried brown stalks and seed heads left behind provide habitat and food for birds, wildlife, and insects, as well as something more interesting than a brownish lawn for your view.

Consider how you want a vegetable garden to blend into or stand out from your other landscaped areas. Chapter 5 covers different planting styles. From neat and orderly row gardens to more meadowlike chaos gardens, there is a vegetable-garden aesthetic for everyone.

Whether you're planting a vegetable garden for maximum production or simply for fun and enjoyment makes a difference in the design as well. Form follows function in growing food.

Planning with Purpose **41**

Edible gardens can be beautiful places that enhance the aesthetics of your yard.

**Design principles.** Designing a garden is different from designing an interior space, because here we're working with living beings. Plants—especially vegetable plants—have certain requirements you can't get around. But your creativity is not constrained in designing a vegetable garden. Unless you're breaking ground on thousands of square feet of vegetables, there's no need to stick to a staid block of straight rows. Straight rows are a holdover from farming and are efficient for producing quantities of produce. If what your heart wants is a spiral garden, an area with a central focal point and garden beds radiating outward, or colorful containers arranged in the corner of a patio, you can design at will.

Here are some basic edible-garden-design principles that apply no matter the size, type, or location of your garden:

- Choose a focal point and plan your garden from there. Tall plants and trellises may be your garden's focal point, or you may pull in ornamental elements, like a topiary or art piece. Adding a third dimension to a vegetable garden makes the space more interesting and—in the case of using vertical growing options such as trellises—makes more efficient use of your growing space.

- Tall plants and trellises belong on the north and east sides of the garden. Direct sunlight comes predominately from the south and west in the summer. Place the tall elements farthest from the sun so their height doesn't shade the other plants. The exception to this is when you're growing vegetables that prefer cooler weather (see Now in Season, page 57) or those that prefer to grow with fewer hours of direct sunlight in the summer (particularly in the southern United States). Plant those in the shade of the tall plants and trellises.

- Plants in the same family tend to have similar water, light, and nutritional needs, and they experience the same pests and diseases. Your garden design should keep plant families in mind. (Read about plant families in chapter 4.)

- Give your plants space. Seeds and seedlings are tiny, and when you put them in the ground, it's hard to envision what they will become. A cauliflower seed packet says the mature plant needs 18 inches; don't be tempted to plant them 12 inches apart. The plants need space so their roots can access nutrients and moisture and the plants can fully develop and remain healthy.

- Give yourself space to access the plants. You will thank yourself later when you incorporate pathways into your vegetable-garden design. At some point, you need to reach each plant for weeding, watering, pruning, trellising, or harvesting. Design your garden so you don't have to reach more than 2 to 3 feet from the pathway to touch each plant.

- Allow yourself space to enjoy the garden. This could be as simple as a wide-open space in one corner to place your garden stool or as elaborate as an elevated patio and dining table surrounded by garden beds.

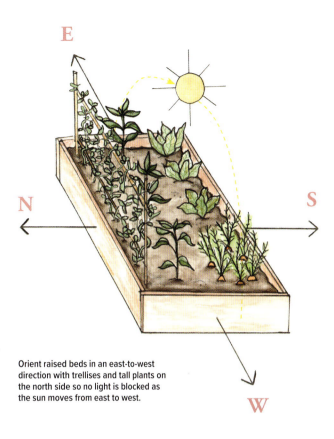

Orient raised beds in an east-to-west direction with trellises and tall plants on the north side so no light is blocked as the sun moves from east to west.

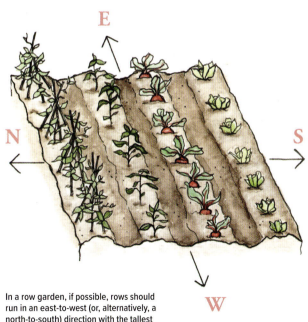

In a row garden, if possible, rows should run in an east-to-west (or, alternatively, a north-to-south) direction with the tallest plants on the north side.

Planning with Purpose 43

**Ecosystem services.** A sustainable vegetable-garden design accounts for all the functions a garden serves. The vegetables, fruits, and herbs you grow provide for your table, but this is just the start of the list of benefits the garden offers.

Wrap in your garden's other ecosystem services with these design factors:

- Include flowering plants for pollinators. Most produce from your garden is the result of pollination—the movement of pollen from the anther (male part of the flower) to the stigma (female part of the flower). Some plants require insects or hummingbirds to visit their flowers for pollination to occur; others are self-pollinated or wind pollinated. Maximize their chance to be pollinated: Invite more pollinators to your garden with ornamental flowers, edible flowers, and flowering herbs in your design. For example, plants with large flowers such as squash, sunflower, and catmint will attract bumblebees, a prime pollinator, into your garden.

- Incorporate flowering plants for beneficial insects. It is a fact of life that for some insects to survive, they must eat other insects. The insects that gardeners consider "beneficial" eat the insects that prey on your garden plants. Beneficial bugs will be attracted to your garden if their favorite pest-insect meal is present, and you can give them another reason to visit by also including the flowering plants they love.

While beneficial insects tend to be less well-known than pollinators, ladybugs are recognizable good bugs. In its lifetime, one small ladybug can eat 5,000 aphids. Even smaller than a ladybug, aphids are voracious, soft-bodied pests comprising more than 1,000 North American species that suck the sap from many vegetables, from arugula to tomatoes.

- Plan for year-round habitat and fodder for birds and insects. You may have stopped to wonder where the insects hide and what the birds eat while the landscape is sparse through the winter. Backyard gardens hold some of the answers.

Mixing flowers and flowering herbs in with vegetables creates a thriving ecosystem where pollinators, birds, and other beneficial creatures are supported.

Create a year-round safe haven for birds and insects. Support wildlife by letting plants stand through the winter.

Find a friendly way to exclude animals from the garden, such as fencing them out or installing motion-activated deterrents, rather than poisoning, shooting, or otherwise harming them.

When putting your garden to bed for the winter, consider how you can support wildlife in this offseason. Cutting back perennials and removing dead flowers and annuals may give the garden a tidy look, but it removes natural forage and habitat useful to birds and insects. Withered fruit and dried seed heads are a food source, and insects will make homes in hollow plant stems. The plants left behind will also add winter interest to the garden space.

- Make plans to add a compost bin to your garden space. Composted kitchen and yard waste reduces organic matter in landfills and allows you to turn your garden "trash" into garden treasure. Healthy plant matter, inedible produce, and other lawn and garden scraps break down into valuable fertilizer. Plus, keeping this organic material out of the landfill reduces the amount of harmful gases released by the decomposing trash in those anaerobic heaps. Read about how to make compost on page 103.

**Wildlife exclusion.** While you just read about how to use your garden to offer creatures a home and forage in the sparse times of year, it's also important to limit their access to your edible plants during the growing season. Birds and wildlife love eating garden vegetables as much as you do, and animal waste left behind can be a hazard to human health.

Depending on the birds and wildlife visiting your space, your design may need to include a fence of varying heights and materials. You may also need to add elements to discourage animal visitors, such as reflective ribbons or pinwheels, motion-activated lighting, or motion-activated sprinklers. It is possible to creatively incorporate exclusion tactics while maintaining the aesthetic you want. Page 202 offers more insight.

**Your commitment.** Sustainability is not just about gardening in an earth-friendly manner. Sustainability relates to your own ability to sustain your garden. You can grow drought-tolerant, regionally adapted plants with the perfect drip irrigation and mulch installation, but if you don't enjoy your time in the garden and can't maintain your outdoor space, there's not much point in "sustainable" gardening.

A vegetable garden requires attention during much of the year, year after year. The activity level ebbs and flows throughout the seasons, but rarely is there nothing to do in a medium-sized or larger vegetable garden. Be realistic in your undertaking. Start small to gauge how much time and effort your garden will require. This careful planning allows you to make changes as you scale up. Growing vegetables can and should be a joy. Let your garden design reflect this idea.

## LET A MAP BE YOUR GUIDE

Maps are important tools in garden planning. They can be simple hand-drawn sketches on blank paper or a more formal professional drawing made to perfect scale. Maps help you in your decision making and keep your garden plans on track.

**Maps for garden placement.** Deciding where to put your garden is the first reason maps are useful. Look at the list of garden-placement considerations on page 39. Your yard may be perfectly flat, receive exactly 10 hours of direct sunlight, and have water spigots at every corner—in which case, you don't need a map to make your decision because you have the perfect garden area. In reality, your yard likely has shady spots, a slope, and water-access considerations—in which case, a drawn map clearly outlines your garden-area options.

In whatever way makes sense to you, put your yard on paper or on the computer screen. This doesn't need to be precisely to scale, but give it a good try. On the map, include:

- The house and other structures, fences, trees, sidewalks, and other landscaping features
- The slope and areas where water stands or flows
- Outdoor water spigots
- Areas that receive less than 8 hours of direct sunlight
- A septic-system tank and drainage field, if you have one

This map highlights the areas that are your ideal vegetable-garden spaces.

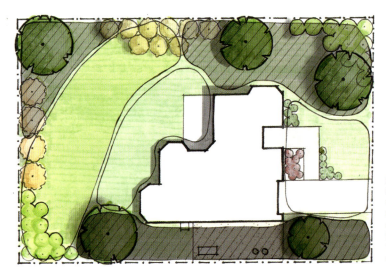

A more formal map like this one shows the placement of the house, driveway, back deck, and larger trees and shrubs. Shaded areas are covered with diagonal lines, while full-sun locations are left unshaded. These are the perfect spots for a vegetable garden.

Once the garden site has been selected, create a more simplified drawing that still shows the house, patio, and larger trees but goes into more detail in mapping out the garden itself. Draw your own map as close to scale as possible, but don't feel like it has to be perfect.

If your design is more complicated and involves perennial trees and shrubs or a forest garden, the map may also need to be more complex. This map shows the back deck, a small patio, a raised-bed vegetable garden, and all of the planting sites for perennial crops.

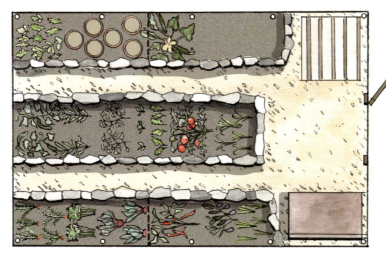

It can also be helpful to draw a plan for a high tunnel or greenhouse plantings. It is a great way to plan what crop goes where and figure out a crop rotation plan.

**Maps for garden design.** Your garden-placement map offers the ideal spot for your garden, and within that space, you can grow your family's favorite vegetables, fruits, and herbs in a style that matches your aesthetic.

In chapter 4, you'll have a chance to consider what to grow, matching your taste buds with your climate and your garden space. In chapter 5, you'll read about different planting styles, from neat and orderly row gardens to less-managed-looking chaos gardens. Use what you learn in those chapters to design your vision for your ideal vegetable garden.

As you form this plan for your garden, keep adaptability in mind. Rigid garden plans rarely work without unnecessary stress and expense. Stay true to the needs of your plants, work with the aesthetic you desire, and have fun with your design.

Planning with Purpose    **47**

# GARDEN-DESIGN TOOLS

### GRAPH PAPER AND PENCIL
are garden-design tools that are as basic as it gets. If you're the type of person who likes the somatic experience of putting ideas to paper by hand, it's hard to beat graph paper and a pencil.

### APPS AND SOFTWARE
focused on garden design can be helpful. If you are looking for more than a sketch-it-yourself design, apps and websites can offer help. Some programs feature garden plants and landscaping elements that you can drag and drop into ready-made templates, and others can design the whole garden based on parameters you enter.

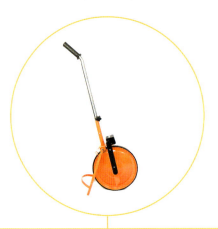

### TAPE MEASURES
are useful when marking garden-bed widths and taking short-span measurements. Plus, a tape measure is an easy tool to keep in your pocket or on your clipboard. Use a landscape pin to anchor the tape to the ground when you need an extra hand while taking measurements.

### A MEASURING WHEEL
is a good investment for garden planning. For larger measurements and those along curved planes, a measuring wheel is the way to go. From the starting point of your measurement, walk and roll the wheel alongside you to calculate a distance. This works best on even ground, as the wheel will take every bump and hole into account for its measurement.

### LANDSCAPING FLAGS
can be used to mark points along the way—irrigation lines, walkways, bed widths, etc. It's hard to beat lightweight and inexpensive landscaping flags. Use different colored flags to signify different points.

### STAKES AND TWINE
are handy for creating edges. Garden twine attached to wood stakes is an easy, reusable marking system. You can continue picking up and moving the system around until you find the configuration that makes you happy. If you're building a series of beds the same length or the same width, you can measure the twine-and-stake system once and then continue to use it as both a measuring and a marking tool.

### MARKING PAINT
is useful for spraying points and edges directly on the ground. It's another easy way to transfer your design plans from paper to your physical space. Some are water soluble and can wash away in the rain, so be sure you know what kind you're working with. Irrigation flagging stakes are another option for marking out beds.

### CALCULATORS
are handy tools for a gardener to have. Successful gardening involves math. In chapter 6, you'll read about soil and amendments. You'll be grateful for a calculator when it comes time to determine the amounts your garden will need.

### GARDEN NOTES
are helpful as well. Whether in notebook, calendar, or electronic form, give yourself a way to take notes about your garden design, decisions, and changes. Record your soil amendments, planting and harvesting dates, pest and disease treatments, and more to get to know what your garden needs as you move through each season and each design iteration.

Planning with Purpose   49

CHAPTER 4

# DECIDING *What to* GROW

NOW THAT YOU'RE in the planning mindset, you understand your climate, and you know where to install your garden, you can explore what to plant in it. This is rarely an easy decision, because there are so many vegetable options: regionally adapted heirloom varieties in fantastic colors, early-season crops that bring green to the garden as the snow clears, varieties resistant to drought and pests, and more.

While we can't tell you exactly what to plant, this chapter will outline how to make your planting decisions. You'll learn about different plants' characteristics, how to source seeds, how to save your own seeds at the end of the season, and the importance of flowers in the vegetable garden.

## GETTING *to Know* VEGETABLE PLANTS

TO THE UNINITIATED, plants are plants. They're green, they grow from the ground, and some of them are delicious. You already know gardening is more involved than this oversimplification. Background knowledge of various plants' growth habits and their temperature, sun, and water preferences is essential for planning and planting your garden.

## PLANT FAMILIES

It might be easiest to start thinking about plants as members of various families. In science, all living things are classified in a standard, seven-level system of taxonomy. The highest level is the kingdom, which for plants, is Plantae. Each level is more specific than the one above. For the purpose of classifying plants to learn about them, the fifth taxonomic level is most helpful: the family.

The plants in any given family share genetics as well as characteristics. This is why cucumbers and pumpkins have such similar leaf shape and flower structure. They're both in the cucurbit family, *Cucurbitaceae*. Most members of the same family will be affected by similar diseases and pests, want the same soil nutrients, and have the same water requirements. There are some exceptions in every family, of course, but once you learn the basics behind family characteristics, gardening decisions will come easier.

# A PLANT-FAMILY AFFAIR

Use this table to get to know your vegetable crops by their plant families. Refer to their plant profiles in chapter 11, and you will notice the similarities between vegetables in the same family.

| *Asparagaceae* THE ASPARAGUS FAMILY | *Asteraceae* THE ASTER FAMILY | *Alliaceae* (Alliums) THE ONION FAMILY | *Apiaceae* (Umbellifers) THE CARROT OR PARSLEY FAMILY | *Brassicaceae* (Brassicas) THE CABBAGE OR MUSTARD FAMILY | *Chenopodiaceae* THE GOOSEFOOT FAMILY |
|---|---|---|---|---|---|
| Asparagus | Artichokes | Chives | Carrots | Arugula | Beets |
|  | Lettuce | Garlic | Celery | Bok choy | Spinach |
|  |  | Leeks | Cilantro | Broccoli | Swiss chard |
|  |  | Onions | Dill | Brussels sprouts |  |
|  |  |  | Parsley | Cabbage |  |
|  |  |  | Parsnips | Cauliflower |  |
|  |  |  |  | Collard greens |  |
|  |  |  |  | Kale |  |
|  |  |  |  | Kohlrabi |  |
|  |  |  |  | Mustard greens |  |
|  |  |  |  | Radishes |  |
|  |  |  |  | Turnips |  |

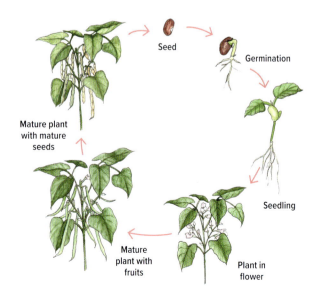

The life cycle of a bean plant, an annual vegetable that grows, flowers, sets seeds, and dies all within a single year.

# ANNUALS, PERENNIALS, AND BIENNIALS

Understanding vegetable plants' life cycle gives you the information you need to choose and place your vegetables each season. Plant life cycles fall into three main categories: annual, perennial, and biennial.

**Annual plants.** Annuals complete their life cycle within a single year. A full life cycle spans from germination to plant growth to flower and seed development to death. Most vegetable plants are annuals or are treated as annuals. Each year, you'll need to replant annuals.

**Perennial plants.** Perennial plants persist for at least 3 years without the need for replanting. Winter-hardy perennial vegetables are less common (think rhubarb and asparagus); more often you'll grow perennial herbs and flowers. Outside of the vegetable garden, trees and grass are two obvious perennial examples.

| Cucurbitaceae (Cucurbits) THE GOURD FAMILY | Fabaceae (Legumes) THE PEA AND BEAN FAMILY | Lamiaceae (Mints) THE MINT FAMILY | Malvaceae THE MALLOW FAMILY | Poaceae THE GRASS FAMILY | Polygonaceae THE BUCKWHEAT FAMILY | Solanaceae (Nightshades) THE NIGHTSHADE FAMILY |
|---|---|---|---|---|---|---|
| Cucumbers | Beans | Basil | Okra | Corn | Rhubarb | Eggplant |
| Melons | Peas | Lavender | | Lemongrass | | Peppers |
| Pumpkins | | Mint | | | | Potatoes |
| Summer squash | | Oregano | | | | Tomatoes |
| Winter squash | | Rosemary | | | | |
| | | Sage | | | | |
| | | Thyme | | | | |

Whether a plant grows as an annual or a perennial is sometimes also influenced by location. Lemongrass is an example of a biologically perennial plant. It grows as a perennial in Sacramento, California, but would not survive the winter in Frankfort, Kentucky, so it is grown as an annual there. Garden staples such as tomatoes and peppers also fall into this category. In the warm tropical climates they are native to, these plants are perennial. But when growing them in regions where frosts are the norm, they are grown as annual crops.

In your garden design, consider that true winter-hardy perennial vegetables and herbs will remain in place for years. Give them a spot where they can stretch out over time and where they will not be in the way as you're planting, pulling, and replanting your annuals.

**Biennial plants.** Plants with a life cycle spanning 2 years are called biennial. They grow foliage in the first year, overwinter, and then produce flowers and seeds before dying in the second year. Generally, biennials don't produce edible fruit, so you'll harvest them in their first year. Many biennials can be kept in the garden over the winter, given the right climate conditions and protection from the harshest elements.

In planning your garden, treat biennials as if they were annuals, expecting to replace them each year. If you were to grow biennials for seed, you would need to give them a place in your garden for 2 years.

The life cycles and growing seasons of common vegetable and herb plants are outlined on page 57 in the Now in Season chart.

Deciding What to Grow **53**

## *A Plus for Perennials*

Perennial plants have always been an important and sustainable food and medicine source for humans. The food-forest concept—layering plants in a garden much the way they are naturally layered in a forest setting (see page 91)—is rooted in cultivating perennial plants. In a food forest, not just vegetables and herbs but also fruit and nut trees, bramble bushes, and edible tubers comprise a self-supporting plant population.

In the garden, the green, leafy part of a perennial vegetable or herb plant dies back in winter, but its extensive root system is still alive so the plant may grow back next year. An obvious benefit of perennial plants is you don't have to replant them each year. Perennials may require pruning or fertilizing, but you only have to plant and help them get established once. Most are hardy within their adapted climate zones and require little attention after their first year.

Perennial plants are also a nice addition to the garden because their appearance changes with the seasons—leaves, flowers, seed heads, etc. This adds to the garden's colors and textures and gives the pollinators something to feed on too.

After a season or two, most perennials can be divided and shared with friends or planted elsewhere in the garden. It's a treat to not have to restart perennials from seed each time you'd like to add more.

In the larger climate-change conversation, scientists are looking at perennial plants as one way to keep the ground covered year-round, lower soil temperatures, reduce soil erosion and runoff, hold moisture, provide stable structure for the soil microbiome, and sequester carbon. In the backyard garden, perennial plants do the same on a smaller scale.

Vegetable gardens that focus on perennial crops are becoming more popular as they are productive and require less maintenance.

Perennial vegetables in gardens are few and far between in cooler parts of the United States and Canada, though they are more common in warmer climates. A number of seed breeders are experimenting with perennial vegetable varieties suited for a wider climate range. In fact, perennial varieties of kale, spinach, and arugula may soon be available commercially.

Lettuce is an annual crop.

Rhubarb is a perennial crop.

Swiss chard is a biennial crop.

## *Perennial Volunteers*

Some garden plants are technically annuals (and sometimes biennials), but they still return to the garden year after year. Reseeding volunteers—or "mock perennials"—come from either self-seeding annuals, underground parts forgotten in harvest, or plants that were mowed but not killed last season.

In some cases, mock perennials are a welcome surprise. In others, they're a nuisance. Their placement and numbers, as well as your perspective, make the difference.

Here are a few common examples of mock-perennial garden volunteers:

- Arugula, lettuce, basil, cilantro, and dill allowed to go to flower and drop their seeds can sprout a whole new crop next year.
- Fruits of melons, pumpkins, summer squash, and winter squash forgotten in the garden will rot, and their seeds can germinate into new vining patches.
- Unharvested potatoes and garlic can grow new plants from the tubers and cloves left behind.
- Biennials like Swiss chard, kale, and turnips you mowed above the leaves' growth point may continue growing leaves the next season.

Dill is notorious for seeding itself around the garden. Some gardeners find it charming; others find it frustrating.

Deciding What to Grow 55

Cabbage, lettuce, and peas are examples of cool-season crops.

## COOL-SEASON AND WARM-SEASON CROPS

In a previous chapter, you read about how climate and weather affect vegetable plants and how to use your climate and microclimate to grow different crops. Gardening doesn't have to stop as the frost approaches, as long as you understand which plants will survive and thrive in which temperatures.

**Cool-season crops.** Cool-season vegetables and herbs are characterized by their ability to withstand frost, but they struggle in hot and dry conditions. These vegetables not only withstand cold temperatures, they require them for germination and growth. Some of the cool-season vegetables benefit from frost, as the frost concentrates the sugars and gives the vegetables an even better flavor. This is true for Brussels sprouts and leafy greens such as kale and collards. On the other hand, when exposed to hot weather, cool-season vegetables will wilt, taste bitter, get tough and starchy, and go to seed. Some cool-season crops are also sensitive to changes in day length. When the days grow longer, they are triggered to flower.

**Warm-season crops.** Conversely, warm-season crops thrive in heat but are vulnerable to frost. These vegetables need warm soil for germination and warm weather for growth. Cool weather and too much rain can make warm-season crops stop producing, turn bitter, and become more susceptible to disease.

Look at the chart titled Now in Season on the facing page, and you'll see a pattern: Cool-season crops aren't fruiting vegetables; they're leaf and root vegetables. Warm-season crops require warmth and sunlight for fruit production.

In your garden design, account for the temperatures of each season, the light and shade during that time of year, and the microclimates available to you. Plan to put in cool-season crops early enough in the year that you can harvest in time to plant warm-season crops right behind them. In the fall, you may be able to do the opposite, putting in cool-season crops after your warm-season vegetables are finished producing. The next chapter has more about planting your vegetables based on your frost dates.

Basil, peppers, and green beans are examples of warm-season crops.

## NOW IN SEASON

Refer to these lists to understand when to include these crops in your garden.

| COOL-SEASON ANNUAL | WARM-SEASON ANNUAL | COOL-SEASON BIENNIAL | WARM-SEASON BIENNIAL | PERENNIAL |
|---|---|---|---|---|
| Arugula | Basil | Carrots | Dill | Artichokes |
| Beets | Beans | Cilantro | | Asparagus |
| Bok choy | Corn | Kale | | Chives |
| Broccoli | Cucumbers | Leeks | | Garlic |
| Brussels sprouts | Eggplant | Onions | | Lavender |
| Cabbage | Melons | Parsley | | Lemongrass |
| Cauliflower | Okra | Parsnips | | Mint |
| Collard greens | Peppers | Swiss chard | | Oregano |
| Celery | Pumpkins | | | Rhubarb |
| Kohlrabi | Summer squash | | | Rosemary |
| Lettuce | Tomatoes | | | Sage |
| Mustard greens | Winter squash | | | Thyme |
| Peas | | | | |
| Potatoes | | | | |
| Radishes | | | | |
| Spinach | | | | |
| Turnips | | | | |

Deciding What to Grow

Radish is an example of a short-season crop that's ready to harvest in just 30 to 45 days.

Brussels sprouts are a long-season vegetable requiring over 100 days to mature.

## SHORT-SEASON AND LONG-SEASON CROPS

In learning about your growing season in chapter 3, you read about using the number of days in your growing season to determine the best vegetable varieties for your garden. We can divide vegetables into short-season and long-season crops, as well as into short-season and long-season varieties within those larger crop groups.

### Short-Season Vegetables

Fast-maturing vegetables are known as short-season vegetables. These crops and varieties are a wise choice for gardens with shorter growing seasons (typically the farther north you go, the shorter your growing season is, with the exception of maritime climates). They may be adapted to wide temperature fluctuations, allowing the cool-season, fast-maturing varieties to be grown in early spring and the warm-season, fast-maturing varieties to be grown in the heat of summer. These short-season vegetables and varieties allow you to harvest while the growing conditions are optimal for that plant, getting peppers in before a frost or pulling radishes before they bolt. Because they're in the ground for less time, short-season vegetables require less total water than long-season vegetables, though they need more soil nutrients available to them immediately.

Another benefit to growing short-season vegetables is that you can pull these from the garden when their season is complete and put something new in their place. This form of succession planting, which you'll read more about in the next chapter, is one way to get more harvests out of limited garden space.

### Long-Season Vegetables

While it sounds like short-season vegetables have all the perks, there are reasons to grow slower-maturing varieties (a.k.a. long-season vegetables). Some heirloom and regionally adapted varieties are long-season crops.

Crops and varieties requiring a longer time to mature develop a different flavor profile. The varieties we find in the grocery store are more likely short-season varieties, having been developed to grow quickly and transport well, losing the emphasis on flavor somewhere along the way.

Sometimes you just can't find the vegetables you want in a fast-maturing variety. Celery and Brussels sprouts, for example, are notoriously slow-growing vegetables, needing 90-plus days for even the fastest-maturing varieties. You can't rush nature.

Long-season crops are most often planted as transplants rather than direct-seeded into the garden. Germinating them indoors shortens the time they need to spend in the garden. They start their life protected from cold weather and pests indoors and can take advantage of outdoor growing during their preferred weather conditions.

In another form of succession planting, you can seed both short-season and long-season varieties of the same crop to have a sustained harvest throughout the season. Carrots are a good example of this: Plant some short-season carrots that will mature in 55 days, and on the same day, plant some long-season carrots that will mature in 80 days. Now you can spread out the carrot harvest over time.

Succession planting allows you to grow a mixture of short-season and long-season varieties of the same crop together to lengthen the harvest period. This bed contains three varieties of carrots—one short-season, one mid-season, and one long-season—giving the gardener months of fresh carrots.

## *Bolting*

To *bolt* means to move suddenly or nervously. In gardening, it also refers to the abrupt shift from a vegetative state to a reproductive one, which causes the plant to flower and set seed, sometimes early or unexpectedly. Creating seeds is the last step in a plant's life cycle, signaling the end of its productive life. A plant can bolt when it is exposed to conditions outside its ideal. For example, cilantro is quick to bolt in hot and dry weather, and spinach will bolt as the length of daylight increases. As plants are exposed to more fluctuations in temperature and precipitation, our gardens are likely to see more bolting than what we've come to know.

Bolting changes plants' flavor and texture. Arugula becomes bitter, root vegetables get woody, and basil loses its flavor. Some plants are still edible and delicious when bolted, including kale and dill. Cilantro that's bolted is creating coriander, the name for cilantro seeds. Bolted radish seeds are crunchy and spicy snacks. However, in most cases, it's best to harvest before bolting.

You can prevent plants from prematurely flowering in a few ways:

- Select varieties that are slow to bolt or "bolt-resistant." This trait will be listed on the seed packet label or transplant tag.
- In some herbs—such as basil, mint, and oregano—pinching or top pruning can delay flowering.
- Schedule planting to give vegetables and herbs the time they need to produce before the weather changes or the days grow longer.
- Use transplants instead of sowing seeds directly into the garden to give plants more time to grow in their ideal weather conditions.
- Mulch the garden and provide adequate water to the plants to reduce soil temperature and plant stress.

This bolted spinach plant has gone to flower.

Deciding What to Grow   59

# VEGETABLES *for* EVERY GARDEN SIZE

**THE VEGETABLES YOU CHOOSE** to grow will also depend on your garden's size. In the previous chapter, you read about the importance of starting out small and building your garden over time. This is important enough to mention again. Having a larger garden means more vegetable varieties are available to you, but it also requires more time, energy, and resources. Take heart in knowing you can grow a lot of food in a small garden. Creative thinking and compact varieties make it possible. As you expand your garden space in future seasons, you can implement larger types of vegetables and more extensive crops.

## SPACE-SAVING DESIGNS

In the next chapter, you'll read about intensive-planting garden styles. These designs allow you to pack more vegetables into smaller spaces. One intensive-planting option that makes sense no matter your garden's size is vertical gardening. While ground-level garden space is limited by the number of square feet your yard has to offer, you just have to look *up* to multiply your plants' growth potential. Vertical supports in the form of trellises, stakes, and other structures let vining plants climb rather than sprawl along the ground, and they bolster bushy plants in their upright growth. See page 86 for more vertical gardening advice.

Using vertical supports offers a way to save space, plus it adds interest to the garden.

# COMPACT VARIETIES

In considering the varieties of vegetables available for backyard gardens, you may have to unlearn some things you were taught by viewing vegetables at the grocery store. Most vegetable varieties—from beets to pumpkins and everything in between—grow in a range of sizes. The vegetable plants, too, can grow in sizes from large to small and in shapes from vining to bushy.

When considering varieties for a small-space garden, read the seed packet label or variety description. Here are some things to look for:

- Varieties described as compact, dwarf, baby, or mini are usually a good bet. These may yield small-sized produce, or they may grow full-sized produce on small, compact plants. Read the description to find out.

- Spacing requirements listed for each variety tell you how large it will grow. Compare a few, and choose the most compact.

- Some vegetables have either a bushy or a vining habit, depending on the variety. If you have the vertical space, a pole bean can take up less garden area than a bush bean. The same goes for a vining versus a bush cucumber.

- Tomatoes are known as determinate or indeterminate. Determinate tomatoes only grow a few feet tall, but they can grow equally as wide. Indeterminate tomatoes are vining and can grow for 12 feet or more. Decide whether you have the trellis space or the ground space to accommodate determinate or indeterminate tomatoes. The tomato profile on page 257 offers more information on the differences. There are also dwarf tomatoes, which are determinate types bred to be extremely compact (only 6 or 8 inches tall in some cases).

- Greens and herbs that can be harvested while small are good for small gardens. This includes cut-and-come-again lettuce, spinach, and the like, as well as cilantro, parsley, Swiss chard, and others that can be harvested at any size. (Read more about how to harvest in chapter 10.)

Compact varieties, such as this 'Fairy Tale' eggplant, are another wonderful way to grow more food in less space.

Compact and dwarf tomatoes are perfect for container growing.

Deciding What to Grow

# YOUR *Favorite* FOODS

**YOU'VE NOW READ** the basics of the biology and physiology of vegetable plants, which helps you understand those best suited to your garden's climate and seasons. Knowing that turnips and spinach will do great in your space is only helpful if you enjoy eating turnips and spinach. One more critical part of deciding what to grow involves listening to your taste buds.

Think about what you and your family love eating. Because you're starting out small, you'll want to prioritize the vegetables you hope to harvest this year. Look through the profiles in chapter 11. These common vegetables and herbs are a good place to start. Get out your garden notebook or your note-taking app and make a list of your favorites.

Your list of favorites may look something like:

- Asparagus
- Lettuce
- Chives
- Garlic
- Carrots
- Cilantro
- Arugula
- Bok choy
- Cabbage
- Collard greens
- Kale
- Turnips
- Beets
- Swiss chard
- Cucumbers
- Summer squash
- Winter squash
- Beans
- Basil
- Lavender
- Lemongrass
- Tomatoes

This is a long list, but—as you've already read—not all of those vegetables and herbs will be planted at the same time. Some of those are cool-season crops, and others are warm-season crops. Use the chart on page 57 to divide your list into cool-season, warm-season, and perennial crops. Now you have a sense of what plants will be taking up garden space in each season. (The perennials are a commitment—they're staying put in the garden until you decide to move them.)

With this list in hand, research the amount of space each crop needs. Cabbage plants require 12 to 18 inches of space between them, whereas carrots need just 2 to 3. Also jot down notes about how each vegetable actually grows. One tomato plant can produce a few dozen tomatoes, but one garlic plant will produce just one head of garlic.

When looking for space-saving varieties, seek out selections with the words *compact, bush,* or *dwarf* as an indication of the plant's mature stature. This bush cucumber takes up significantly less space than its full-sized counterparts.

62 American Horticultural Society | *Essential Guide to Organic Vegetable Gardening*

Be sure to grow the foods your family loves and eats the most of.

Now circle your must-grow plants for each season. Be realistic about the garden space available.

With limited space, plant choice might come down to growing fewer types of vegetables or growing fewer plants from each category.

There are two ways to look at this:

1. Each family of vegetable or herb has its own maintenance, soil, water, and harvest requirements. The more plant-type diversity, the more details to manage.

2. A vibrant garden features diversity, and by bringing many types of plants together, you're creating a more sustainable garden ecosystem.

Neither of these options is necessarily right or wrong—just be sure there's a little plant diversity, otherwise you run the risk of being overrun with pests targeting one plant family.

While whittling down your must-grow list is hard, it is a necessary part of your garden planning. In the next chapter, you'll read about types of garden design, and you can use this list to map out the design that you choose.

Deciding What to Grow

# SEEDS *for* THOUGHT

There are so many types of seeds to choose from!

**WITH A BETTER IDEA** of what you want to put in your garden, you can focus on where to get these seeds or plants. You'll have the opportunity to decide on the types of seeds you want, the region and breeder they come from, and whether to plant seeds or transplants.

## TYPES OF SEEDS

Before gardening became an industry, seeds were open-pollinated and could be shared among and between communities. Today's gardeners can choose from heirloom, hybrid, open-pollinated, and even genetically modified seed types.

### Hybrid Seeds

Hybrid seeds result from controlled breeding between parent plants. The seeds may be labeled as *F1 hybrid,* meaning they are the first-generation result of a specific plant breeding. Hybrid plants are bred from parent plants carefully selected for specific characteristics. Hybrid examples include tomatoes resistant to tomato mosaic virus, larger-sized cantaloupes, and onions resistant to root rot.

Hybrid breeding may take place in a laboratory, on a plant-breeding farm, or in another controlled environment. It is labor-intensive and done by hand, thus the seed is typically more costly. Hybrids are bred through cross-pollination to produce specific characteristics, and humans have been hybridizing plants since the dawn of agriculture. Plant breeders and hybridizers spend years perfecting their hybrid crosses before offering the seeds for sale.
If you plan to save your garden seeds, hybrids are not a good choice, as they will not "breed true" and result in the exact same crop the next season. Seeds you saved from a dwarf, multiheaded F1 hybrid sunflower may grow to be a tall, single-headed sunflower next year. There's no guarantee hybrid genetics will be replicated. In fact, you can almost count on them not being replicated.

### Open-Pollinated Seeds

While hybrid seeds come from careful plant crossing by seed breeders, open-pollinated seeds have resulted from genetic development over time. Open-pollinated varieties (known as strains) have mostly stable traits, and they breed true to type. You can save and replant open-pollinated seeds, and for the most part, you'll grow the same thing you grew last year, with some natural variation that may be related to your climate and gardening habits.

Hybrid varieties are bred for disease resistance, early maturity, drought tolerance, or any number of other beneficial traits. They are typically more costly due to the labor-intensive task of creating them.

Open-pollinated varieties have stable traits and breed true to type. They are great for seed saving (see page 68).

Deciding What to Grow   65

## Do You Need Organic Seeds for an Organic Garden?

Because the word *organic* is regulated by the U.S. Department of Agriculture, nothing offered for sale can be called "organic" unless it meets the National Organic Program standards and is inspected and labeled as such.

USDA NOP guidelines require organic producers to use organic seeds, seedlings, and planting stock. The regulations do permit growers to use nonorganic seeds and planting stock when the equivalent organic variety is not available. For example, if a farmer is looking for 'Fat Horse' heirloom pole bean seeds and cannot find a source that's certified organic, they can document their search for organic seeds and then plant nonorganic seeds. The nonorganic seeds must not be genetically modified or otherwise treated with a prohibited substance, according to the NOP standards.

For seeds to have USDA NOP certification, they must:

- Not be genetically modified
- Not be treated with any NOP-prohibited substance
- Come from certified-organic plants

If a packet of seeds is not labeled "certified organic," don't assume the worst. It could simply mean the seed producer did not pursue USDA organic certification. Contact the seed seller if you'd like to know for sure.

Heirlooms, such as this Charentais melon, are classic selections that have been grown for generations.

### Heirloom Seeds

All heirloom varieties—sometimes called landrace varieties—are open-pollinated, but not all open-pollinated varieties are considered heirloom. Heirlooms are old, standard varieties that were selected for specific traits generations ago and have continued to be grown by home gardeners to keep these varieties alive, along with their associated community heritage. The heirloom seeds you grow today may have resulted from a plant your great-grandmother grew 50 years ago.

### GM Seeds

Genetically modified (GM) seeds are those from plants that have had their DNA modified to achieve a desired trait. Scientists identify a specific DNA segment that makes up a gene—sometimes from organisms other than plants—and insert the DNA segment into plant cells. Whole plants are grown from those cells using tissue culture. Seed from those plants or from those plants' offspring is collected and sold as GM crop seed.

While more than 90 percent of corn, cotton, and soybeans grown commercially in the United States is produced from GM seeds, few GM vegetable seeds have been approved for sale. Even fewer of those vegetable seeds are available for home gardeners. As of this book's publication, only one GM vegetable seed—a purple tomato—can be purchased for use in a home garden. All GM seeds, including the home-garden GM tomato seeds, require purchasers to sign an agreement that outlines what they're allowed to do with the seeds, the plants, and the produce.

It's important to point out that in the USDA National Organic Program standards, the use of genetically modified seeds is prohibited.

# REGIONAL AND ANCESTRAL VARIETIES

It's easy for today's gardener to look at seeds as a means to an end. You need a seed to grow a plant to eat a vegetable. Gardening—although largely known today as a hobby—was once a necessary means of survival. For most of human existence, 24/7 grocery stores were not an option. Your ancestors—wherever your lineage began—grew and foraged for their own food.

Now that seed production has become a business, purchasing seeds from a big-box store and ordering seeds from a website that offers the largest selection are the most convenient ways to get seeds for all of the vegetables you want to grow. For some gardeners, their regional seeds, the seeds of their ancestors, and the seeds of their culture—and the stories behind them—are more valuable than the seeds you can purchase off the shelf. These seeds may be important for reasons of heritage as well as for adaptability. Seeds from vegetables grown in a region over time are more suited to that region's growing conditions. These seeds may also be more suited to the changing climate conditions and pest pressures we are experiencing now.

People are forming regional collectives, called seed commons, to bring together farmers and gardeners growing locally adapted, resilient varieties with those who also want to grow these varieties. Seed libraries are even smaller groups that collect and share seeds from area gardeners. Some smaller seed companies focus on regional and culturally important seeds as well.

# USING TRANSPLANTS

While this part of the book has focused on seeds, the same facts you learned here apply to vegetable transplants (also known as starts). You can find heirloom, open-pollinated, and hybrid transplants that have been adapted to your region for many types of vegetables. You'll learn how to decide between seeds and transplants for your garden in chapter 7.

Ancestral varieties have been passed down in families and between friends since before grocery stores and seed catalogs existed. The Italian tomato 'Costoluto Fiorentino' is one of thousands of heritage varieties grown around the world. It has been passed between members of the Italian and Italian American community for generations.

Deciding What to Grow  **67**

Saving your own seeds is a sustainable way to continue your garden from year to year, but some seeds are easier to save than others.

## Saving Your Own Seeds

A full-circle moment will arrive for you as a gardener when you grow a plant, allow that plant to go to seed, save the seed, and grow another plant from that seed the next season. Being able to save seeds is a true measure of sustainability. Some seeds are easier to save than others, and you can build your seed-saving confidence over time.

By saving seeds, you're carrying forward the genetics of your crops from one season to the next. As you choose the plants whose seeds you want to save, look for the flavor, hardiness, and pest-resistance characteristics you want to strengthen.

### SEED SAVING FOR BEGINNERS

Look to the biology and physiology of each plant to determine how easy it will be to save its seeds.

### Pollination Type

**Self-pollinating plants** such as beans, peas, and tomatoes, which feature flowers that have both male and female parts, are the place to start. Because pollen from other plants isn't needed, other genetics aren't mixed in, and seeds saved from self-pollinating, nonhybrid plants will be more likely to grow to be just like their parents.

**Cross-pollinating plants** require pollen from another flower (or sometimes another variety entirely) in order to create seeds. Cross-pollinating plants may have flowers with both male and female parts, or they may have separate male and female flowers. Both require a visit from a pollinator (or, in some cases, a gust of wind) to move pollen from the male to the female flower part, and that pollinator (or the wind) can introduce pollen from plants of a different variety. This commonly happens within the cucurbit family. These cross-pollinating plants may produce seeds that grow into plants with different traits than the parent. If you grow just one variety of each species (for example, only one variety of cucumber), you have a better chance of saving seeds that breed true. However, pollinators may have visited a different variety in the neighbor's garden.

**An important consideration.** It's important to remember all of this only matters if you plan to save your own seeds. Cross-pollination does not negatively impact the current year's fruit production. In other words, if you plant a green-fruited 'Black Beauty' open-pollinated zucchini and it cross-pollinates with a yellow-fruited 'Goldy' hybrid zucchini, the fruits produced on the 'Black Beauty' plant this season will still be green and those on the 'Goldy' zucchini will still be yellow. The genetic repercussions of the cross only come into play if you save seeds from one of those 'Black Beauty' or 'Goldy' fruits and plant them next year. Because of the cross-pollination, the new plants from those saved seeds could be yellow or green or some combination of both. The fact that 'Goldy' is a hybrid variety throws another genetic roll of the dice too.

### Seed Production

Plants that produce seed pods or seeds not surrounded by a fleshy fruit are a good place to start. Seeds from an ear of corn, a radish, or a pea or bean pod are obvious and ready to save after drying at the end of the growing season.

Seeds developing inside a fleshy fruit often require processing before storage. Tomato seeds benefit from fermentation to remove the gelatinous seed coating. Pumpkin and winter squash seeds require washing and separating the flesh from the seed.

## Crop Life Cycle

Annual plants are easier than biennial or perennial plants because they set seed in the same year they're planted. Biennial plants require more patience because they won't set seed until the next season. Plant division is usually the most efficient way to regrow perennials.

## Plant Breeding Type

Be sure to save seeds from plants that are open-pollinated, not hybrid. A hybrid plant's seeds will not grow true (see page 275).

## SEED-SAVING TIPS

Whatever kinds of seeds you're saving, a few tips always apply:

- ↪ Allow the seeds to fully ripen on the plant before collecting.
- ↪ Seeds in pods, such as beans and okra, should dry on the plant before harvest.
- ↪ Store saved seeds in a cool, dry place that's out of sunlight and sealed away from moisture.
- ↪ Label saved seeds right away so there's no confusion about what's in the packet when it comes time to plant next season.

# SEED-SAVING CROPS FOR BEGINNERS

| CROP | POLLINATION NEEDS | SEED REQUIRES PROCESSING | LIFE CYCLE | DIFFICULTY |
|---|---|---|---|---|
| Arugula | Insect | No | Biennial | Beginner |
| Beans | Self | No | Annual | Beginner |
| Broccoli | Insect | No | Biennial | Beginner |
| Cilantro | Insect | No | Annual | Beginner |
| Dill | Insect | No | Annual | Beginner |
| Eggplant | Self | Yes | Annual | Intermediate |
| Lettuce | Self | No | Annual | Beginner |
| Melons | Insect | Yes | Annual | Intermediate |
| Mustard | Insect | No | Annual | Intermediate |
| Okra | Self | No | Annual | Beginner |
| Peas | Self | No | Annual | Beginner |
| Peppers | Self | No | Annual | Beginner |
| Pumpkins | Insect | Yes | Annual | Intermediate |
| Radishes | Insect | No | Annual | Beginner |
| Tomatoes | Self | Yes | Annual | Intermediate |
| Winter squash | Insect | Yes | Annual | Intermediate |
| Zucchini | Insect | Yes | Annual | Intermediate |

# FLOWERS FOR *the* VEGETABLE GARDEN

A vegetable garden that includes plenty of flowers boosts biodiversity and is welcoming to all.

**FLOWERING PLANTS ARE IDEAL** companions for vegetable plants. A number of flowering herbs and ornamentals are easy to care for tucked among vegetable plants. You may want to have something blooming in the garden throughout the growing season to take advantage of what flowers can offer.

Letting your vegetable and herb plants go to flower has some of the same benefits as intentionally placing flowers among your vegetables. If you aren't in a hurry to replant that spot, you could leave a bolting lettuce or basil plant to add more blooms to the garden.

## WHY FLOWERS

You read a simplified explanation of the importance of insects for pollination on page 44. Pollination is just the beginning of the benefits that flowers bring to a vegetable garden. Flowering plants also provide the following benefits.

### *Cucurbit Pollination*

Having flowers around is particularly good for cucurbit crops. Members of the cucumber family (*Cucurbitaceae*), including cucumbers, squash, melons, gourds, pumpkins, zucchini, and more, have separate male and female flowers on the same plant (botanically they're known as monoecious plants). Insects are required to move the pollen from the male flowers to the female flowers in order for fruits to be set. When you have lots of flowers around, you have more pollinators around to move this pollen and enhance fruit set. If you find your cucurbit crops are not setting fruit, you may have a lack of pollinators in your garden. In this case, hand-pollinating is a helpful practice. Use a paintbrush or cotton swab to move pollen from the male flowers (those with a straight stem) to the female flowers (those with an immature fruit at the base) in the morning.

Female cucurbit flowers have a swollen, unfertilized fruit at their base. Male flowers have a straight stem.

Flowering herbs, such as this dill, support beneficial predatory insects, including this syrphid fly, whose larvae consume aphids.

**Boost biodiversity.** The more diverse your garden space, the better, in terms of plant health. Pests are attracted to spaces with concentrations of their food source. In the summer, when your garden is packed with nightshade vegetables (*Solanaceae*) and cucurbit vegetables (*Cucurbitaceae*), it's a good idea to add some other plant families to the mix to disrupt the pests' ability to find their targets.

**Attract beneficial insects.** Predators are a natural part of any ecosystem, and the garden is no different. You want to attract pest insects' predators (also known as their natural enemies) to the garden. Certain flowers provide nectar and egg-laying opportunities for beneficial predatory insects like syrphid flies, hover flies, lacewings, and ladybugs (see page 197).

**Add more edible options.** It's not just the insects that come to the flowers for food. Many flowers are edible additions to salads and baked goods. Herbalists look to these plants as valuable additions to their medicine cabinets and tea blends as well.

**Bring texture and color to the space.** This point goes without saying. Flowers are beautiful. Their foliage is also interesting. Flowering plants make the garden an even more pleasant place to spend time. Plus, it's nice to grow a few colorful blooms to cut and bring inside now and then.

Some flowers tend to reseed themselves in the garden. If you do not want this, stay on top of deadheading them to remove the spent flowers before they drop seed. You can also save the seeds to share and to replant next year.

Also be aware that flowering plants that spread by rhizomes or runners can spread far and wide. A yarrow you planted in one corner of the garden might pop up in another corner the next spring. Prepare to be ruthless in your spreading-plant control, or confine those with a spreading tendency to containers. It's the price you pay for the pleasant atmosphere they bring.

Deciding What to Grow  71

# FAVORITE FLOWERS

You may already have in mind your favorite flowering plants to add to the vegetable garden.
For inspiration, some that blend seamlessly among vegetables are outlined in this chart.

| FLOWER | PLANT FAMILY | LIFE CYCLE | RESEEDS OR SPREADS |
|---|---|---|---|
| Bee balm (bergamot) | *Lamiaceae* | Perennial | Spreads |
| Borage | *Boraginaceae* | Annual | Reseeds |
| Calendula (pot marigold) | *Asteraceae* | Annual | Reseeds |
| Chamomile | *Asteraceae* | Annual | Reseeds |
| Cosmos | *Asteraceae* | Annual | Reseeds |
| Echinacea (coneflower) | *Asteraceae* | Perennial | Reseeds |
| Lavender | *Lamiaceae* | Typically perennial; depends on the variety | No |
| Marigold | *Asteraceae* | Annual | Reseeds |
| Nasturtium | *Tropaeolaceae* | Annual | Reseeds |
| Nepeta (catmint) | *Lamiaceae* | Perennial | Spreads |
| Sage | *Lamiaceae* | Perennial | No |
| Snapdragon | *Plantaginaceae* | Perennial | Reseeds |
| Sunflowers | *Asteraceae* | Garden sunflowers are typically annuals | Reseeds |
| Sweet alyssum | *Brassicaceae* | Annual | Reseeds |
| Yarrow | *Asteraceae* | Perennial | Spreads and reseeds |
| Zinnia | *Asteraceae* | Annual | Reseeds |

| SEASON | BLOSSOM COLOR | EDIBLE |
|---|---|---|
| Blooms in summer and fall | Purple or pink | Yes |
| Frost tolerant; blooms in summer and fall | Blue or white | Yes |
| Blooms in early summer and fall; doesn't prefer heat | Yellow or orange | Yes |
| Blooms in summer and fall; foliage is frost tolerant | White flowers with orange centers | Yes |
| Blooms spring through fall | Range of colors | No |
| Blooms in summer | Typically purple; other colors are available | No, but roots are used in teas |
| Blooms in summer | Typically purple; sometimes pink or white | Yes |
| Blooms in summer and fall | Typically yellow or orange; sometimes a range of colors | Yes |
| Blooms spring through fall | Range of colors | Yes |
| Blooms spring through fall | Purple or white | Yes |
| Blooms spring into summer | Purple | Yes |
| Blooms summer into fall | Range of colors | Yes |
| Blooms in summer and fall | Typically yellow; available in a range of colors | Yes |
| Blooms spring through summer; established plants are frost tolerant | White or purple | Yes |
| Blooms summer into fall; frost tolerant | Typically white or purple; range of colors available | Yes |
| Blooms spring through fall | Range of colors | Yes |

CHAPTER 5

# EXPLORING *Planting* STYLES

**PLANTING STYLE AFFECTS** both form and function, and while it's certainly possible, even encouraged, to play around with different planting styles in the same garden, it's helpful to choose your styles before planting, at least at the beginning of the gardening year. Some styles will be more permanent, such as a food forest that uses foundational plantings, including perennials. Others, like block planting, you can try for a year, and if they don't work for you or your space, you can move on to try something else. Gardening is about experimentation and finding your own way; there's no right or wrong answer when it comes to planting style.

When choosing a planting style, consider a few key factors of your garden: overall size, bed type, and whether you'll focus on annual vegetables or a mix of annuals and perennials, possibly even herbs and flowers mixed in with your veggies. A large garden (1,000 square feet or more) allows room for traditional row planting, where lots of space is given between plants, while a small garden (500 square feet or less) will benefit, especially in terms of yields, from intensive techniques such as matrix and succession planting (see page 84).

It's unlikely you'll choose just one style, though. Instead, mix it up! Here are some examples of mixing planting styles in your garden.

- If you're growing in rectangular raised beds, block planting (including square-foot gardening) would be a logical approach, and you could also try vertical planting with a trellis along one side.

- With an in-ground garden, play with a more layered planting style throughout, mixing taller plants with shorter and vining crops; you can also interplant herbs and flowers, which add beauty and help with pollination.

- Just because you grow systematically in rows or blocks in one raised bed doesn't mean you can't try chaos gardening—randomly scattering seeds and seeing what happens—in another. Allow yourself the flexibility to try new things.

Planting style does determine, in part, the look of the garden. If you prefer a more orderly aesthetic, rows or blocks are a good pick. If you like a looser look, you might start planting in a layered style. But perhaps more important than looks, planting style also determines how the garden is maintained, and it can also affect what and how much the garden produces. Plant spacing varies significantly among styles, and as some plants can be spaced closer together than others, some styles are more suitable to one plant or another.

Casual vegetable gardens like this one offer a lot of opportunity for layered plantings and combining a variety of plant sizes, textures, and growth habits together.

Structured garden layouts like this one are perfect for formal homes or highly visible areas.

Soil prep will also be different in one style versus another. For example, in an edible landscape each individual planting hole can be amended with compost, whereas in a row garden compost can be turned in or layered on a long bed. It will be easier to employ row covers for insect control or frost protection in a row garden or raised beds planted in blocks than in a matrix garden with layered plantings. How the garden is watered will also be affected. Many irrigation systems, including highly efficient drip tape, are best employed with more ordered, straight planting styles.

All of these considerations are discussed in the following descriptions of planting styles. Remember, you can mix and match in your garden, but some styles may be better suited to your space. Work with what you have, but don't be afraid to test out new things.

# GROWING *for* ORDER

**STYLES BASED ON ORDER** and tidiness include row planting, block planting, and container planting. Typically, in these styles, each plant has its own space, and multiples of a plant are placed all together in one area, whether it be in a line (row), rectangle (block), or circle (container). Grouping plants in this way creates a regimented look and feel that extends to the maintenance, which is simplified in terms of scheduling. But simplified scheduling doesn't necessarily mean less maintenance in the acts of weeding, watering, or plant protection. While these styles may be precise, there are upsides and downsides to every planting style.

## ROW PLANTING

Row planting is a classic style, reminiscent of a farm—it's often called a conventional garden. Tidy and orderly, rows can be ideal when you have plenty of space and when your terrain is relatively flat. Row beds are typically evenly spaced, 1 to 2 feet in width, with enough path room between to allow for walking, kneeling, and pushing a wheelbarrow to work in the garden. Paths are often mulched to prevent weeds, and the row itself is the cultivated soil for growing plants. Row planting offers simplified cultivation.

If rows are narrow, such as 1 foot wide, and paths are at least 2 feet wide (enough space for a wheelbarrow), then much of the overall space is given to paths rather than to growing. Wider rows of 2 or 3 feet are a good option for maximizing growing space using row planting.

Some of the benefits of row planting include:

**Plenty of airflow:** Evenly and amply spacing plants allows plenty of airflow between them. Airflow can help prevent the spread of disease that happens when plants are cramped and the leaves aren't able to dry out; disease and fungus, such as powdery mildew, often spread through wet leaves. This open space, though, can allow weeds to creep in, so staying on top of weeding is essential in a row garden.

Traditional row planting makes seeding, cultivation, and harvesting easier thanks to walking space in between rows. Mulching the walking paths is a good idea to reduce weeds.

**Simplicity of planning:** In row planting, multiples of the same plant are typically grouped together. So, all your tomatoes together within a row, all beans together, squash together—you get the idea. Taking it further, you can plant by plant family; tomatoes, peppers, eggplant, and potatoes could be placed together because they are related (*Solanaceae*). There is some belief that this can create mini monocultures, making your plants recognizable and attractive to pests, but the simplicity of planting in this manner is undeniable.

Exploring Planting Styles   77

Tall, indeterminate tomatoes like these are easy to harvest when planted in rows and secured neatly to hardwood stakes.

You can also mix and match row width depending on the crop. Adjusting row width to the crop can be a good way of using space more efficiently and effectively.

- **3-foot rows** are good for leafy crops like lettuce, spinach, kale, chard, and mustard. They grow well (and are easy to harvest) when planted intensively.
- **2-foot rows** work for tomatoes, corn, summer squash, and other larger plants that need more space.
- **1-foot rows** suit root and bulb crops like onions, garlic, beets, and carrots.

In the Northern Hemisphere, the preferred way to orient rows is east to west (or, alternatively, north to south), with taller crops planted on the north side and shorter plants toward the southern end. This will help prevent the taller plants from shading out the shorter ones. But when planting on a slope, keep rows perpendicular to the slope to avoid erosion, regardless of the direction.

Any crop can be grown in rows, and spacing of plants will vary widely and depend on the plant. While rows are typical for in-ground gardens, you can take the row approach in raised beds as well.

## BLOCK PLANTING

Similar to row planting, the block planting style satisfies the need for order, but when compared to row gardening, blocking suits smaller gardens and can be more efficient in terms of growing space. Blocks are essentially short, wide rows or rectangles, and they can run across a longer bed, whether an in-ground or raised bed. Here are some examples of the block planting style:

- Four 2- x 4-foot blocks in a 4- x 8-foot raised bed will make it easy to access all of the plants from each long side (in the raised bed, paths aren't necessary)
- Multiple 2- x 3-foot to 6- x 3-foot blocks with 1- to 2-foot paths in between, in a larger, in-ground garden

Compared to row planting, block planting can reduce weeding by minimizing the amount of bare ground. Setting up irrigation may be a bit more complicated than with row planting, though not by much; the linear style is still suitable for drip irrigation (see page 169). As with row planting, the systematic nature of this planting style, and its emphasis on planting the same plant (or plants of the same family) together, lends easily to crop rotation. The number of plants per block depends on the plant.

**Easier crop rotation:** Planting in groups in rows makes crop rotation much simpler, and rotating crops can be an effective way to avoid insect issues and disease. In crop rotation, crops of the same family are grouped together and rotated around the garden season after season so that plants of the same family aren't planted in the same spot for at least a few years, sometimes longer depending on the plant and the size of the garden. Rotating crops helps prevent the buildup of soilborne diseases and pests, which often affect plants of the same family. It is much easier to keep track of crop rotation when plants are grouped together by family.

Some gardeners will use the row style but also plant intensively in wide rows about 3 feet across, getting the benefits of row-style planting while lessening the potential drawback of space inefficiency. With rows 3 feet wide, it's still easy to reach the center of the bed from either side without straining or needing to step into the growing bed, which can compact soil.

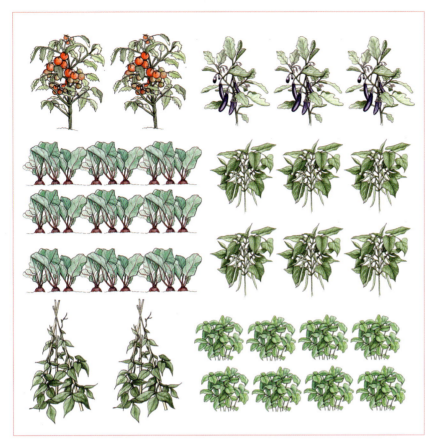

This illustration shows block planting in a square garden. Each crop is planted in its own section of the bed, simplifying maintenance, harvesting, and crop rotation.

What grows best in a block:

- Beets
- Broccoli
- Cabbage
- Carrots
- Corn
- Greens
- Lettuce
- Eggplant
- Peppers
- Radishes

Corn grows particularly well using this method because it is wind-pollinated. Growing corn in a block at least five rows wide and deep helps ensure that pollen travels from plant to plant as the wind moves through.

What doesn't grow best in a block:

- Beans
- Cucumbers
- Peas
- Tomatoes

Because they need trellising, tomatoes and cucumbers are less suited to block planting, though they can be integrated into a block-style garden. Beans and peas, because they need to be trellised and harvested from each side, are better suited to row planting—though again, the block and row styles are similar and can be employed together.

## *Square Foot Gardening*

A specific and popular method of block planting is square foot gardening. Designed and coined by Mel Bartholomew in his early 1980s book *Square Foot Gardening*, the system is organized around 1- x 1-foot squares, or blocks, using carefully determined spacing. The goal of square foot gardening is to grow the maximum amount of produce in a space, with less maintenance (such as weeding) than a row garden. Beds are ideally 4 x 4 feet with paths at least 2 feet wide between. Each bed is divided into 16 squares, and each square holds a different vegetable, flower, or herb.

The number of plants per square depends on the plant, but the method outlines specific numbers and spacing per plant—for example, 1 pepper plant per square, 4 lettuce plants, or 16 carrot plants. In the square foot method, all vining plants are grown vertically to maximize space. This style claims to produce the same amount of produce as a row garden in one-fifth of the space! Square foot gardening originally was meant to move gardeners away from the row method and the modeling of home gardening after agriculture; its efficiency appealed to an increasingly suburban population, and still does today.

# CONTAINER PLANTING

For anyone without an in-ground garden space, container gardening provides the ideal planting style. Containers can be grouped or scattered around a patio, arranged on a balcony or rooftop, or even lined up along a driveway. The plant spacing for the block planting style can be used as a general guide for planting in containers, although containers tend to dry out more quickly than in-ground gardens or raised beds, so bigger—meaning more soil in the container—is usually better. Also consider plant roots; shallow-rooted plants like lettuce can grow in only a few inches of soil, while deeply rooted plants like tomatoes need more soil depth.

If your space gets full sun, it's possible to grow almost any vegetable in a container—as long as the container is large enough. Here are general guidelines for pot sizes by plant:

- 10 to 14 inches wide and 6 or more inches deep for shallow-rooted plants like lettuce, greens, cabbage, and strawberries

- 18 inches wide and 12 inches deep for medium plants like broccoli, cauliflower, large cabbage, eggplant, peppers, or compact tomatoes

- 24 inches wide and 18 inches deep for summer squash, tomatoes, cucumbers, artichokes, or a mixed planting

Material is another key factor in container gardening success. Unglazed terra cotta pots dry out the fastest, while glazed clay and plastic retain water better. The color of the pot affects the soil temperature; black or dark-colored containers retain heat, while white or light-colored pots reflect heat. So consider the plant's soil, temperature, and water needs when choosing container material. Some ideas:

- Plant eggplant—which needs a lot of heat and a good amount of water—in a large black plastic pot to give it the best possible conditions, or in a metal container that would also retain heat.

- Choose a small terra cotta planter for your thyme, as this Mediterranean herb needs the soil to dry out between watering.

- Upcycled half barrels are a good option for larger plants such as tomatoes. They dry out, but not too quickly, and they hold a lot of soil.

Growing vegetables in containers large or small yields excellent (and beautiful!) results.

Whatever container you choose, be sure it has good drainage, including an unobstructed drainage hole, as no vegetable plant wants a waterlogged pot. Soil needs to drain well, but plants will also need to be watered more often than in other gardening styles, sometimes twice daily (morning and night) in the heat of summer, particularly if you live in a hot Southern climate. Self-watering planters can help with this increased watering schedule, and tube irrigation can also be run to individual containers.

This rooftop container garden is growing in fabric grow bags, a lightweight way to grow.

Perhaps more than any other planting style, container planting lends itself to myriad visual styles. The gardener's choice of container colors and materials not only serves a function but also suits one aesthetic or another. And planting choices within the containers also create a visual effect. For example, you could plant one plant per pot, with the pot size and material suited perfectly to the individual plant—a good approach to maximize yield of harvest. Or you could mix plants together in the same pot, choosing a pot large enough to suit the combination of plants.

One popular method, or recipe, for container planting uses three plants in a container, each chosen for their growth habit. The recipe calls for:

- 1 thriller (a tall, upright plant) in the center or back
- 1 filler (a mounding plant) in the side or center
- 1 spiller (a trailing or vining plant) along the rim of the pot

Plants will be spaced closer together than in a row or block garden. Also, you'll need to account for any plant supports—such as a stake for a tomato plant (a thriller)—in your plan at planting time, whether using the single plant per pot method or mixing plants together.

Exploring Planting Styles   81

# GETTING INTENSIVE

**IN VEGETABLE GARDENING,** planting intensively allows you to make the most of the space you have. The goal is to increase yields without sacrificing soil health, even boosting it if possible. In intensive gardening, as much soil as possible is covered with plants and put to use. The look of this planting style veers away from those traditional, tidy rows to a more full, and perhaps less orderly, look.

So, what classifies as intensive planting style? We'll discuss many methods, but it starts as simply as spacing plants more closely than is generally recommended on plant tags or other guides. A little secret is that most spacing requirements for vegetables are based on field trialing, meaning testing the performance and yield of specific varieties grown in a farm-style setting using row-style planting. The spacing of plants in rows is farther apart, allowing for airflow between plants and making harvest—by hand or by machine—easier. There are definite advantages to row planting and wide spacing, but there are advantages to planting closely too.

## ADVANTAGES OF INTENSIVE PLANTING

Consider the advantages of intensive methods to decide if this style is right for you. Space constrictions may force you into planting intensively, but the other advantages may help you come to love this style of growing.

**Maximizing space.** Planting closely allows you to grow more plants in a given area, making it useful in small spaces like urban gardens.

**Reducing weeds.** Covering the bare soil with plants you intend to grow makes less space for plants you don't intend to grow: weeds. Having fewer weeds saves you time and effort.

**Protecting soil.** As vegetable plants shade out weeds, they also shade the soil and keep it in place, preventing soil from drying out or eroding.

**Helping with insects.** Methods of intensive gardening that use mixed plantings can attract beneficial insects that prey on other insects aiming for your crops. A mix of plants can also confuse insects that may harm your plants.

**Increasing the harvest.** Comparing close planting to row planting, a well-managed intensive garden may grow more in the same square footage.

Additionally, a closely planted garden has a lush look many gardeners love. Add in mixed planting methods and layering, and an intensive garden can achieve a natural style that's usually reserved for perennial plantings.

Intensive planting involves close spacing and incorporating an array of plant heights and structures together to maximize production from small spaces.

When using the intensive planting style, be sure to leave room to step into the garden for maintenance and harvesting.

## DISADVANTAGES OF INTENSIVE PLANTING

Of course, there are disadvantages to intensive planting too. Rows are rows for a reason, and when you abandon more orderly planting styles, you should know the potential pitfalls.

**Increased work.** Though not guaranteed, intensive planting could mean more planning and maintenance to keep closely planted crops in check.

**More water and nutrients.** Since plants are competing for resources, you may need to water and feed plants—and soil—more often.

**Ineffective watering.** When plants are tightly packed, it can be tempting to water overhead, which leads to foliage diseases on many plants. Instead, think ahead and consider installing drip irrigation or soaker hoses before planting (see page 169).

**Stepping on plants.** If you are growing intensively in the ground, it's important to leave some bare space where you can walk. In raised beds (which we'll discuss on page 125), make sure you can reach all your plants—generally, a 4-foot-wide bed allows you to reach the center.

**Disease issues.** Close spacing of plants means diseases—and insects that spread them—can travel quickly from plant to plant. Wet conditions make diseases more likely to spread, so it's vital to water from below.

Exploring Planting Styles  **83**

This gardener has planted a succession planting of carrots in place of spring peas that were recently pulled from the garden.

Staggered sowings of cucumber seeds in this garden have resulted in a row of slightly older seedlings on the outside of the trellis, with a younger planting on the inside of the trellis. Succession planting like this results in a more extended harvest.

## SUCCESSION PLANTING

To increase your harvests, rely on succession planting. Succession planting is the practice of staggering plantings to provide a continual harvest through the growing season or year. Succession planting can mean planting smaller quantities of the same crop at staggered intervals. This is especially helpful with root crops such as radishes that produce one harvest per plant—you pull them up and they're done—as opposed to fruiting plants that continue producing even after the first harvest. It can also be helpful with lettuces and other greens and herbs that are prone to bolting, such as arugula and cilantro. If you stagger planting by a few weeks, as soon as the first crop bolts, your second crop of leaves will be ready for harvest.

Some crops that are good for this type of succession planting—staggering sowings every 2 to 3 weeks for a continual harvest—include:

- Arugula
- Beets
- Bush beans
- Carrots
- Cilantro
- Lettuce
- Peas
- Radishes
- Spinach

Succession planting can also mean staggering plantings of different crops in the same spot. As you start to see the growing seasons as more than just separate pieces (spring, summer, fall, winter), and instead see the seasonal cycle as one continuum, you'll see opportunities for this type of succession planting.

For example, you might grow snap peas in a spot in early spring, then pull those plants as the weather warms in late spring and replace them with peppers that grow through summer. After the pepper harvest starts to wane in early fall, you can pull those plants and grow a quick crop of fall lettuce in the same spot before winter comes. Be sure to consider plant families and crop rotation as you succession plant through the year; avoid growing crops of the same family in the same spot over and over. It's better to mix it up.

# INTERPLANTING

Interplanting basically means planting multiple crops together in the same place rather than separating them out one plant per spot. Most other landscapes and gardens not meant for production have a mixed style, but vegetable gardening traditionally has kept the same plants together in the same place for ease of planning and harvest.

Interplanting can also be called intercropping, mixed planting, or—a more orchestrated version—mixed matrix planting. Mixed matrix style purposefully incorporates a variety of plants chosen to vary their colors, heights, textures, bloom times, and fruiting or harvest times through the growing season.

Benefits of interplanting include:

**Diversified harvests.** You can grow more types of plants in the same space. This is especially useful for small gardens.

**Increased biodiversity.** Growing a mix of plants invites a mix of other creatures into your garden, including many pollinators and other beneficial insects. Biodiversity can lead to better resilience in the face of pressures like diseases.

**"Gardeny" style.** Mixed planting makes a vegetable garden look and feel more like other types of gardens, such as perennial gardens and cottage gardens, and less like a mini farm.

Interplanting results not only in more plants in a given space but also in a beautiful garden environment.

Exploring Planting Styles 85

Simple bamboo teepees are great structures for vertical growing, particularly for pole beans, whose twining vines easily wrap around the poles.

When choosing crops to interplant, consider their light, water, and nutrient requirements—plants with similar requirements can be mixed together. But it can be helpful to also consider their roots and mix plants that have different root depths. Shallow-rooted plants like spinach, lettuce, corn, and cabbage can be mixed with more deeply rooted plants like cucumbers, tomatoes, peppers, beans, and squash. But try to avoid mixing deeply rooted crops together, because they will compete for water and nutrients. That also goes for crops grown specifically for their roots, such as carrots, radishes, and beets—they grow well with shallow-rooted plants, but it's best not to grow them with other root crops or deeply rooted crops.

## VERTICAL AND LAYERED PLANTING

Another version of intensive style is vertical gardening. There are so many ways to grow vertically! Adding trellises and other structures enables you to grow many plants up, saving lots of garden space. It also gives a garden height and visual interest. There's the added benefit of being able to care for and harvest crops without bending and kneeling, so vertical gardening can be useful for anyone with limited mobility. And growing plants vertically improves airflow, preventing many fungal diseases caused by cramped plants, and enables them to get plenty of sunlight, potentially increasing yields.

Support structures for vertical growing include:

- Trellises
- Stakes
- Cages
- Netting
- Arches
- String
- Wire
- A-frames

It's important to plan ahead when growing plants up trellises and other structures. Install the support before you plant; this avoids damaging roots by sticking a stake or cage in the ground after the roots have already developed. Knowing you will be growing plants vertically also helps you plan for interplanting. For example, you can install a trellis, sow peas at the base to climb the trellis, and then plant lettuce on the other side; the lettuce will get a little shade from the pea trellis, which may help the lettuce produce longer before bolting when the weather warms.

Peas produce small tendrils from their nodes; these allow the plants to grip onto trellises and climb.

Cattle panel arches are a popular way to grow heavier climbing vegetables, such as winter squash, pumpkins, melons, and cucumbers.

Exploring Planting Styles **87**

Vegetables suited to vertical growing include tomatoes, cucumbers, squash, pole beans, peas, and smaller-fruited melons and winter squash. Unless it's a dwarf or container variety, tomatoes really do need to be grown with some kind of vertical support, as do peas and pole beans. Growing the others vertically is optional, but they really benefit from vertical growing—and look great while doing it. If trying melons and squash vertically, they need a heavy-duty trellis like steel mesh, as well as additional support from slings or netting as the heavy fruits grow.

While trellising techniques used in vertical gardening can also be used in layered planting, there's a bit more to layered planting. In a layered planting, plants are organized to take advantage of various levels of light. Taller plants should be planted in the back or on the north side, medium-height plants in front or around the taller ones, and shorter plants in front or on the edges. Plants tolerant of light shade can also be placed below taller plants to create layers.

Combining vertical growing with layered planting, as this gardener has done, is yet another way to maximize space. The combination of tall tomatoes with medium-height lettuce and cucumbers that cascade down over the edge of the bed results in greater production from the space.

## Living Mulch

A type of interplanting, underplanting, and layering (with intensive planting, it's all related!) is called living mulch. Mulches perform a vital function in the garden by shading soil to prevent evaporation, erosion, and growth of weeds, and to slightly lower soil temperature (you'll learn more about mulches on page 159). As opposed to regular mulch made of bark, straw, or compost, a living mulch is a plant chosen to perform the same functions.

Living mulches are typically low-growing selections like lettuce, strawberries, and radishes. They can also be vines such as sweet potatoes, cucumbers, Southern peas, and winter squash. Some herbs make good living mulches, including chamomile and thyme. Using a living mulch rather than a static one increases the harvest, supports biodiversity, and can improve the soil; as nitrogen fixers, living mulches that are legumes (like Southern peas) actually boost soil fertility.

A note on cucumbers: If you use cucumber as a living mulch, be sure to plant the taller plant (like tomato or eggplant) first, as cucumbers produce chemicals that can prevent seeds from germinating. That makes it good for preventing weeds, but it can also hinder growth of other crops, especially if planting them from seed.

Employing a living mulch, such as the clover beneath these pole beans, helps protect the soil from erosion and reduces weeds.

While the height of vegetables varies by variety and growing technique, here's a general list of vegetables organized by their height, which is useful when considering planting in vertical layers.

**Taller Vegetables**
- Artichoke
- Asparagus
- Corn
- Beans (on trellis)
- Cucumber (on trellis)
- Okra
- Peas (on trellis)
- Tomato (on trellis)
- Winter squash (on trellis)

**Medium-Height Vegetables**
- Broccoli
- Brussels sprouts
- Cauliflower
- Collards
- Eggplant
- Kale
- Pepper
- Potato
- Rhubarb
- Summer squash
- Swiss chard

**Shorter Vegetables**
- Arugula
- Beets
- Cabbage
- Melon
- Cucumber
- Garlic
- Lettuce
- Mustard greens
- Onion
- Pumpkin
- Radish
- Spinach

Exploring Planting Styles

# ALTERNATIVE STYLES

Edible landscaping involves incorporating edible plants into your overall landscaping, as this gardener has done in their front yard. The benefits are obvious!

**PART OF WHAT MAKES** vegetable gardening fun is the opportunity for innovation. Consider the history of crops. Most of them didn't start out being great to eat, even if they were edible, but over years and generations of innovation, human gardeners and farmers developed the amazing-tasting plant-based foods we now love to eat and grow. It's the same with planting styles. Necessity breeds innovation, and cultures all over the world have developed planting styles out of necessity—and sometimes just out of creativity. Let's explore some you may want to try at home.

## EDIBLE LANDSCAPING

While it became popular in America in the late twentieth century, edible landscaping isn't necessarily a new idea. British gardeners have mixed ornamental and edible plants for centuries, and ancient Persian gardeners were known for incorporating edibles in with ornamentals too. Edible landscaping takes the principles of landscape design and incorporates productive plants, such as vegetables. This doesn't sound too rebellious, but it may be for many suburbanites in the United States. Those living in neighborhoods with restrictions that ban vegetables from front yard gardens—considering them too messy—take a risk (albeit a small, social one) when sneaking peppers in beside their peonies.

With full-blown edible landscape plans, fruit trees, nut trees, berry shrubs, and grape vines can all be incorporated. But it's also possible to add a few vegetables and herbs here and there to a traditional landscape that features nonedible trees and shrubs. It's important to still consider the light, water, and soil needs of your plants. Though you may not be able to give them ideal conditions like in your vegetable garden, do the best you can.

Find spots with full sun, even if the sun is only available for a few months in early spring until a deciduous tree's leaves return. When planting annual vegetables, incorporate some compost into planting holes to give them the nutrition they need. You may also need to water extra if your landscape doesn't have irrigation, as neighboring tree roots could sip up all the water. Also, be sure you're not using any fertilizers, herbicides, or other additives in your landscape that you wouldn't want used on your organic crops!

Here are a few more tips for planting veggies into your landscape.

**Go for color.** Choose annual vegetables to fill in and add color around trees and shrubs the same way you would use annual flowers. Good low-growing options include Swiss chard, lettuce, and purple kale. These cool-season crops grow best in spring and fall, but they may also grow into summer if provided partial shade. Beautiful upright options include peppers and eggplants; their jewel-like fruits add surprising pops of color.

**Incorporate herbs.** Some perennial herbs—including thyme, rosemary, lavender, and oregano—work well as groundcovers or border plants. Annual herbs such as basil also work well in sunny spots, and some selections have beautiful color and form; look for columnar basils with an upright habit and purple basil varieties with showy leaves and flowers.

**Hide in plain sight.** Small root crops and edible bulbs can be interplanted in a landscape and barely noticed. Tuck garlic, onions, beets, and radishes in wherever you find the space. As a cold-season crop, garlic can add some green to an otherwise drab winter landscape. And quick-growing radishes will be ready to harvest before the neighbors even know.

## FOOD FORESTS

Forest gardening has been practiced by Indigenous woodland people all over the world for thousands of years. This style of gardening works with the forest rather than against it, and proponents of permaculture (a system of agriculture based on mimicking natural ecosystems and eliminating waste) adapted this genius idea to create the style of planting known as a food forest. A food forest mimics natural woodland ecosystems with food plants such as fruit and nut trees, berries, perennial vegetables, and annual crops.

Like in a natural forest, considering layers—and how they interconnect—is essential to planning and caring for the food forest. Unlike a typical vegetable garden, most plantings are permanent, so it's vital to have a solid plan in place before planting. If you're interested in biodiversity and sustainability—as we all should be—research food forests more. Here's a basic overview of the layers in a food forest planting scheme.

- **Canopy:** large fruit and nut trees
- **Sub-canopy:** smaller, dwarf fruit trees
- **Shrubs:** fruit-bearing shrubs, including berries
- **Herbaceous:** perennial vegetables and herbs
- **Ground cover:** low, spreading plants that prevent weed growth
- **Root zone:** root crops in the top layer of soil, called the rhizosphere
- **Vertical:** vines that grow on trees and other structures

Food-forest gardening combines edible annuals, perennials, vines, root crops, and even woody plants like trees and shrubs together to create a forestlike environment for long-term food production.

Exploring Planting Styles  91

Food forests and other permaculture gardens also sometimes employ a historic planting style called hügelkultur. The German name denotes its European origins, and it makes use of woody material rather than discarding it as most vegetable gardening styles would. Gardeners create hügelkultur raised beds by piling up branches, prunings, and brush, adding compostable material such as straw, compost, and soil, and watering it well. Eventually, the free-form beds decompose to form a spongy medium that's good for growing potatoes, squash, and melons.

## CHAOS GARDENING

Far afield from the traditional row-style vegetable garden, chaos gardening—also called random gardening—relies on virtually no planning at all. Chaos gardens usually include a mix of flowers, herbs, and vegetables sown by scattering seeds randomly and allowing them to sprout and grow at will. A chaos garden is not about how much food can be produced. It's more about being surprised that food can be produced at all with so little intention or attention! Chaos gardens are also about supporting wildlife and the natural ecosystem.

To start your chaos garden, prepare the soil, whether in-ground or in a raised bed. You'll want the soil to be as loose and well-draining as possible, so it's a good idea to add a layer of compost. Mix flower, herb, and vegetable seeds together, then scatter them over the plot. Tamp down the seeds, making sure they make good contact with the earth; you can also lightly cover them with additional soil. Water

Chaos gardening is a more casual way to grow. It is entirely random and typically involves mixing edibles and flowers that are sown from scattered seed. It's less predictable than other methods of growing, but it can also be lower maintenance.

# DESIGN STYLE QUICK REFERENCE

| | SPACE | BED TYPE | VISUAL STYLE | PRIMARY PLANT TYPES | MAINTENANCE | PRODUCTIVITY |
|---|---|---|---|---|---|---|
| **ROW** | Large | In Ground | Ordered | Annual | High | High |
| **BLOCK** | Any | Any | Ordered | Annual | Medium | High |
| **CONTAINER** | Small | Container | Ordered | Annual, Biennial, Perennial | Medium | High |
| **SUCCESSION** | Any | Any | Varies | Annual, Biennial | High | High |
| **INTERPLANTING** | Any | Any | Mixed | Annual, Biennial, Perennial | Medium | Medium |
| **VERTICAL** | Any | Any | Mixed | Annual | Medium | Medium |
| **EDIBLE LANDSCAPE** | Any | In Ground | Mixed | Annual, Biennial, Perennial | Light | Medium |
| **FOOD FOREST** | Large | In Ground | Mixed | Perennial | Medium | Medium |
| **CHAOS** | Small | Any | Random | Annual, Biennial, Perennial | Light | Low |

lightly and occasionally as seeds sprout and begin to grow. That's really it! But here are some additional things to think about with this random planting style.

- **Consider light conditions.** Mix sun-loving seeds together or shade-loving seeds together.

- **Choose shallow-sown seeds.** Lettuce, greens, and basil can be sown ¼ inch or less and still grow.

- **Know your climate.** If you have a long warm season, tomatoes and peppers may have time to mature if sown directly outdoors. Areas with shorter growing seasons require faster-maturing crops for chaos gardening.

- **Know your neighbors.** Communicating with neighbors about this style can help them understand your goal.

- **Grow nearly wild varieties.** For tomatoes, try 'Matt's Wild Cherry' and let it ramble without trellising.

- **Let plants bolt and bloom.** Don't intervene when plants bolt or self-sow. It's part of the chaos.

- **But do pull some weeds.** If crabgrass or other weeds creep into your chaos garden, take the time to pull them out, or they'll take over.

No matter which gardening style (or combination of styles) you choose, know that it will change and develop over time. As the years pass and you become more familiar with your space, adaptations will undoubtedly be made. Now that you know the different planting style options and which vegetables you want to grow, it's time to dig in and get your garden started. The next chapter covers the essential task of preparing the site for planting.

Exploring Planting Styles **93**

CHAPTER 6

# SOIL *and* SITE PREP

**THERE IS NO SUCH THING** as perfect soil; the properties you relish depend on the soil's intended purpose. To an engineer, supreme soil provides a solid foundation to build on. To a pedologist (soil scientist), exemplary soil contains many layers of decomposed rock that reveal the stories of an ancient Earth. But to gardeners, the ultimate soil is light and airy, drains well, and is rich in nutrients.

This chapter dives into the nitty-gritty of soil. You'll learn about fundamental properties, such as texture and structure, that give soil its unique personality. This chapter also covers the vibrant living world beneath your feet and the importance of nurturing this soil ecosystem. By the end of the chapter, you'll discover how to create high-quality garden soil and identify the factors that indicate soil health. Chapter 8, Garden and Plant Care, returns to the subject of garden soil to offer advice on maintaining healthy soil throughout each gardening season. The current chapter also covers the preparation of garden sites, including growing in the ground, raised beds, or containers.

# The NITTY-GRITTY ABOUT SOIL

**A BASIC DEFINITION** of soil is that it is a matrix of solid fragments, air, water, and living organisms. The solid bits are a combination of inorganic minerals intertwined with organic plant and animal remains known as organic matter. The unique blend of minerals and organic matter imparts specific soil properties that influence the movement of air, water, and nutrients. Some properties are intrinsic, while others adapt with the proper ministrations over time.

Soil formation is a long process in which solid rock (bedrock) is weathered by wind, rain, and ice into primary soil minerals. These minerals are classified by size, from the tiniest specks of clay to larger grains of sand. Over time, they accumulate in place or are transported by wind or water. As soil settles, distinct layers—called horizons—develop. The top layer, or A horizon, is the foundation for all plant life and is highly regarded by gardeners.

The quality of topsoil largely depends on the amount of organic matter present to support an essential community of soilborne organisms that naturally build soil over time. The soil-building practices outlined in the rest of this chapter hinge on supporting and nurturing this community. After mastering the basics of soil-building, you'll be able to leverage your soil's strengths instead of fighting its weaknesses.

## THE LIVING SOIL

The mineral, air, and water components of soil account for more than 90 percent of its composition. Although organic matter makes up only a small fraction (typically ranging from 5 to 10 percent of the soil's total composition), it plays a crucial role as it is home to the living soil. Ecologists estimate that soil is home to nearly 59 percent of all living creatures on Earth, from the smallest bacteria, fungi, and protozoa to larger worms, snails, and bugs. Experts agree this is likely an underestimate, given how little we know about this critical habitat.

The definition of living soil varies, but for organic gardeners, it is best to think of it as a community of soil organisms that work together to break down organic matter to build soil health and provide plant nutrition. This breakdown of organic matter—be it twigs, leaves, or dead animals—is the basis of decomposition.

Decomposition is a cycle driven by groups of organic matter gatherers, shredders, and eaters that comprise the soil food web. At the end of the process, animal and plant remains are broken down to such a degree that they resemble their most basic molecules.

What remains is often called humus, a dark, spongy material that fertile soils have lots of. While some experts argue over the true definition of humus, gardeners say you can't buy it, but you can build it. Humus is created in place only through the extraordinary action and connection of soil organisms.

This soil horizon diagram shows the different layers that make up the upper portion of the Earth's crust. From bottom to top, the layers are: bedrock and parent rock, subsoil, topsoil, and the organic humus layer.

Healthy soil doesn't happen overnight. Fertile growing areas are the result of regular additions of organic matter and help from the soil food web.

An active part of the soil community lives in and around plant roots—a zone known as the rhizosphere. This area is a hot spot for teamwork. Plants ooze a sugary substance from their roots to encourage a collection of microbes, fungi, and insects to stay close. In turn, these organisms provide the plant with certain nutrients, fend off underground pests and diseases, reduce watering needs, limit erosion, and aerate the soil.

There is also evidence that soil organisms play a key role in carbon storage, a meaningful way to draw down atmospheric carbon dioxide to mitigate the impacts of climate change. While the amount of soil carbon storage is still disputed among experts, there is no denying that fostering a thriving community in your garden soil will lead to success in many ways. Therefore, understanding how to support a diverse, well-fed, and active soil community is more than a nerdy pleasure—it's vital.

Adding organic matter, such as this compost, to garden beds provides food for the many soil organisms that live in partnership with our plants.

Soil and Site Prep  **97**

# Meet the Living Soil MVPs

Living soil is the driving force behind the decomposition process, which is vital in enhancing soil health, recycling nutrients that plants require, and generating carbon-stable humus. Despite scientists acknowledging soil as one of the planet's most diverse ecosystems, they have yet to uncover even a fraction of its community and fully comprehend the range of services it provides.

## BACTERIA

Did you know that a tiny amount of soil—just one teaspoonful—can contain between 100 million and 1 billion of these single-celled organisms? Amazingly, most bacteria remain unnamed and undiscovered. Among these tiny creatures, there are two types: aerobic bacteria that thrive in oxygen-rich environments and anaerobic bacteria that prefer habitats with low oxygen levels.

**Role:** There are four main functional groups of bacteria: (1) Decomposers that break down organic matter, (2) Mutualist bacteria that form relationships with plants and include nitrogen-fixing bacteria, (3) Disease-promoting bacteria, like blights, and (4) Lithotrophic bacteria that consume minerals (rather than organic matter).

**Habitat:** Bacteria live in the thin films of water surrounding soil particles or along the edges of mineral particles and organic residue.

**Benefits:** They support nutrient cycling and availability, improve soil structure, and enhance water retention. A diverse population of soil bacteria also helps produce antibiotics to protect plants from pathogens.

## FUNGI

Fungi are neither plants nor animals and represent their own kingdom. Experts cannot pinpoint how many species of fungi reside in the soil, but roughly 170,000 species have been identified, and many more are expected.

**Role:** Fungi play a significant role in the decomposition of organic matter. They break down materials other organisms cannot. More than 80 percent of plants form a symbiotic relationship with mycorrhizae, a type of fungi that forms long filaments, creating a complex network. These filaments release enzymes that decompose organic matter into nutrients, which fungi then absorb and transport to plants. In return, plants exchange those nutrients with fungi in exchange for sugars.

**Habitat:** Fungi compose 10 to 30 percent of all biomass in and around plant roots.

**Benefits:** Fungi are crucial in capturing carbon, cycling nutrients, improving soil structure, and retaining water. It is now believed plants can communicate with each other and share nutrients through the vast network of mycorrhizae.

## PROTOZOA

Protozoa are known as single-celled animals. These tiny and motile creatures can be as small as 1 micrometer or several millimeters long. Around 1,600 species of soil protozoa have been identified with distinct adaptations to survive on land, in contrast to their aquatic counterparts. Once again, experts anticipate discovering many more species over time.

**Role:** These creatures graze on bacteria and fungal spores.

**Habitat:** Protozoa live in the thin layer of water between soil particles and organic matter, sharing the same habitat as their primary food source.

**Benefits:** They regulate bacterial populations and release nutrients for plant growth that would otherwise remain locked up in microbial biomass.

## NEMATODES

Nematodes are tiny, wormlike creatures found in soil. According to some studies, there can be up to 10 million nematodes in 1 square meter of soil. These creatures play an important role in soil-building, but this aspect of their biology is not well explored by scientists. While scientists have studied parasitic nematodes that attack plant roots, little is known about the beneficial nematodes that feed on bacteria and help improve soil health.

**Role:** They feed on many soil organisms, including bacteria, protozoa, insect larvae, and other nematodes.

**Habitat:** Like many of the smallest soil organisms, nematodes live in the thin films of water that surround soil particles or along the edges of minerals and organic residue.

**Benefits:** They help control the population of soil pests and diseases. They build soil fertility by increasing nutrient availability.

## EARTHWORMS

Earthworms are long, slender, segmented, soil-dwelling invertebrates. Some earthworms have up to 100 separate segments that work independently to relax or contract, which allows them to move through the soil.

**Role:** Worms excrete nutrient-rich soil as castings (worm poop) and create tunnels that aerate and loosen the soil and percolate water.

**Habitat:** Earthworms are abundant in fertile and moist soils as they require moisture to survive.

**Benefits:** They provide soil aeration, nutrient availability, nutrient cycling, and improved soil structure.

*Important note: Some regions of the United States are facing negative impacts from invasive earthworm species such as the Asian jumping worm. These species are capable of quickly consuming leaf litter and other debris, resulting in dramatically increased rates of nutrient cycling and the rapid leaching of soil nutrients.

## INSECTS

There are more than 1 million named species of insects, many of which impact soil in some way. Despite their differences, all insects share some common characteristics. For instance, insect bodies must include a head, an abdomen, a thorax, antennae, and six legs. Some insects have wings for flying, while others have a hard protective exoskeleton.

**Role:** When it comes to soil health, insects are responsible for shredding large pieces of organic matter into smaller pieces, which is an important first step in decomposition. They also consume smaller soil organisms and leave their waste behind, and they tunnel and burrow through the soil, aerating it as they go. Predatory insects can also help control soil-dwelling plant pests.

**Habitat:** Insects crawl through the different layers of soil horizons but are most active in the topsoil.

**Benefits:** This diverse group promotes soil aeration, nutrient availability, nutrient cycling, pest prevention, and improved soil structure.

## SOIL TEXTURE

When you grab a handful of soil, it may feel coarse, like sandpaper, or silky smooth between your fingers. All soil has an inherent texture created from broken-down rock hammered by wind, rain, or waves. The type of rock and the unique weather conditions that degrade the rock create distinct sand, silt, and clay particles.

The size and combination of these particles lay the foundation of your soil's distinct behavior. You may notice your soil drains quickly or remains waterlogged for an extended period after a storm. Your plants may grow abundantly without much attention or struggle to produce a significant yield. The texture of your soil determines these characteristics to some extent.

Scientists highlight the significance of soil texture as an intrinsic factor that plays a crucial role in maintaining a thriving soil ecosystem. For instance, coarse and sandy soils tend to contain a meager amount of organic matter, which is essential for supporting life. These types of soils drain rapidly, leaving both plants and soil organisms dehydrated.

Fine-textured soils, on the other hand, are made from sticky particles of silt and clay. Nutrients, water, and organic matter easily cling to clay particles and provide a welcoming habitat for soil life. The downside is that fine soils are easily waterlogged and squished together, making it difficult for soil organisms and plant roots to prosper.

Luckily, soils are rarely pure sand or clay; they are a mixture. The golden standard of garden soil is loam: roughly 40 percent sand, 40 percent silt, and 20 percent clay. Loam contains plenty of organic matter and nutrients that resist washing away. Loam also holds on to water, but not too long—so soil organisms and plant roots do not suffocate.

Soils have varying textures and structures, depending on the source of their parent materials and how much organic matter is present. Top left is a granular, sandlike structure, and top right is a blocky aggregate structure typical of loam. Bottom left is a prismatic structure, and bottom right is platy, which is typical of clay-based soils.

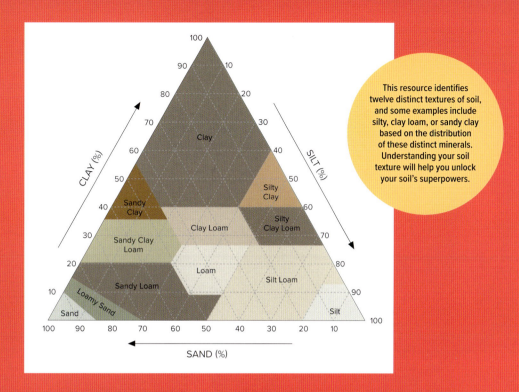

This resource identifies twelve distinct textures of soil, and some examples include silty, clay loam, or sandy clay based on the distribution of these distinct minerals. Understanding your soil texture will help you unlock your soil's superpowers.

## Determining Your Soil Texture

### HOW TO DO A MASON JAR TEST

To determine your soil texture, conduct a simple Mason jar test. Start by filling a Mason jar with at least 2 inches of soil. Next, add water to the top of the jar and mix in a squirt or two of liquid dish soap to help separate the sand, silt, and clay particles. Shake the jar vigorously and leave it to sit for 24 hours. By doing this, the soil will settle into three distinct layers—sand (bottom layer), silt (middle layer), and clay (top layer). After a day has passed, measure the thickness of each layer. Divide the width of each layer by the total height of the original soil sample to reveal the percentages of sand, silt, and clay that make up your soil's texture.

Once you have calculated the percentage of each mineral in the soil, use the soil texture triangle above to chart your soil texture with impressive accuracy. Draw a dot on each axis to mark the percentage of the individual minerals you calculated, forming the sides of the triangle. Use the charted lines within the triangle to connect the dots, and you'll land on your specific soil texture.

Another way to determine your soil's texture is by using the ribbon test, which relies on touch and feel, so no calculations are required.

### HOW TO DO THE RIBBON TEST

Start with a golf ball–sized clump of soil. If your handful is dry, slowly add a drop of water at a time, mixing as you go, until you have a ball of soil with the consistency of sculpting clay. If you have extremely sandy soil, you may never reach this point.

Once your sample is adequately moist, gently roll the ball into the shape of a cigar, using both hands if necessary. Hold the cigar in the palm of your hand and start to press the soil between your thumb and forefinger. Slowly press down the length of the cigar to form a flat ribbon of soil. Keep at it until the ribbon breaks.

If your soil does not form a ribbon at all, it's sandy. If you've grown your ribbon an inch long before it breaks, you may have loam. If your ribbon is 2 or more inches long, you likely have clay soil. Finally, rub the soil between your fingers to hone in on a specific texture combination. If the soil is smooth, it has silty elements. If you feel anything coarse or gritty, it's sand.

Soil and Site Prep

The aggregates in this soil are of various sizes, which means the structure has adequate pore space and is suitable for supporting plant roots.

Poorly structured soils may not drain easily—or they may drain too quickly. Raising planting areas into berms can help overcome soil structures with poor drainage.

## SOIL STRUCTURE

While your soil's texture cannot be changed, its structure is something you can—and should—improve. Soil structure is the arrangement of sand, silt, and clay particles into clumps known as aggregates. Aggregates, glued together by sticky clays, plant roots, and glomalin (a gluelike substance that some beneficial fungi ooze), form even larger masses called peds. Peds can be round with smooth edges, blocky, jagged, or columnlike, and how they stack on top of each other creates different soil structures.

Soils with good structure have many aggregates jumbled on top of each other. This pattern creates plenty of open pockets, known as pores, for water and air to fill. Large pore spaces are the perfect habitat for soil organisms to occupy, especially if there is ample organic matter to feed on. Well-structured soils are also easy to dig, promote adequate drainage for plant roots, and generally resist erosion (the loss of topsoil).

Poorly structured soils possess the opposite properties. Individual soil aggregates sit on top of each other in tightly packed layers. This structure limits the open pore space and the suitable habitat available for soil organisms. Soils with poor structure generally drain slowly and impede root growth.

You can study your soil's structure by grabbing a handful of soil and squeezing it into a ball. Observe how it breaks apart when you push down on it with your index finger or thumb. If it crumbles softly when probed, you have a good structure. If it stays firm in the shape of a ball, your soil structure may need improvement. The good news is you can enhance soil structure by nurturing the community of organisms that help aerate the soil and glue aggregates together.

# BUILDING SOIL *with* COMPOST

**IN NATURAL ENVIRONMENTS,** plants grow and die back, leaving stacks of leaves and stems to decompose in place. Soil organisms work to transform them into spongy, black organic matter—the backbone of living soil. Gardeners often disrupt the natural decomposition cycle by removing debris and uprooting vegetables during harvest.

Gardeners can support the accumulation of organic matter by leaving plant roots in the ground after harvest or by planting between last season's garden debris. However, each garden is different, and these suggestions may not be viable options for every gardener. Digging through root-dense soils can be challenging, and seeds can struggle to germinate through a mat of debris. Instead, adding organic amendments (see page 124 for a complete list of soil-building amendments) and materials such as compost can replace any lost organic matter.

Composting is a process and a product made by piling raw materials such as leaves, grass clippings, and garden remnants into bins or piles. As the material sits, it heats up, shrinks in volume, and breaks down into soil-building organic matter. Gardeners who are earnest about cultivating, supporting, and maintaining living soil will love the benefits compost provides, and you'll soon learn (if you haven't already) that it is a resource you can't live without.

Adding compost builds soils that act like a damp sponge, allowing water to drain freely without drying out the soil. Compost also improves the structure of soils, making more room for soil organisms to gather. With the right food, moisture, and feedstocks (compost ingredients), the compost heap becomes the perfect breeding ground for soil organisms, which you reintroduce into the garden with each application. Continuous use creates a positive feedback loop of soil-building benefits that last longer than a simple dose of fertilizer.

A compost heap allows gardeners to just pile materials on as they become available. It is informal but often takes longer to yield finished compost.

Layering green and brown materials together and turning them regularly results in the fastest rate of decomposition.

Soil and Site Prep 103

Compost tumblers are a tidy way to make compost, though they hold a limited volume of materials.

Making compost is a beautiful way to recycle kitchen waste, yard debris, and other organic materials you once saw as a nuisance. If you have the space, freestanding piles take the least effort, but they can look messy and have no defense against curious critters looking for an easy meal. Many backyard composters use simple wooden constructions or ready-made plastic bins, often designed to spin for easy turning.

## How to Purchase Quality Compost

Making compost isn't ideal for everyone. It requires space, mounds of organic materials, and extra maintenance. If composting doesn't fit your lifestyle, you can purchase it in bags or in bulk from your local garden center.

If you use a lot of compost in your garden, choosing a high-quality product is essential. When buying bagged compost, avoid products that bake in the sun for weeks. Exposure to high temperatures can kill the soil organisms essential for creating a quality product. While you'll still be adding soil-building organic matter, you may miss out on all the benefits of good compost.

When it comes to purchasing compost, it's a good idea to buy in bulk if you need more than one-third of a pickup truck bed. This is because buying bagged products can add up quickly. Not only is buying in bulk more affordable, but it also ensures you get a better product when compared to compost stored long-term in plastic bags. Bulk compost sits in large, open piles, providing an ideal environment for soil organisms. This makes it the best product available when it's time to pick it up.

Municipalities and garden centers often have bulk compost for sale. This is a fantastic resource, but do your homework before adding it to your garden. Ask what kinds of materials they accept and where they come from. Confirm how they make their compost and how hot it gets during production. Safe compost should reach over 130°F for at least 3 days to kill off pathogens.

Don't be afraid to walk away if you notice any red flags. The last thing you want is weed-ridden or plastic-filled compost throughout the garden. An easy way to ensure quality compost is to look for the seals of approval you trust. The U.S. Composting Council website offers a database of trusted composting companies. There is also the Organic Material Review Institute (OMRI), which lists approved composting products that meet the regulations for use in organic agriculture. Seasoned gardeners trust these products, and you can too.

When compost bins are filled with the right combination of ingredients, the compost breaks down quickly.

In this partially decomposed compost pile you can see the ingredient layers. Mixing helps speed the decomposition of the pile.

## COMPOSTING BASICS

A well-balanced compost is all about having the right ingredients, and the best recipe is a mixture of compost feedstocks. Composters often describe feedstocks in broad categories depending on the nutrient content they provide. Green materials, such as grass clippings and garden debris, are rich in nitrogen, while brown materials, such as shredded paper, straw, or leaves, are carbon rich.

Soil organisms break down feedstocks in a ratio of 20 to 30 parts carbon to 1 part nitrogen. This is called the carbon-to-nitrogen ratio (C:N). The right C:N ratio provides microorganisms with what they need to multiply and, in turn, encourage rapid decomposition. If the C:N ratio is too high, nitrogen-rich materials are lacking, and the composting process grinds to a halt. If the C:N ratio is too low, temperatures within the pile can become so hot that microorganisms suffer.

Individual compost feedstocks rarely possess this golden ratio, so a blend of brown and green materials is preferred to achieve a balance. Home composters are left to make their best guess when mixing materials, which can discourage those looking to build the perfect pile. Don't let this hold you back; it's more about troubleshooting issues as they come up during the process (for more on troubleshooting, see page 108).

If you have trouble gathering enough debris for a good-sized pile, collect materials throughout the season or ask friends and neighbors for their unwanted yard clippings. Alternatively, you can purchase straw, but be wary of materials sprayed with pesticides, as these chemicals tend to accumulate in the compost over time.

Additionally, backyard compost heaps often do not generate enough heat to kill pathogens or eliminate weed seeds. For this reason, it's best to avoid adding pet wastes, diseased plants, or plants that have gone to seed. You may also wish to avoid adding tasty ingredients that attract unwanted critters, such as fatty oils, meat, and dairy products.

Soil and Site Prep

# COMPOST FEEDSTOCKS

| FEEDSTOCK | TYPE | TIPS | C:N |
|---|---|---|---|
| Dry Leaves | Brown | Shred dried leaves to prevent matting, which can prevent water and air from reaching the center of your pile. | 30:1–80:1 |
| Straw/Hay | Brown | Straw typically contains fewer weed seeds than hay. Ensure no chemical pesticides or herbicides are used to treat the hay before harvest. | 40:1–100:1 |
| Wood Chips | Brown | Wood chips are very high in carbon. If you use them, add more green materials to balance them out. | 100:1–700:1 |
| Cardboard | Brown | Remove all tape and staples. Avoid any cardboard with high-gloss ink. | 60:1–200:1 |
| Household Paper Products | Brown | Newspapers, brown paper bags, napkins, or paper towels can all be thrown in. Larger pieces should be shredded or ripped. Avoid any paper with high-gloss finishes. | 50:1–150:1 |
| Coffee Grounds | Green | Toss in the unbleached filter, too. Enormous amounts of coffee grounds can lower the pH of your pile. | 20:1–40:1 |
| Grass Clippings | Green | Fresh clippings turn up the heat with plenty of nitrogen. Avoid clippings treated with chemical herbicides or fungicides that can harm microorganisms | 15:1–25:1 |
| Fruit and Vegetable Scraps | Green | Collect kitchen scraps in a bin or pail while preparing meals. Tossing them into your pile is a perfect way to recycle kitchen waste. | 12:1–20:1 |
| Green Plant Trimmings | Green | Avoid any debris with visible signs of disease. | 20:1–30:1 |
| Sawdust/Wood Shavings | Brown | Both materials are very high in carbon. If you use them, add more green materials to balance them out. | 200:1–500:1 |
| Seaweed | Green | Check in with local authorities for harvest restrictions, and rinse off the salt before adding. | 15:1–25:1 |
| Manure (Cow) | Green | Manure mixed with animal bedding provides a near-perfect ratio of C:N. | 20:1–40:1 |
| Manure (Chicken) | Green | Manure mixed with bedding provides a near-perfect ratio of C:N. | 6:1–12:1 |
| Woody Brush | Brown | Large branches and woody perennial trimmings decompose slowly. Chop them into smaller pieces before you throw them into the pile. | 100:1–500:1 |

Things to avoid: fatty oils, meat, dairy, diseased plants, invasive weeds, pet waste, and plants that have gone to seed.

**Please note: The C:N ratio of individual feedstocks is tricky to nail down because it varies based on moisture and degree of degradation. For example, fresh grass clippings will have more nitrogen than those mowed down a few weeks ago. Tree leaves from various species each have their own C:N ratio.

Compost needs the right amount of carbon-rich brown and nitrogen-rich green materials to keep microbes active and well-fed. Roughly speaking, mix one part green material with two parts brown material to achieve the right C:N ratio. Or a 50/50 mix works fine, depending on what you have on hand.

# How to Build and Manage Your Compost Heap

Composting is an approximate science. The simpler your system, the more likely you'll use it in the long run. Follow these instructions to build, layer, and manage your heap.

**1 Establish the location.** Consider placing your compost pile on a slightly elevated area to allow for proper drainage after rain. Setting the pile close to your garden area is also important for easy access.

**2 Create the foundation.** Clear the footprint of your pile by removing any sod or weeds. Loosen the first inch of soil with a garden fork to encourage the native microbial flora and fauna to invade your pile. You may lay down a rugged plastic tarp if runner weeds are prevalent in your area. You'll want to do anything to prevent them from creeping into your pile from the soil below and taking over.

**3 Construct your bin.** You can build a simple three-sided bin from scrap wood, concrete blocks, or straw bales. The bin should be at least 3 feet wide, 3 feet tall, and 3 feet deep; otherwise, the compost may not get hot enough to encourage breakdown. Line the bottom with a base of wood chips or brush for aeration.

**4 Layer feedstocks.** Now it's time to layer your brown and green materials. Add a pitchfork of green waste, followed by two forkfuls of brown waste. After you pile a few layers, water the heap to give the decomposition process a head start.

**5 Turn the pile.** Compost management is about keeping your pile aerated to encourage active aerobic microbes. Probe the center of your pile occasionally to gauge the inner temperature. After the initial 2 weeks, you'll find the pile has cooled. Reactivate your compost by turning it over. Bring the inside of the pile outward and the outer materials to the center with a pitchfork the best you can. If you're not interested in this step, you can let your pile sit after the initial build. It will break down much slower, but eventually, you'll still make compost.

**6 Keep your pile damp.** The right amount of water for your compost heap is a Goldilocks situation. You need enough moisture to keep decomposers active, but not so much water that the pile is soggy and waterlogged. Grab a handful of compost and squeeze to test if your pile is right. The texture should feel damp but not dripping wet.

**7 Enjoy.** Compost piles built with the proper ratio of brown to green materials, kept moist, and turned over regularly are ready in 2 to 3 months. Finished compost can be added to the garden when the pile is no longer warm after turning, is odor-free, and has a uniform brown appearance.

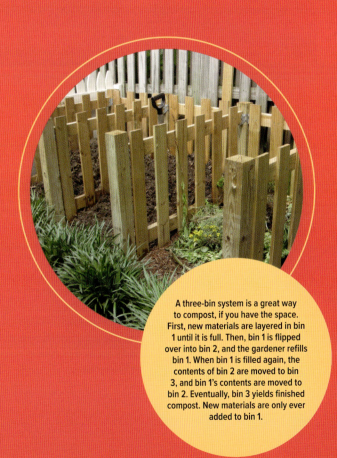

A three-bin system is a great way to compost, if you have the space. First, new materials are layered in bin 1 until it is full. Then, bin 1 is flipped over into bin 2, and the gardener refills bin 1. When bin 1 is filled again, the contents of bin 2 are moved to bin 3, and bin 1's contents are moved to bin 2. Eventually, bin 3 yields finished compost. New materials are only ever added to bin 1.

Compost piles are notorious for sprouting surprise volunteer plants from discarded seeds and pits. These melons may prove to be a good surprise or a not-so-good one.

## TROUBLESHOOTING COMPOST ISSUES

For successful composting, you must meet three basic principles: proper aeration, adequate moisture, and the correct mixture of ingredients. Don't worry. You can improve any troubled pile once you identify the problem. Your compost pile may need attention if it is cold or slimy, or if it smells bad.

Slimy compost is usually the result of an environment that lacks oxygen. When piles are not turned or materials mat together, aerobic microbes (oxygen-loving microbes) move out. They are replaced by anaerobic microbes that thrive in oxygen-poor environments and create the slimy conditions you observe. Anaerobic piles eventually break down into compost, but this takes years rather than months.

If your compost pile is dry and crusty, it may need supplemental moisture. If the composting conditions don't improve after you turn and add water, you may lack nitrogen-rich materials. For a quick fix, tear your pile apart and layer in more green feedstocks.

You may notice plants starting to grow in your pile. This is common if you throw in unwanted fruits and vegetables. Seeds can sprout and grow. Some plants are truly weeds, and you'll want to pull them out before they go to seed. But you may see a tomato seedling or a bean sprout you can transplant into your garden.

The most problematic issue with compost is a foul odor, which can be caused by several culprits. Nauseating ammonia smells waft from piles stacked with too many nitrogen-rich materials or overloaded with raw manure. The work of anaerobic microbes is to blame as well, especially if your pile is too wet.

In most cases, aerating the pile by turning it over to dry it out, as well as adding brown feedstocks, should bring the smell under control. Very large compost piles should be regularly monitored for temperatures capable of causing the pile to spontaneously combust. This is typically not a problem in a home compost pile, but it is a safety concern with large piles or windrows.

## COMMON COMPOST PROBLEMS AND SOLUTIONS

| PROBLEM | ROOT CAUSE | POTENTIAL SOLUTION |
|---|---|---|
| It stinks! | • Too much moisture<br>• Heavy and compacted<br>• Too much nitrogen | Add dry, lightweight materials like dried leaves, wood chips, or straw to your pile. |
| It won't break down | • The pile is too small<br>• Lack of moisture<br>• Lack of nitrogen<br>• Cold climate | Make your pile bigger and insulate the sides with straw bales if possible. Add some green feedstocks* and turn your pile to blend. |
| It's scorching (>170°F) | • The pile is too large<br>• Uneven ventilation | Split your pile in two and turn it over. |
| There are unwanted critters | • Attractant feedstocks | Remove meats and fatty food from the pile. Reinforce the bottom and sides of the bin with hardware cloth to prevent access. |
| It's a soggy mess | • Too much moisture<br>• Rainy climate | Stop adding water to the compost. Cover your pile with a tarp to keep out the rain. |
| There are swarming bugs | • Fruit flies or fungus gnats call the compost home | Cover all food scraps on the top of the pile with leaves or straw. Check the moisture, as these bugs thrive in wet environments. |

Composting issues can crop up throughout the season. Troubleshoot any problems to speed up the composting process.
*If greens are hard to come by, add a high-nitrogen amendment like blood meal or fish meal to take their place.

# HOW *Do You* IDENTIFY HEALTHY SOIL?

The color of your soil can tell you a lot about it, especially the amount of humus present.

**SOIL QUALITY DESCRIBES** the soil's capacity to do what we want it to do. Soil quality indicators are specific characteristics used as a metric to monitor the beneficial physical and biological properties that matter the most. For any gardener, suitable indicators would be those properties that contribute to growing nutrient-dense food.

The first quality indicator that comes to mind may be soil fertility, which makes sense. Without plenty of nutrients, you won't have a lush garden ripe with cherry tomatoes and plump peppers. However, focusing on the soil's nutrient content alone treats soil as a means to an end rather than the star of the show. But don't worry. Plant nutrients and how to add them to the soil are explained in chapter 8. Instead, properties like drainage, structure, and biological activity—important properties to keep tabs on—are better indications of soil quality. Observing these indicators will help you understand the soil below your feet and help you determine the best site for a new garden. These indicators are also easy to test yourself, so keeping track of your soil-building progress over the years is straightforward.

## COLOR

Soils come in a variety of colors, and these colors can reveal a lot about them. Beige to brown soils generally indicate a healthy amount of organic matter. And you don't need much; soils that contain 5 percent organic matter look dark when wet. The darker the soil, the more humus—an indicator that your soil is biologically active. Dark soils also have an intoxicating earthy smell.

In contrast, soils lacking organic matter take on the hue of their mineral composition and appear pale in color. They tend to be poorly structured and provide a lackluster environment for plants and soilborne organisms.

Distinct colors also clue you in to potential environmental issues, such as drainage. Uniform blue/gray colors point to soils that fluctuate between times of waterlogging and periods of complete dryness. This flip-flop between extremes places a lot of stress on plants. Conversely, soils with intricate patches between lighter colors and red splotches indicate soils that drain slowly and are consistently waterlogged. Black soil can indicate mucky, anaerobic conditions.

### *How to Do a Color Test*

**Assessment:** Take a trowel and dig a small trench 1 foot wide by 1 foot deep. Examine the overall color of the soil as you scoop. If the soil is dry, spray it lightly with water to better indicate soil color. Examine the walls of the hole too. You may see different layers of soil, which are the different soil horizons. Or you may see mottled patterns that clue you in to potential environmental conditions specific to your site.

Soil survey experts use the Munsell color scale to determine the specific color of the soil. The Munsell system is a group of color chips—think paint swatches—divided by hue, brightness, and intensity of color. Color identification using the Munsell color scale is so specific that forensic scientists use it to match soil to a particular crime scene. This level of specificity may be excessive for your purpose. Still, if you have a keen interest in soil, *The Munsell Color Soil Book* might be available at your local library.

The biological activity of a soil, both visible and microscopic, is a significant indicator of its quality.

## BIOLOGICAL ACTIVITY

One of the most significant indicators of soil quality is the level of activity of both small and large soil organisms. An active community implies that your soil has the basics of food, water, and shelter these organisms need to thrive, indicating your soil is well structured and has a healthy dose of organic matter.

However, it can be challenging to assess the presence of some of the most important players, because many are hard to see with the naked eye. Lab tests that identify microbes and fungi through genetic sequencing are available for those teeny-tiny microbes. Other tests measure the respiration rate (a metric decomposition) to get an idea of the level of microbial activity.

However, these lab results are expensive and difficult to interpret because they are sensitive to the impact of rain, temperature, and organic matter supply. Results vary widely depending on soil type, topography, and plant cover. Instead, an easy at-home measure of general activity is the calico test. Calico or muslin is a type of cotton textile that can be purchased by the yard; in a pinch, a strip of 100 percent cotton clothing can also do the trick.

### How to Do a Calico Test

**Assessment:** Dig a small hole, roughly 4 inches deep by 6 to 8 inches wide. Place a piece of unbleached calico cotton (or unbleached cotton material) into the hole and cover. Make sure to mark the location so you can find it again. After a couple of weeks, dig up your cotton swatch and examine the level of deterioration. The greater the decay, the greater the biological activity. The best-case scenario would be to find no cotton strip at all.

You can also search for larger creatures like earthworms by digging a hole. They are easy to spot, and this can be a fun activity for children. You'll want to do this when the soil has warmed to at least 55°F so the worms will be active. If the soil is too cold, they could retreat deeper down out of sight.

Dig a hole about 1 square foot wide and 1 foot deep. Shovel the soil onto a tarp to keep things tidy. Gently comb through the mound of scooped soil in search of earthworms. Having at least ten worms is a good sign you have other soil dwellers and all the benefits they provide. Once you're done, toss the soil and worms back into the hole. See note on page 99 about aggressive invasive earthworm species.

Taking a drainage test is essential for understanding how quickly your soil drains.

# DRAINAGE

Soil drainage is a metric of soil structure because of its effects on soil porosity (the volume of available pore space between individual soil clumps). Porosity impacts the movement of air and water, which plants and soil organisms depend on for growth, nutrient transport, and overall soil quality. High-porosity soils have lots of space for air and water to fill, while low-porosity soils have hardly any space at all.

In addition to soil structure, your garden's topography can impact drainage. Low-lying areas or trenches may not drain as well as elevated spaces. High water tables can also impede drainage if there is nowhere for the water to go. Likewise, if rock ledges or hardpans are just beneath the surface, your soil will probably be easily waterlogged by rainfall or routine watering.

## *How to Do a Drainage Test (a.k.a. a Perc Test)*

**Assessment:** Dig a hole approximately 1 foot wide by 1 foot deep and fill it with water. Wait until the water has completely drained and fill the hole again. After 15 minutes, measure the drop in water with a measuring tape or ruler. This measurement will tell you the hourly drainage rate when multiplied by 4.

Soils that drain less than 1 inch an hour are considered poorly drained. You're in the sweet spot if the soil drains between 1.5 and 6 inches an hour. Soils that drain more than 6 inches an hour are considered drought-prone.

# SOIL pH

Soil pH measures the acidity or alkalinity of your garden soil. The pH scale ranges from 0 (very acidic) to 14 (very alkaline or basic). For reference, acidic lemon juice has a pH of 2 or 3, while alkaline bleach ranges from 11 to 13 on the pH scale. Plants and soil organisms generally prefer a slightly acidic to neutral pH around 6.5 to 7.

Soil pH that is too low or too high impacts soil microbes' activity and nutrient availability. Soil pH can be increased with lime or decreased with sulfur applications. Just how much depends on the measured pH, soil texture, and organic matter content (for specifics, see page 157).

It is crucial to remember the pH scale is logarithmic. A change in one unit of pH represents a tenfold difference in the soil's acidity or alkalinity. For instance, soil with a pH of 3 is ten times more acidic than soil with a pH of 4 and a hundred times more acidic than soil with a pH of 5. Therefore, even minor alterations in soil pH can result in substantial changes in soil quality.

## How to Take a Home pH Test

**Assessment:** Testing your soil pH is simple if you have a pH probe; purchase this tool at any local garden center. However, at-home pH kits or a professional lab service provides more precise measurements of soil pH. At-home tests take practice because they require mixing various reactants and comparing colors to get a reading. But once you are comfortable following the labeled instructions, these tests are great—they are inexpensive, and you get immediate results.

Conversely, it takes time to ship a soil sample off to the lab and wait for the results. Depending on the lab, you could wait up to a month to hear back. Despite these factors, many gardeners prefer this approach because the results come with specific instructions for lowering or raising your soil pH that at-home tests do not provide.

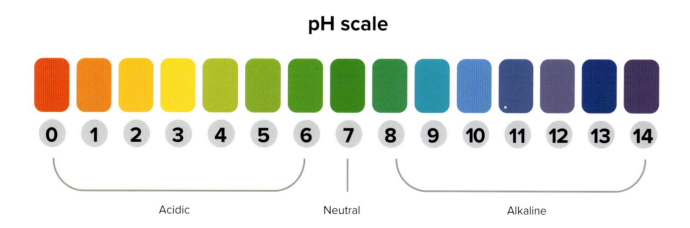

Soil and Site Prep

Compaction can become an issue when heavy equipment is used to grade or prepare your garden site.

## SOIL SALINITY

Sodic soils have elevated concentrations of salt that can dramatically stunt plant growth. Salty soil can also discourage seed germination and provide unfavorable conditions for soil organisms. Soils can be naturally salty or accumulate salts over time from heavy fertilizer use or lack of drainage.

### How to Test for Salinity

**Assessment:** A salinity meter measures the electrical conductivity of the soil. This tool is jabbed into the soil and uses an electric current to measure the salt content. Expected results read as a value between 0 and 50,000 millisiemens per meter (a siemens is a unit of electrical conductance, whereas an ohm is a unit of resistance). The higher the reading, the saltier your soil. This tool can be expensive, so if you don't want to invest in it, you can also observe the character of your soil. Salty soils usually appear crusty and dry, with deep cracks; imagine a parched desert playa.

## COMPACTION

Soil compaction is an indicator of soil structure. Any soil can become compacted by an external force that pushes soil particles together and collapses the pockets of space between soil aggregates. As a result, compacted soils are hard, dense, and difficult to dig.

Monitor soil compaction closely—it can completely destroy the soil ecosystem and prevent plant roots from taking hold. Also, check for compacted soils before establishing a new garden space, especially near home foundations. These areas are often heavily compacted due to construction activities.

### How to Evaluate Soil Compaction

**Assessment:** You can quickly evaluate soil compaction with a simple tool from the hardware store—a wire flag. Push the base of the flag into the soil and observe how far it goes before it stops. Loose, fluffy soil will have little to no resistance; the flag will drive right in. Soils with moderate compaction will take more pressure to push the flag through the soil, and you may feel some resistance. Severely compacted soils will prevent the flag from going much of anywhere at all, and you will see the metal wire bend under pressure.

# SOIL QUALITY PROGRESS REPORT

Use this worksheet to track your soil-building progress from season to season.
This soil progress report was adapted from the Michigan Soil Health Progress Report Recording Sheet.

| SOIL QUALITY IDENTIFICATION | | INDICATOR OBSERVATIONS | | |
|---|---|---|---|---|
| Indicator | Your Score (1–10) | 0–3 | 4–7 | 8–10 |
| Biological activity (soil moisture and temperature may impact observations) | | 0–5 earthworms are detected. Very little to no deterioration of buried fabric | At least 5 worms are detected. Visible tattered remains of buried cotton fabric | 10+ worms are detected, or there was no sign of buried cotton fabric |
| Color | | Pale-colored soil with a yellowish tint | Light brown | Dark-brown or black soil |
| Compaction | | Metal wire bends under pressure, or you are unable to push the wire deeper than 1 inch underground | There is some resistance as you push the wire underground | There is little to no resistance, and you can push the flag deep underground |
| Drainage rate | | Less than 1 inch an hour | Over 6 inches an hour | Between 1.5 and 6 inches an hour |
| Drainage after rainfall | | • Water pools on the soil surface for an extended period after a storm • Soil forms hard crusts when finally dried • Prolonged muddy season in the spring | • Minor pooling that disappears after 24 hours • Some muddy spring conditions that last a few weeks or less | No surface pooling or muddy spring conditions |
| Texture | | No ability to form a ribbon | Soil ribbon extends over 2 inches or is difficult to break | Soil ribbon reaches about 1 inch before it crumbles |
| Soil cover (mulch/cover crops) | | Less than 50% of the soil is bare during the season | Around 50%–70% of the soil is covered | Over 70% of the soil is covered |
| Soil disturbance | | Constant repetitive tillage | Single-pass or minimal tillage. Moderate disturbance of the top 6 inches of soil | No-till or minimal disturbance of the top 6 inches of soil |
| Soil erosion | | Visible dust in the air or active gullies created by water | Some dust or old signs of rain-formed gullies | No airborne dust and no signs of water erosion |
| Soil structure | | Powdery soil when dry, or large, hard clods make it difficult to prepare a seed bed. Soil crusts after a rain and roots grow horizontally. | A ball of soil crumbles under pressure. Some visible signs of organic matter and root growth. | Very crumbly, with a granular or blocky texture. Roots grow vertically without restriction. Preparing your seedbed for planting is very easy. |
| TOTAL SCORE | | Poor soil health 0–30 points | Fair to good soil health 31–70 points | Excellent soil health 71–100 points |

# Understanding Soil Contamination

Soil contamination is a widespread issue that affects both urban and rural areas. Exposure to soil toxins can occur through inhaling contaminated dust, absorbing chemicals through the skin, or consuming vegetables grown in contaminated soil. If there is a suspicion you have contaminated soil, it is crucial to take special precautions.

Heavy metals—such as lead, arsenic, and cadmium—are common soil contaminants. Hot spots of heavy-metal contamination occur near industrial activity, conventional farmland, and high-traffic areas. Household sites can also be contaminated depending on what the land was used for previously and what construction practices were used during building.

If you are concerned about potential contamination, a heavy-metal soil test will tell you if there is a cause for concern. Send a soil sample to your local university or Extension office (learn how to gather a soil sample on page 161). The results take time, so postpone any digging until you receive your report.

While this bathtub makes a cute planter, that may be lead paint flaking off its side, which could lead to contaminated soil.

If test results show problematic contamination levels, action may be required. For highly contaminated sites, **always seek professional advice.** If test results indicate mild contamination, building raised beds and filling them with contaminant-free soil is a good option.

To do so, cover the ground with a thick protective barrier, such as heavy-duty landscape fabric or mulch. This prevents toxic dust from kicking up while you work in the garden. Your raised bed should be at least 18 inches deep to prevent plant roots from accessing the contaminated ground.

## POTENTIAL CONTAMINANTS

| MATERIALS OF CONCERN | POTENTIAL SOURCE | LIKELY CONTAMINANT |
|---|---|---|
| Paint (pre-1978) | Old houses, landfill operations, manufacturing sites | Lead |
| Exhaust fumes | Heavily trafficked roads or highways; any road built before leaded gas was prohibited in 1996 | Lead, zinc, polycyclic aromatic hydrocarbons (PAHs) |
| Treated lumber | Wood-lined planting spaces | Arsenic, chromium, copper |
| Burning waste | Old landfills or backyard bonfires | PAHs, dioxins, heavy metals |
| Sewage sludge | Municipal treated sewage sludge used as a soil amendment | Heavy metals, per- and polyfluoroalkyl substances (PFAS), persistent bioaccumulative toxins (PBTs) |
| Contaminated manure | Copper and zinc salts added to animal feed | Copper, zinc |
| Pesticides | Previous agricultural areas with widespread pesticide use; heavily saturated residential properties | Lead, arsenic, mercury, and chlorinated products |

# GARDEN *Site* PREPARATION

If possible, create a level garden space to avoid low-lying areas where water pools.

**THE TYPE OF GARDEN** you want to create determines the site preparations required. If you plan to grow directly in the ground, it is essential to consider your native soil carefully. On the other hand, if you are thinking about raised beds or growing in pots, your focus shifts to selecting suitable containers and sourcing high-quality soil to fill them (see page 128). In any case, good preparations shepherd good results, and the first step is laying the groundwork.

A fundamental aspect of groundwork concerns controlling and accessing water. As discussed in an earlier chapter, consider how water moves through and within your potential garden site. Do you notice dips and dents where water pools, or slopes that quickly shuttle water away? Eliminating these landscape features promotes uniform watering when you are ready to grow, whether in the ground, raised beds, or large containers.

If achieving a perfectly level space is difficult, concentrate on your site's drainage. Investigate depressions where water may pool during the next heavy rainfall. Look to see where water collects, how it flows over the landscape, and how quickly these areas dry out. If one spot stays wet for longer, this could indicate the location of potential drainage issues. These types of large-scale considerations should be dealt with before you dig in.

It's also important to consider how accessible water is on your site before you begin growing. Some gardeners may be lucky enough to receive plentiful rain throughout the growing season, but most of us need to water plants regularly. Seasonal gardening tasks can be taxing, so avoid adding hauling water to your to-do list.

## LEVEL IT OUT

For extensive projects, a skid-steer loader is a valuable tool for moving large amounts of earth, digging out big rocks, or flattening large areas with big bumps and dips. Steeply sloped land requires carving out flattened terraces supported by bermed land or a retaining wall. You can rent the necessary machine from your local home improvement store or hire a professional to do the work.

Using a machine to do the heavy lifting is convenient but likely compacts the soil you wish to cultivate. If possible, prevent using heavy machines when the soil is wet. If you live in a cold climate, it is better to do this work when the ground is frozen and the soil can better resist compaction.

If the best site for your garden is sloped, consider building terraces that cut into the hillside to keep the growing areas level.

If you have a smaller project and need to level the ground, use a shovel and a sturdy metal rake. Simply move the soil into any slight depressions and smooth out any bumps to create a level surface. Alternatively, you can pile on extra soil until the entire area levels out. Once you have a level surface, you can amend and improve the soil as needed.

It's okay to leave a gentle slope rather than fret over perfectly level ground. A gentle slope with a 1 percent grade or less can be a precious asset in wet or snowy climates. During spring, when snow starts to melt, the sloped terrain allows excess water to drain off the garden. Gentle slopes are also helpful for regions with heavy rainfall, which is becoming more common and increasingly intense due to our changing climate.

## ADD DRAINAGE

If you identify soggy areas of concern, install underground drainage pipes to direct water away from the garden. Adding sufficient drainage could be a straightforward task you can do yourself. Advanced projects that require careful slope calculations and the need to avoid underground hazards could require professional planning and skills.

Digging a trench around your garden's perimeter with a gentle slope can direct excess water where it needs to go. Aim for a 6-inch decline for every 100 feet to keep the water moving downhill. You can then lay down perforated tubing and fill the trench with loose gravel. When it rains, water will collect in the trench and move away from your crops.

However, for areas with extensive drainage issues or high water tables, installing a complex network of underground pipes may be necessary, for which professional help is strongly advised. You want to perfect your drainage system the first time to avoid digging up your garden *again* to correct any errors later on.

## ACCESS TO WATER

Plants uptake water laden with dissolved nutrients to grow roots, shoots, leaves, and fruits. On average, plants require 24 to 120 gallons of water for every pound of dried leaves, roots, or shoots produced. Water requirements vary dramatically depending on the crop, climate, and soil type.

Issues with water scarcity are increasing in much of the United States. It is not uncommon for local municipalities to restrict water use during the growing season to preserve resources. Your ability to use municipal water may also come at a cost. Across the United States, the average water bill is increasing as more pressure is put on our water resources. Consider how big of a growing area your water resources can support.

You can use rainwater collection systems to provide supplementary water. However, it is important to check with your local authorities regarding permits. In some western states, collecting rainwater may be prohibited by the law.

Finally, consider your setup. Do you plan to install irrigation or water by hand? Whichever you choose will influence the proximity of your water source to the garden. Laying hundreds of feet of irrigation line can add up, and wrangling a 300-foot hose is a nightmare.

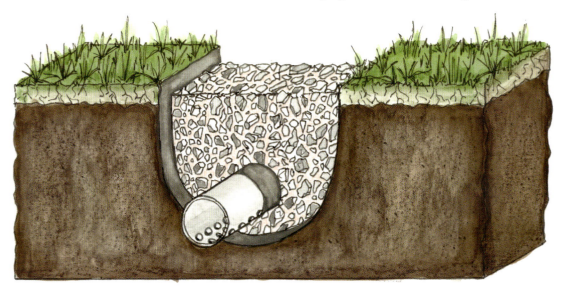

For areas with larger drainage issues, installing a French drain may be necessary. Perforated pipe surrounded by landscape fabric is located at the bottom of a gravel-filled ditch to let water freely drain down and be funneled away from the area.

# GETTING RID OF WEEDS *and* GRASS

**NOW THAT YOU'VE PICKED YOUR SITE,** it's time to prepare the ground for planting. The thought of breaking new ground may evoke images of backbreaking work and long days toiling under the sun, but it doesn't have to. How you break new ground or rehabilitate a neglected garden depends on what you plan to grow and the state of your soil.

The most significant decision is whether to use no-till or till methods to prepare your soil. Soils untouched for many years need little help besides removing the existing grass and weeds. In this case, no-till methods that smother weeds without turning over the soil work well and preserve the natural living soil already at work.

In other cases, your soil may need major rehabilitation to jump-start the soil-building process. Compact or imbalanced soil, for example, benefits from a preliminary till to loosen the soil and mix in organic matter or pH-stabilizing amendments. This can help to quickly nip significant issues in the bud before you plant in a way that no-till options can't achieve (read more on the case against tilling on page 153).

However, rototillers or tractors apply force to the soil, and regular use can ultimately lead to a compaction issue known as plow pan later on. Therefore, reserve tilling for those soils that need the extra muscle. Once you delve into no-till methods, you'll be impressed by how quickly your soil can improve.

Whichever process is right for you, starting well before planting is best. It takes time for weeds to disappear and for added soil amendments to take effect. Start in the fall to give your efforts time to take full effect. Come spring, you'll be ready to get your seeds in the ground.

Solarizing is a slow but effective way to use the sun's heat to kill weeds in new planting areas.

## SCORCH WEEDS BY SOLARIZING

Soil solarization is a no-till method that uses rugged plastic tarps to retain the sun's heat and scorch weeds. The best time to solarize the soil is in June, July, or August, when temperatures are the hottest for most regions.

A thick (1.5 to 2 millimeters) clear plastic tarp works well for most gardeners. The clear plastic allows the sun's heat to pass through the tarp and get trapped underneath, similar to the effect of greenhouse gasses in the atmosphere. However, gardeners in cooler or coastal areas may have better luck using a black silage tarp. While this material doesn't trap as much heat, it works by blocking sunlight so weeds don't continue to grow while you wait for the soil temperature to heat up.

Many plastic sheets intended for this use come ready-treated with UV protectants to prevent degrading in the baking sun. You must monitor plastic sheets without UV protection closely and remove them before they degrade; otherwise, they will be difficult to remove without littering your garden with scattered bits of plastic.

Composting in place (also known as sheet mulching) is a great no-till way to make a new planting bed. Layers of organic matter are placed on top of a base of cardboard or newspaper and left to decompose in place. A top layer of compost creates the perfect site for planting.

Some studies show that in hotter climates, overheating the soil can harm the living soil you wish to support. However, experts found that when the tarp is removed, the soil ecosystem quickly rebounds, especially if you add compost before you plant. The benefit of heating the soil to an extreme temperature is you kill off not only weeds but also their seeds and hidden soil pathogens.

Start by cutting down tall weeds as close to the ground as possible with a mower, weedwhacker, or scythe. Water the ground and cover the entire planting area with a heavy-duty plastic sheet. Anchor the plastic with weighty objects like sandbags, rocks, or concrete blocks—anything to prevent the tarp from becoming a sail in the wind. The soil is ready to plant in hot and sunny climates in about 4 to 6 weeks. If your climate is rainy or cool, the process could take as much as twice that time.

# COMPOST IN PLACE

Composting in place (also known as sheet mulching) is a standard no-till method for smothering weeds and building soil from the ground up. It's like building a compost pile directly where you want to plant. This technique involves layering materials like cardboard, mulch, and any organic waste at your disposal. Think of all those broken-down boxes or stacks of old newspapers waiting to be recycled—they now have a new purpose in the garden.

You can sheet mulch a wide area or choose to sheet mulch in rows separated by permanent pathways. Either approach requires a hefty amount of materials and plenty of time to break down. If you want to plant directly into your sheet-mulched area, add several inches of topsoil or finished compost to create a surface suitable for planting.

Get started by mowing down tall weeds and grass. Cover the ground with a barrier of wetted cardboard, newspaper, or thick paper bags. Overlap pieces by at least 4 inches, or new weeds will work through. The thicker the layer, the better it will serve as a weed barrier. Avoid using paper materials with glossy inks or lots of color, and remove tape and staples as you go.

Some gardeners shovel on a layer of wood chips to help secure the cardboard barrier, while others start piling on nitrogen-rich materials right away. There is no exact recipe for your remaining layers, but the same principles for building a quick-to-decompose compost heap apply here too. Continue the process until your heap is at least 6 to 8 inches tall. Top it off with a layer of compost or topsoil. If the bed looks too tall now, remember it will shrink down as it decomposes into garden gold.

# ORGANIC HERBICIDES

The term *herbicide* has a lousy reputation among organic gardeners because it conjures up images of unwanted synthetic chemicals. However, a variety of commercially made organic herbicides are made from natural substances like acetic acid (vinegar) and clove oil. Unlike synthetic weed killers, these products pose less of a personal and environmental risk.

Organic herbicides work on contact, so an even application is best. They work well on newly sprouted weeds but are nearly ineffective on perennial weeds with long taproots or extensive root systems. Therefore, organic herbicide applications are most effective when combined with other

# COMMON ORGANIC HERBICIDES

| TYPE | ACTIVE INGREDIENT | HOW IT WORKS |
|---|---|---|
| Acids | Acetic acid (vinegar) and citric acid<br><br>Note: The acetic acid concentration for effective herbicidal use is 10 to 20%. Culinary vinegar is only 5% acetic acid, so it isn't effective for controlling most weeds. | When used as a soil drench, products can lower the pH to unsurvivable levels.**<br><br>When sprayed on leaves, they remove the waxy coating, making the leaves vulnerable to desiccation. |
| Essential oils | Clove, cinnamon, citrus, and eugenol | These oils damage plant tissues, causing cellular membranes to collapse. |
| Soaps | Pelargonic acid + fatty acids, ammonium nonanoate, and sodium lauryl sulfate | These compounds infiltrate plant cells and cause membranes to rupture. They also strip the waxy leaf coating, which leads to dehydration. |

Common organic herbicides include soaps, oils, and vinegar products. Always read and follow the labeled instructions for safe use and product storage. Look for products with the OMRI seal to guarantee they are approved for use in organic agriculture.

**Soil drenches are best left for pathways and uncultivated spaces. Altering your garden soil pH to extremely acidic levels will harm your crops long-term.

weed-removal strategies outlined in this chapter. Despite their limitations, studies show that using a high volume of product mixed at lower concentrations is more effective than using a small volume of spray mixed at high concentrations. Experts also recommend using these products when it's hot and sunny for the best results.

Efficacy also improves when used with an adjuvant (a substance added to herbicide sprays to enhance the herbicide's performance). Adjuvant products help herbicides stick to plant leaves and stay there longer. Always follow the labeled instructions for use and mixing protocols.

Organic herbicides can be used to kill turfgrass. Just be sure to use them according to label instructions on a hot, sunny day for maximum effectiveness.

Soil and Site Prep  121

Good old-fashioned sod stripping is another way to start a garden in a patch of lawn. Sod can be removed by hand using a shovel or with a mechanical sod stripper.

# BUILDING *Garden* BEDS

**ONE IMPORTANT DECISION** you must make early in the planning process is whether to grow your plants directly in the ground or in raised beds. Raised-bed gardening is well-defined and convenient, which is why it's popular among many gardeners. However, in-ground growing has a lower start-up cost and provides you with more flexibility. If you need help figuring out where to start, consider the advantages and disadvantages of each style. You never know, a combination of both strategies might be the best approach.

The main benefit of constructing raised beds is they are a practical solution for growing in areas that might not be suitable otherwise. They provide a fresh start and allow you to choose your soil rather than working with what you've got. Raised beds solve problems such as soil contamination and shallow soil over rock ledges. Moreover, the elevated planting area reduces the need to bend over, so it's easier to maintain.

But the benefits don't stop there. The clear boundaries created by raised beds help prevent weeds from creeping in from the wild edges of the garden. The exposed sides help the soil warm quickly in the spring, allowing for earlier planting in cool climates. They also provide excellent drainage and prevent soggy soils even in the rainiest regions.

## STRIP SOD

Removing sod is hard work. You can avoid the backbreaking effort by renting a powered sod cutter from a local equipment-rental company. These machines make deep cuts that remove most grass roots. They are the perfect tool for tough-to-rip-out grass species with long runner roots or thick mats of turf. Pulled strips of sod are great to reuse around the yard to fix blemishes or add turf to new areas.

If you choose to remove sod by hand, here are a few tips that make it easier. First, use a sharp spade or half-moon edger to cut a perimeter around your garden area. Clear sod from inside your cut perimeter in manageable strips that are small enough to lift comfortably.

Use a shovel or pitchfork to pry each layer of sod from the ground. If you cut deep enough, this should be reasonably easy. If the sections are hard to pry back, take your edger and make deeper cuts through the mat of roots. Once you free a strip of sod, gently shake off loose soil and repeat.

## TILL…BUT SPARINGLY

Even though organic gardening practices focus on no-till techniques for the health of the living soil, some tilling might be required when breaking new ground. Heavy clay soil benefits from a one-time till to loosen the hard soil and mix in organic matter deeper underground. Sandy soil can also benefit from the power of tilling to mix in large volumes of compost to increase the organic matter content of the soil quickly before planting. However, it's best to ditch the tiller once you accomplish these initial benefits.

Amending planting areas with organic matter is a seasonal ritual that offers tremendous value.

122 American Horticultural Society | *Essential Guide to Organic Vegetable Gardening*

# Building Bermed Bed Spaces in the Ground

Establishing dedicated bermed bed spaces or rows with in-ground gardens helps you reap the same benefits provided by raised beds, such as improved drainage and prevention of soil compaction from foot traffic. Even a slight elevation of a few inches can help your growing space warm quickly in the spring so you can get planting sooner.

A dedicated bermed bed in the ground is also great for soil building. Using the same layout of beds and pathways each year allows you to know exactly where to apply soil amendments and compost without wasting any on areas without plants. Plus, it saves you the work of raking out new beds each year—it's already done!
To get started, rope off the perimeter of the bed you want to make. It doesn't have to be a traditional row; you could make a kidney shape, a spiral, or any other shape you want.

One tip: Beds wider than 4 feet are difficult to tend, so ensure you can easily reach the middle of your bed space. If you plan to garden in a large area, arrange it into smaller bermed spaces with pathways in between.

Once you establish the outline, shovel soil from the area just outside the bed's perimeter into the center of the bed. All this shoveling can be a lot of work, but if you keep the same layout year after year, you only have to do it once. Soon, you'll see a mound take shape in the middle of your outlined bed. Take a rake and level the mound by spreading the soil within the bed's perimeter to flatten it. Add a few inches of compost to top it off and aim to create at least 5 or 6 inches of elevation compared to the surrounding ground. Secure the sloped sides of your berm by firmly tamping them with a metal rake to help the soil stay put when it rains. Over time, your bed may settle, but annual applications of compost will keep it mounded.

Of course, you can always plant directly in the ground with little fuss if you've done the site and soil prep to set you up for success. It takes time and patience to build soil, but the reward of planting directly in the ground is additional room and the added flexibility to grow what you want where you want. Plants also benefit from growing in the ground because their roots can stretch deep in search of groundwater and untapped nutrients. Plus, there's a better chance of mutually beneficial interactions with the living soil.

## SOIL-BUILDING AMENDMENTS

Soil amendments are organic or inorganic materials used to improve the physical soil properties that affect plant growth, such as soil structure, water retention, and aeration. The best amendments also add organic matter to feed the living soil. You can incorporate them into your native soil or rejuvenate depleted raised beds or containers.

Organic amendments—such as compost, manure, or fallen leaves—are highly valuable for attracting and nourishing beneficial soil organisms. However, particular plant and animal products can introduce unwelcome pathogens or parasites if not prepared correctly. If you have any concerns, purchase plant or animal products from a reputable supplier.

Inorganic amendments—such as lime, gypsum, or vermiculite—are mined from the earth. While they don't provide organic matter, they can rectify saline soil, improve aeration, and stabilize soil pH. However, they take time to break down, so you shouldn't expect instant results.

Every garden plot has a unique soil texture, structure, and biome, so providing specific amendment recommendations and application rates is impossible. Instead, it's more important to understand your unique soil type, how to work with it, and what amendments will help you achieve your soil-building goals.

# ORGANIC SOIL AMENDMENTS

| AMENDMENT | DESCRIPTION | IMPROVEMENT PROVIDED | NOTES |
|---|---|---|---|
| Bird/bat guano | Aged excrement from seabirds or bats | Enhances soil structure, aeration, and microbial activity | It is important to avoid using raw guano as it poses a risk to human health. Instead, opt for composted or dried products that limit your pathogen exposure. |
| Mushroom compost/ mushroom soil | Used mushroom-growing substrate | Adds organic matter, improves soil structure, enhances microbial activity | This amendment is steam pasteurized prior to use so it's free of weed seeds. "Fresh" mushroom soil may be high in soluble salts, "weathered" products less so. It has an alkaline pH between 6.0 and 8.0. |
| Manure | Excrement from cow, sheep, chicken, horse, or llama | Reduces compaction and enhances water permeation and retention | To use manure safely, see page 125. Pig, dog, cat, and human waste should be avoided due to the risk of potential parasites. |
| Worm castings | Excrement from earthworms | Improves soil structure and water retention to provide habitat for a wide range of microorganisms | "Castings" refer to the organic matter that has already decomposed, which then becomes a source of readily available nutrients for plants. |
| Greensand | Mined rock | Absorbs excess moisture in clay soils and preserves soil moisture in sandy soils | This product provides more than thirty trace minerals and nutrients that are essential for supporting plant growth. |
| Lime | Mined rock | Adjusts and maintains soil pH | Learn more on page 157. |
| Gypsum | Mined rock (calcium sulfate) | Improves soil structure and mitigates salinity issues in the soil | Large quantities of calcium sulfate can lead to nutrient imbalances. |
| Compost | Decomposed organic debris | Improves all aspects of soil quality | You can make your own or purchase ready-to-use products. |
| Cover crops | Living plants grown with the intent of improving the soil, adding nutrients, or providing mulch | Prevents soil erosion and provides a source of organic matter deep underground, enhancing soil structure and aeration | For a list of cover crops, see page 174. Learn how to plant a cover crop on page 173. |
| Sulfur | Mined mineral | Adjusts and maintains soil pH | Learn more on page 210. |
| Biochar | Woody organic debris processed with high heat in low-oxygen environments | Reduces compaction and improves aeration and nutrient retention | This charcoal-like material is resistant to further decomposition, which allows it to last for an extended period. |

Soil amendments are best mixed into the soil before planting to improve any soil quality indicators that are lacking. Their continued use can help maintain quality soil over time.

## *Animal Manure Safety*

Manure is more than just manure. It's a blend of animal excretions, feathers or hair, undigested food, and bedding materials. This mixture raises some safety concerns because, like other animal wastes, it can carry harmful pathogens such as fecal coliforms and salmonella and even spread parasitic worms. However, the benefits of using manure in the garden far outweigh the risks if you take the proper precautions. For example, keep stockpiled raw manure in a protected area away from pets and children.

If you plan to use manure in your garden, mixing it into your compost pile can help eliminate potential pathogens or diseases. To successfully eliminate the risk, your pile must reach temperatures over 130°F for at least 3 days. You can monitor the heat of your pile daily with a temperature probe. However, it's common for backyard compost piles to fail to reach these temperatures, so buying precomposted manure is a better option for some.

Another alternative is to let manure sit and age over time. While this method doesn't eliminate existing pathogens, it prevents them from reproducing by drying out the pile, leading to a reduction in population over time.

To ensure a safe harvest, apply manures at least 90 days before harvest, regardless of the method you use to process it. Avoid using raw manure when possible, but if necessary, apply it at least 120 days before harvest. It is important to wear gloves while you spread manure and wash your hands thoroughly after each application. Additionally, washing any vegetables before bringing them inside is a good practice.

## BUILDING RAISED BEDS: OPTIONS AND IDEAS

Rows of evenly spaced, wooden, rectangular boxes come to mind when you think about a raised bed garden. However, a raised bed can be much more than a square wooden box, although it is always an excellent option. You can be as creative as you like and use what you have on hand to keep expenses low.

Gardeners often prefer to use long-lasting materials like rot-resistant wooden boards, stone, metal, or concrete so their beds will last a long time. On the other hand, there are advantages to using materials that decompose quickly, such as straw. Although you may need to rebuild them often, straw beds do not require tools to construct and are easily moved. This is a significant benefit if you need to change the location of your garden or if you are not permitted to build a permanent structure on rented land.

Take time to contemplate what material will provide the look, function, and longevity you're after. You should also take into account the cost of the materials you choose. It's also worth noting that neighborhoods may have strict homeowner associations (HOAs) that prioritize aesthetics over function. If so, research which materials your HOA approves before proceeding with your construction plans.

There are innumerable ways to build raised beds, and plans abound online. Find what works for you.

Soil and Site Prep 125

Straw bales make excellent frames for temporary raised beds. They'll last a few years before decomposing in place.

Wood is one of the most popular materials for framing raised beds. For a longer life, choose a naturally rot-resistant wood like cedar, black locust, or redwood.

Natural stone can be used to create attractive raised beds that last for generations. Stone can be dry stacked or mortared.

## *Straw*

Constructing a raised bed using straw bales is an easy and affordable option. However, it is important to choose the right type of bales. Though straw and hay bales may seem alike, there is a crucial difference. Straw bales are made of dried grain stalks used for animal bedding and mulch. Hay, on the other hand, is cut from dried grasses and legumes to be consumed as feed. As a result, hay often contains a hidden enemy—weed seeds, and lots of them.

Don't be afraid to ask questions when you search for straw bales. Some fields are treated with chemical herbicides before the straw is cut and baled, and these chemicals can remain active when you bring the straw home. Some vegetables—such as root crops, greens, legumes, and tomatoes—are sensitive to residual herbicides, which can leave you wondering why your garden is a flop.

Building straw-bale beds is a cinch, regardless of your building abilities. Once you've gathered your bales, arrange them in any pattern you'd like, as long as you create an enclosed area to fill with soil. Over time, the bales will start to decompose, but they should last a season or two. Some gardeners plant directly into straw bales by creating pockets filled with extra scoops of soil, which works too. However, this approach requires a lot of excess water to keep plant roots from drying out.

## *Wood*

Raised beds are frequently made out of wood, and you can create your own designs or purchase premade kits from retailers. Although any type of lumber can be used, it's best to choose naturally rot-resistant varieties. Avoid chemically treated lumber as much as possible. Although it is often cheaper and more durable outdoors, the preservatives used in the treatment process can seep into the soil.

Most of the worst chemicals used to treat wood—such as arsenic—have long been banned, but heavy metals such as copper are still used today. If you opt for using treated lumber, install an impervious plastic liner before filling your bed. This barrier will prevent preservatives from coming into contact with your soil.

If you are going for naturally rot-resistant woods, look for Atlantic white cedar, western red cedar, white oak, black locust, Osage orange, or redwood. Check your local hardware store for availability and price. Some lumber can become rather costly depending on the size and amount of raised beds you aim to build.

## *Stone*

Building raised beds using stone can be a substantial investment, but it is a durable and long-lasting material. Stone beds are also an excellent option for cool-climate gardeners because the material can help warm the soil through radiant heat. During the day, stones absorb the sun's heat, which is slowly released at night to help maintain elevated soil temperatures despite the cold. However, in hot and sunny climates, this benefit may become counterproductive if the radiant heat causes the soil to reach dangerous temperatures that can harm plant roots.

Although you can assemble stone beds on your own, they may require specialized drills or machinery, so you might need to hire a professional. If you are in the planning phase, keep this added installation cost in mind.

## *Urbanite*

Some gardeners are opting to use urbanite as a unique way to build raised beds. Urbanite is broken, recycled concrete paving, and it's often available on construction sites and through websites like Craigslist or Facebook Marketplace. It's usually free, though you'll have to do the hauling, and it can also be used to make walkways, patios, and retaining walls. Repurposing materials like urbanite keeps them out of landfills and eliminates the need for the energy consumption and materials required to make new products.

## *Concrete Blocks*

Concrete blocks are another long-lasting and durable option that is often more affordable than stone constructions. You can lay blocks out in a single layer or stack them on top of each other to add height. If you go for the stacked option, consider using mortar to secure your blocks, because they tend to move around as the ground shifts from moisture or temperature swings. Concrete bed enthusiasts also recommend driving rebar through the hollow cores of each block and into the ground to hold them in place.

This material is often linked with safety concerns due to its resemblance to cinder blocks. However, the two materials are not the same. Concrete blocks are made from a mixture of stone or fine crushed sand, whereas cinder incorporates toxic coal ash into the mix. Even though cinder blocks haven't been manufactured for the last 50 years, the name still persists, leading to the source of confusion.

## *Metal*

Galvanized steel or corrugated metal beds have gained popularity among gardeners looking for durability and strength with a modern aesthetic. Metal beds are easy to install if you purchase a handy kit; if you are more of a

This clever gardener has filled gabions with urbanite (broken, recycled concrete paving) to create a garden wall. Such a structure can also be used to create framing for a raised bed.

Concrete blocks, pre-fab landscape blocks, and even bricks can be used as edges for raised beds.

Galvanized steel or corrugated metal beds are very popular choices, though care should be taken in hot southern climates where the soil temperatures can grow very hot and potentially damage plant roots.

Soil and Site Prep   **127**

DIYer, you can construct them with the help of a wooden frame to which you can attach metal panels. Metal livestock troughs are also gaining popularity in the gardening world because they are easy to find and take minutes to install (remember to remove the drain plug).

The convenience of this material can be diminished in hot climates where metal can magnify the sun's heat and zap moisture from the soil. In the worst instances, the soil temperature can quickly climb and damage plant roots on the hottest summer days. You can minimize this risk by shading the sides of your bed with spilling or vining plants. Alternatively, lining the interior wall of your raised bed with an insulating layer of cardboard can reduce the amount of heat transferred to the soil.

## FILLING RAISED BEDS

Once you've selected your materials and worked hard to build your raised garden beds, it's time to start planting. But before that, you need to fill your beds with soil. The good news is you don't have to worry about breaking up heavy clay soils or fret over sandy soils that are difficult to irrigate. You can create well-structured, well-aerated soil that is rich in organic matter and full of life!

You might have assumed that the benefits of living soil are only available for in-ground gardening. Luckily, raised garden beds can also sustain their own soil ecosystem if they have the right support. Building your own garden soil can create the perfect conditions for soil organisms to thrive. It's also a great way to use the garden debris you have on hand.

If you choose this approach, it's similar to sheet mulching or composting in place (see page 120). Layer green and brown materials until they fill your entire bed. If you want to plant right away, top the pile off with at least 4 inches of compost or topsoil. As the material decomposes throughout the season, don't be surprised to see the soil level shrink. You'll be able to add more compost and debris the following season until the soil level stabilizes. Keep in mind the basic principles of composting (see page 105) to build a balanced heap that will decompose into garden gold.

You can also haul in bulk soil to fill your beds if you want instantaneous results. If you do purchase soil, look for a reputable supplier that produces soil specifically for gardening. This way, you know it's safe, light, and fast draining. Otherwise, you may end up purchasing topsoil scraped from construction sites during a build, which is often low quality and may contain toxic chemicals.

Filling raised beds can be a costly affair, though it only needs to be done once. Bulk soil is less expensive than bagged and eliminates plastic waste.

It's convenient to purchase bulk soil if you have a few raised beds to fill. However, hauling in enough new soil can be expensive for larger raised-bed gardens. Instead, use what you have, but only after amending it with plenty of compost to bring it to life. If this approach fits your needs, aim to mix 50 percent topsoil with 40 percent compost and 10 percent soil-building amendments (see page 124 for a complete list).

Exploring different ways to build healthy soil and foster a healthy community of living organisms is key to successful vegetable gardening. Learn how to tend your soil properly, and a healthy and productive garden is sure to follow. In the next chapter, we'll explore the planting process and discuss growing from seed and transplants.

# TOOLS *for* SOIL *and* SITE PREP

### A HALF-MOON EDGER
is a semicircular metal tool with a long handle. The top of the metal semicircle may have a small shelf to stand on so you can use your body weight to drive the tool into the ground. They help slice through thick mats of sod or create clean perimeter lines around your garden beds.

### HAND SPRAYERS
are a great way to apply herbicides, pesticides, and liquid fertilizers (although you should have separate sprayers for fertilizers and weed/pest killers). They have a handle pump that pressurizes the liquid for a continuous flow when you press the trigger.

### BOW RAKES
are a true workhorse of the garden. Their sturdy and durable metal base and tines have countless uses. Use a bow rake to level ground, spread mulch, aerate the compost pile, or tamp down the sides of your in-ground bermed garden beds.

### TEMPERATURE PROBES
are helpful tools to measure the activity of your compost heap. Piles that are above 100°F indicate happy microbes; piles hotter than 130°F can kill off weed seeds and potential pathogens. Compost temperatures below 70°F could indicate it's ready to use or it may be time to troubleshoot.

### A pH METER
is a handy tool to measure your soil pH with instant results as soon as you insert the probe into the soil. Before you purchase a meter, check the tool's specifications to determine the accuracy of the implement.

### SOLARIZATION TARPS
are for those gardeners ready to dive into no-till cultivation. They are either clear or black plastic tarps ordered for any size plot you have in mind.

Soil and Site Prep 129

CHAPTER 7

# THE ACT *of* PLANTING

**SEEDS ARE TRULY MIRACULOUS.** Despite their small size, they contain all the necessary nutrients and genetic information to develop into healthy seedlings once the conditions are just right. This wonder of nature brings joy to gardeners and serves as a reminder that life is precious, and when we treat even the smallest of seeds with reverence, remarkable things can happen.

It takes some experimenting to start seeds right, whether you are an experienced gardener or a complete beginner. This chapter covers the basics of seed starting, whether you grow seedlings indoors or directly sow seed outside. It delves into the benefits of both approaches and offers guidance to prevent any seed-starting bloopers. Once your seeds start to grow, this chapter explains how to care for seedlings and includes advice on grow lights, hardening off, and transplanting them outside. The chapter ends with a list of tools to help you become a seed-starting expert.

## PLANTING *Possibilities*

**IT IS INCREDIBLE** how much a single seed can produce once you plant and care for it. You can experience this gift by sowing seeds directly in the ground or in containers to transplant later. However, you can also enjoy the benefits of growing food without planting any seeds at all by purchasing ready-to-plant starts from your local garden center or community farm.

Many gardeners choose to sow seeds because they offer a broader range of plant cultivars than what is typically found at a nursery. Seeds are also a more economical and abundant option compared to the higher cost of purchasing nursery starts. For instance, a single packet can contain up to 250 seeds at the same cost as a single nursery seedling. Sowing seeds is a cost-effective choice if you plan to cultivate a large area. You can always supplement with a few plants later to fill in gaps or experiment with a new crop. However, if your garden is limited to a few raised beds, buying seedlings might be a more practical option.

Planting from seed directly into the garden (known as direct sowing) is the easiest way to grow, though it isn't the best fit for every crop.

Some crops need to be grown from transplants, especially if you garden in a zone with a short growing season.

## SHOULD I DIRECTLY SOW SEEDS OR PLANT INDOORS FIRST?

If you choose to grow from seed, planting directly in the ground is simple and efficient, but you have to hope the weather cooperates. Seeds sown too early can be hit by an unexpected frost or fail to sprout because the soil is too chilly. Additionally, as our climate patterns continue to change, early-season growing conditions are becoming more unpredictable, making it difficult for gardeners to rely on historical patterns.

Starting your plants indoors is a great way to manage the chaos of early-season planting by using a heat mat, artificial light, or a sunny windowsill. Not only does this practice protect your plants from unpredictable weather, but it also allows you to maximize your garden's potential. By starting warm-season crops such as peppers and eggplant indoors in pots, you can use your garden space for an early harvest of spinach or radishes while you wait for the soil to warm. Moreover, it gives you the time to prepare your soil and do some weeding in the spring, just in case you're off to a late start.

However, not all seeds benefit from being started indoors. Cool-season root crops such as turnips, radishes, carrots, and beets have delicate tap roots that can be damaged if transferred from a pot into the ground. Additionally, vining crops like cucumber, melon, and squash quickly grow extensive roots that are easily restricted by containers. This can set them back if seedlings are not swiftly transplanted. Starting these crops indoors to set out later may result in stunted roots and weakened plants.

How do you decide what's best for your situation? In general, look to your climate and the length of your growing season. In regions with short growing seasons, crops like peppers, tomatoes, and eggplant have a hard time ripening before the first fall frost, and gardeners benefit from starting these slow-to-grow crops indoors first. You'll also want to consider how much space you have indoors and whether you're willing to invest in additional equipment. In most cases, a combination of direct sowing seeds and planting indoor starts does the trick.

# THE BENEFITS AND DRAWBACKS OF SEEDS VS. STARTS

| | SEEDS | STARTS |
|---|---|---|
| **PRO** | Requires fewer resources and less space | Controlled environment |
| | Better suited for root crops | Protection from pests |
| | Minimal root disturbance | Extended season |
| | Natural adaptation to climate | Increased flexibility in planting timing |
| **CON** | Vulnerable to weather conditions | Transplant shock |
| | Weed competition | Labor-intensive |
| | Exposure to pests | Initial start-up cost |
| | Less control over the timing | Space requirements indoors |

Whether you choose to direct sow or seed starts indoors will depend on your crop selection, seasonal climate, and individual planting preferences. If you are new to growing indoors, start small and work your way up.

## Buying Quality Starts

If you want the benefits of planting starts (also known as transplants) but don't have the room or the opportunity to sow seeds indoors, you can purchase them from a garden center, farm, or online seed company.

The best advice is to purchase starts in person whenever possible because it lets you get a good look at a plant before buying it. If a transplant has any signs of discoloration, it could indicate potential disease or insect activity you don't want to bring home and risk spreading. Discolored leaves could also imply a nutrient deficiency, leading to more significant problems later. If the plant selection doesn't pass this initial scan, move on and try a new establishment. After all, buying starts is meant to simplify the process and should allow you to hand-select the cream of the crop.

Aside from inspecting the leaves, it's crucial to examine the roots. Check if the plant is rootbound, a condition where roots form a dense, tangled mat, signifying they've outgrown their container.

You can quickly check for rootbound transplants by gently turning the pot over to see if roots are growing through the container's drainage holes. While healthy seedlings haven't yet reached this stage, you can rescue some rootbound plants by untangling them. However, be cautious—some plants, such as cucumbers, may not respond well to this type of manipulation, and you may see signs of shock after planting. If you notice dark or mushy roots, it's also best to move on. These signs can imply decay or disease.

If you find starts with healthy foliage and roots, your last easy check is to see if they are in flower. Flowering plants are more vulnerable to transplanting shock and may stay small and underdeveloped. Plants that bloom too early are often stressed. Early blooms strip young seedlings' energy to develop roots and foliage.

If you are still looking for a reliable local resource that provides high-quality transplants, search for an online seed company with good reviews that also delivers plant starts to your door.

The Act of Planting   133

# SOURCING SEEDS

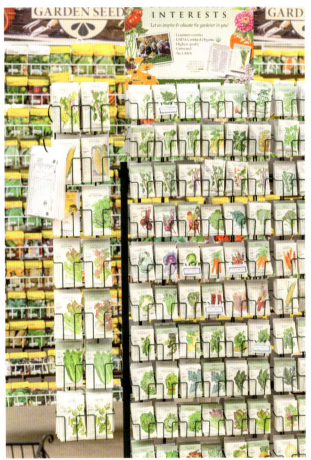

When shopping for seeds, follow your plan so you don't buy more seeds than needed.

**IT IS EASY TO BE MESMERIZED** by the racks of seed packets that appear each spring at your local garden center or hardware store. The colorful packages are alluring and can persuade you to purchase on a whim. Although it's okay to grab a packet or two that catches your eye, it's always better to take some time and plan out what you need beforehand. You'll also want to confirm the seed packets on display are labeled with the current year to ensure you'll have the freshest seeds and the highest possible germination rates.

When you shop for seeds online, you have the luxury of planning ahead for what you need. Most online seed companies send out beautifully designed seed catalogs that provide helpful information such as planting tips, plant profiles, and recommendations. If you don't receive these catalogs in the mail, you'll want to subscribe to these incredibly valuable resources.

Whether you purchase seeds from a store or online, look to source them from a respected regional seed company. When you buy local seeds, you increase the chance of growing plants well acclimated to your area. A surefire way to find local seeds is to pick them up at a community seed swap event. These events are great ways to meet fellow gardeners, exchange growing tips, and build community around the craft of growing food.

There are a few additional seed-sourcing tips to share. For starters, always check the date on the seed packet. Similar to food products in the grocery store, seeds have a packaging date. Seeds older than a year may still sprout, but the odds go down with each passing season. Second, choose organic seeds (collected from plants cultivated organically), because they will produce plants well adapted to growing in organic conditions, and it ensures they haven't been treated with synthetic seed coatings, such as fungicides. Finally, if you want to save seeds at the end of the season, you'll need to find open-pollinated seed varieties marked "OP" on the seed packet (see page 68 for tips on seed saving).

While some seeds last for several years when stored properly, it's always best to plant seeds purchased during the current year to ensure the highest germination rate.

# WHAT *Do Seeds* NEED?

Seed-starting mix is typically a blend of peat moss and vermiculite or perlite. It is light, fine-textured, and well-draining.

**IF YOU ARE NEW TO GARDENING,** it can be comforting to know there is no mystery to growing plants. While plants will thrive or fail depending on the temperature, quality of soil, or amount of rain or sun they get, all you need to remember is every plant needs the same fundamental things—warmth, water, and soil. By providing these basic necessities, you can give your plants the best chance to thrive.

## SOIL

When you start seeds indoors, you have the opportunity to plant them in a perfect potting mix that enables their tender roots to expand quickly. It may come as a surprise, but the best mixes don't contain any soil at all. Instead, they are a mixture of lightweight and porous materials, such as peat, vermiculite, and perlite.

Over the years, peat-based products have faced criticism, as some consider them unsustainable. Harvested from peat bogs, peat is an essential natural resource that takes thousands of years to regenerate. Removing peat to add to potting mix also releases carbon dioxide, a potent greenhouse gas, into the atmosphere that would otherwise remain locked underground.

While the environmental impact of using a few bags of potting mix is small, the increasing popularity of gardening means more and more peat is harvested each year. Now, peat alternatives like coconut coir, aged bark, rice hulls, and other plant materials are available on the market. However, some gardeners maintain that peat alternatives do not perform as well and require more attention to rear healthy seedlings.

### *Make Your Own Potting Mix*

Making a custom potting mix isn't necessary if you'd rather purchase the many quality products available. However, homemade mixes are significantly cheaper than ready-made store-bought options because the individual ingredients are less expensive when purchased separately. If you're planting a high volume of seedlings, making your own mix will lower your expenses. Creating custom mixes also allows you more control over the quality of ingredients. Plus, you can save resources by revitalizing your old potting mix by adding fresh components each year to bring it back to life.

**Recipe:** Makes five gallons
    2.5 gallons of peat or coconut coir
    1.5 gallons of compost
    1 gallon of perlite, vermiculite, or small pumice stone

**Directions:** Pour the ingredients into a large bucket or wheelbarrow. You'll want plenty of room to blend the mix thoroughly. Use a shovel to mix the ingredients uniformly. Fill containers and store excess potting mix in a sealed bin for future use.

You can also create your own potting mix by replacing peat with compost, but there are potential risks involved. Typically, most potting mixes are sterile, which minimizes the chance of disease during the early stages of growth. Still, some gardeners think the risk is worth it because compost has beneficial bacteria and plant nutrients that can improve seedling growth.

Seeds require the right temperature for germination, regardless of whether they are sown indoors or out. The seed packet will share the ideal soil temperature for each vegetable. Use a soil temperature probe to ensure you are hitting the target when direct sowing.

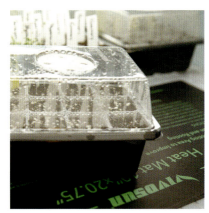
Indoors, seedling heat mats placed beneath seed-starting trays raise the soil temperature just enough to encourage rapid germination.

When starting seeds indoors, use a spray bottle to ensure the top of the soil surface stays moist until germination takes place. From that point on, water from the bottom or use a fine-nozzle watering can.

If you're sowing seeds outdoors, you won't have the luxury of picking the perfect potting mix. Instead, your focus shifts to preparing your native soil. For an in-depth look at preparing your soil to plant, go to chapter 6.

# WARMTH

Most seeds need soil temperatures between 55°F and 70°F to sprout. If you sow seeds in cool soil, they may fail to germinate unless you plant cool-season crops like peas or lettuce, which can tolerate soil temperatures as low as 40°F. On the other hand, when the soil temperature gets too hot—around 86°F to 90°F—seeds suffer, resulting in poor germination rates.

Gardeners often wait patiently for the soil to warm up after a long winter chill, but it's possible to speed up the process. If you're concerned about the temperature of your soil and want to start planting, remove any mulch to allow your soil to absorb more sunlight. Alternatively, cover your planting area with durable plastic sheets at least 4 to 6 weeks before planting to trap the sun's heat and accelerate the warming process.

If you plan to grow plants indoors, your home's ambient temperature is likely warm enough to encourage seeds to sprout, especially when they are placed in a sunny window. However, if you're starting seeds in a greenhouse or unheated garage, you can artificially warm the soil by using a heat mat. These mats are placed beneath seeded containers to warm the soil to a preset temperature that won't damage seeds. Once the seeds sprout, remove the containers from the heat mat to make room for more.

If you plan to use a heat mat, remember this one drawback—they tend to dry the soil. You can prevent this by covering your seed tray with a plastic dome or plastic kitchen wrap to trap moisture while you wait for the seeds to sprout. Once they have germinated, remove the cover to reduce condensation, which can lead to damping-off issues, resulting in seedling death (learn more about damping-off disease on pages 138 and 145).

# WATER

Seeds germinate best when the soil stays consistently moist; fluctuations between bone-dry and soggy soil can prevent germination. Therefore, maintain consistently moist soil that is never soggy. Think of it like a wrung-out sponge—damp but not dripping wet.

Maintaining soil moisture can be difficult, especially for seeded containers that tend to dry out quickly indoors. To overcome this issue, you may need to water pots daily using a spray bottle or a fine-nozzle watering can. Remember, you're not alone in this struggle; many gardeners face the same challenge as they tend to their indoor seedlings.

When it comes to planting seeds outdoors, the main issue is often too much water. Tiny seeds can easily be carried away by heavy rains or strong streams of water from a hose. In addition, if your garden bed is accidentally flooded by a poorly timed irrigation system, seeds can move around as water begins to pool. To prevent this from happening, water your seeds with a very fine mist or a gentle sprinkler and set any automated irrigation to turn off once the soil is wet to a depth of 1 inch.

# SOWING SEEDS
## *in the* GROUND

**DIRECTLY SOWING SEEDS** in the ground is a simple and efficient way to start your garden. There is no need to fuss around or make room for trays of seedlings indoors. Directly sowing seeds also helps maintain a consistent harvest of quick-to-grow crops such as lettuce, radishes, and arugula. Simply plant seeds every few weeks to replenish what you harvest.

No mandate demands you plant in rows, but if this is your approach, it's helpful to use a marked row as a guide. Create a straight line by staking the start and end of your row with two sticks connected by a string. Dig your seed furrow directly below the string before dropping in your seeds.

Planting in rows is a popular approach, but as discussed in chapter 5, you have the freedom to be as creative as you wish with your garden design. You can grow your plants in blocks, swirls, or any other pattern you like. However, tracking where you have sown your seeds with this free-for-all approach can be challenging. Therefore, mark your seeded areas to avoid accidentally pulling out newly emerged seedlings you mistook for weeds.

The depth of your furrow will depend on the size of your seeds. For example, plant small seeds as shallow as ⅛ inch; larger plant parts, like tubers, bulbs, or crowns, require a depth of 6 inches or more. Some seeds are so small you don't need a seed furrow at all. Instead, they are better scattered over the ground and gently raked in or covered with a light layer of compost.

Always consult the labeled instructions on the back of a seed packet for crop-specific guidance. Don't worry too much about spacing now; you can always thin plants once they sprout (see page 138). It's better to have too many seedlings at this stage than to wish you had planted more.

Planting large spaces with small seeds can be tedious, as it is hard to pick them up individually. However, several tools are available to help you achieve an even distribution of seeds. Handheld seed dispensers, for instance, allow you to tap out the right amount of seeds more easily into your planting furrow. Some are even battery-powered and vibrate, making the flow of seeds that fall to the ground effortless. Another popular option is the walk-behind seeder. There are many makes and models, but they all accomplish the same task of depositing perfectly spaced seeds as you push them along. It's worth mentioning, however, that walk-behind seeders work best for straight rows and may be less effective for planting in unique patterns. The planting tools spread at the end of this chapter shares more about these tools.

The ideal seed-planting depth varies by the type of vegetable, but the seed packet will share the ideal target.

Aim to follow the spacing guidelines on each seed packet, but also plan to thin seedlings as necessary. Properly spacing very small seeds, such as these carrot seeds, can be a challenge, making thinning essential. See sidebar on page 138.

# TROUBLESHOOTING OUTDOOR SEEDLING ISSUES

| OBSERVATION | POTENTIAL CAUSE | POSSIBLE SOLUTION |
|---|---|---|
| Poor germination | Old or expired seed | Test your seed viability. |
| | Cold soil temperatures | Wait for the soil to warm or encourage warmer temps by removing mulch or laying down plastic sheets. |
| | Uneven watering | The soil is too wet or too dry. |
| Seedlings falling over/damping-off | Poor air circulation | Thin crowded plants to improve airflow. |
| | Powerful overhead watering | Avoid watering seedlings directly with a strong water flow. |
| Yellow/brown leaves | Nutrient deficiency | Apply diluted (to half the recommended dose) liquid fish emulsion fertilizer during your next watering. |
| | Overwatering | Improve drainage or reduce the length of watering time. |
| Stunted growth | Cold temperatures | Cover seedings with an insulating floating row cover (see page 195). |
| | Lack of light | Wait for the days to grow longer, and seedlings will catch up. |
| | Uneven watering | Maintain consistent soil moisture. |
| Curled/drooping leaves | Uneven watering | Maintain consistent soil moisture. |
| | Pest pressure | Treat for pests. |

Planting outdoors can give you little control over the seeds' environment. However, you can control a few things like seed spacing, consistent watering practices, and protecting seedlings from the cold.

## *Thinning Seedlings*

Thinning is a necessary evil because it's challenging to seed precisely. Many gardeners also intentionally sow more seeds than recommended to increase their odds or to compensate for poor germination rates.

Once small seedlings emerge, wait a few weeks before thinning your crop. This might feel challenging, but it's a necessary step to provide the remaining plants with enough space, nutrients, and air circulation to thrive. Overcrowded plants are susceptible to disease, and the lack of space can stunt growth.

If you find yourself with overcrowded plants, quickly thin tiny sprouts by gently taking hold of the stem below the leaves and pulling them slowly from the soil. However, pulling larger sprouts can disturb the soil and potentially impact the neighboring plants you want to keep around. Use scissors to snip extra plants off at the base, below the lowest set of leaves.

In almost all cases, thinning your seedlings to the recommended spacing found on the seed packet is necessary if you want productive crops. However, if you plan to grow greens and harvest them when they are young and tender, thinning is optional if you harvest them regularly.

**138** American Horticultural Society | *Essential Guide to Organic Vegetable Gardening*

Some vegetable crops are easier to grow from vegetative plant parts, such as bulbs, sets, crowns, and cuttings. Garlic is best planted from cloves in the autumn for harvest the following summer.

Perennial asparagus crowns are planted in a long trench. It will be several years before a harvest can be made, but the plants will go on to produce for decades.

Once your seeds are in and covered, water them often. The challenge with direct sowing is keeping the soil moist without drowning seeds, especially in locations with little rainfall or intense sunshine. At this point, quick and frequent waterings are better than a long, deep soak (although this changes once your seedlings start to grow). Monitor your soil and water frequently until the seeds have sprouted.

If you find yourself watering multiple times a day, an effective way to keep the soil moist is to use any lightweight fabric soaked in water to cover the seeded ground. By shading the earth with wet material, you can prevent soil moisture from evaporating quickly. Once the fabric dries out, simply soak it again and drape it over the soil. But be sure to check on your seeds daily and remove the fabric as soon as they sprout to avoid smothering the delicate seedlings.

## PLANTING BULBS, SETS, CROWNS, OR CUTTINGS

Although planting seeds is the most common method for growing crops, this may not be the most efficient option for some. For example, crops that produce tubers underground, such as Jerusalem artichokes or potatoes, are better grown by planting saved or purchased tubers from last season instead of sowing from seed. Additionally, certain crops grow quicker by planting a clove, set, or root crown (the part of the plant where the stem and roots meet).

A successful garlic harvest begins with a planted clove saved from the last season or purchased from a supplier. While it is possible to grow garlic from the tiny bulblets that hardneck garlic plants produce on their flowering stalks (known as scapes—see page 245), it will take a few years to see a harvest. For that reason, most gardeners grow garlic by planting cloves.

Onions can also be grown from last season's immature bulbs, called sets. Sets (see page 249) are underdeveloped onions harvested the previous year with the intention of planting them the following season. Planting from sets produces a quicker harvest, but the plants tend to bolt prematurely. If your onions do bolt, you can still harvest them, but their shelf life may decline.

Perennial crops that grow year after year—such as asparagus, rhubarb, or horseradish—are easier to grow from a root crown. You can purchase one-year-old plant crowns from seed companies to speed up the growth process of these crops, which typically take longer to mature. After the roots take hold, you can expect to harvest these crops for many seasons without replanting.

If you want to grow perennial herbs, you can propagate them using root or stem cuttings. For soft-stemmed herbs such as mint, basil, and lemon balm, you can clip a few sprigs and root them in water before planting them in the garden. On the other hand, woody herbs like rosemary, thyme, and lavender can be easily propagated by planting their cuttings directly into the soil.

# Winter Sowing

If you're interested in growing plant starts but don't have the space or resources to do so indoors, winter sowing may be the perfect solution. This technique involves converting old milk jugs, two-liter soda bottles, or clear takeout containers into mini-greenhouses that you fill with premoistened potting mix and seeds. As the name suggests, you place these containers outside during the cold months, and as the soil warms, your seeds will germinate; no heat mat or artificial lights are required.

Winter sowing is a set-it-and-forget-it seeding practice, but some preparation is involved to make sure your seeds are protected. First, you'll need to prepare your containers and make sure they have plenty of drainage holes to prevent water from pooling inside and drowning your seeds. If you have trouble poking holes through thick plastic, soften it with a flame so it is easier to punch through with a knife or screwdriver. You'll also want some holes near the top of the container for ventilation.

After creating the holes, the next step is to fill your containers with at least 3 inches of potting mix. A fast and easy method to prepare gallon jugs or soda bottles for filling is to cut around the jug's circumference approximately 6 inches from the bottom. However, make sure that you don't cut all the way around the container—leave a 3-inch hinge so the two pieces are still connected. This way, you will be able to open and fill the container easily while retaining a protective "lid" to cover your seeds.

Once your containers are filled and seeded, place them outside, exposed to snow and rain. You do not need to worry about watering them, as nature will take care of it for you unless you live in a dry region that experiences warm winter temperatures. Choose a location with diffused sunlight, since placing the containers in direct sun could cause the soil to warm and the seeds to sprout too quickly for the frigid winter conditions. Keep an eye out for "false springs," where a brief warm-up is followed by a plunge in temperature that can kill newly sprouted seeds. If you time it right, your seedlings will quickly grow and be ready for the garden once you've prepared the soil for planting.

It's important to note that winter sowing is only suitable for certain garden vegetables. Warm-season crops like tomatoes, peppers, and cucumbers will not germinate when the soil temperature is below 60°F. Instead, look for seeds described on the seed packet as self-sowing, cold hardy, or sown when cool. Popular choices include salad greens, kale, chard, broccoli, cabbage, and peas. Flowering perennials like coneflowers, black-eyed Susans, and verbenas are also reasonable choices.

Winter sowing is a method for starting seeds outdoors in winter. It's best for cold-season crops and perennials.

# PLANTING *Seeds* INDOORS

**THERE ARE COUNTLESS CONTAINERS** you can use to start your seeds, as long as they hold potting mix and allow excess water to drain out. You can use old egg cartons, leftover clamshell containers, toilet paper rolls, or folded newspaper pots, all of which are commonly used by thrifty gardeners. If you prefer to buy something, plastic cell flats that fit neatly in standard 1020 nursery trays are a good option. These cell flats come in different sizes—typically ranging from ½ inch to 2 inches wide, with varying depths—and can help you maximize your space on a sunny windowsill or heat mat.

Eco-conscious gardeners can ditch the plastic and choose to seed in biodegradable pots. Pressed peat pots are the standard, but you can also find biodegradable pots made of coir, composted manure, and paper. Biodegradable pots are handy for starting crops such as cucumber, squash, peas, and corn—all of which have sensitive roots that do not appreciate being disturbed. These pots can be directly planted into the ground right along with the plant, eliminating the need to remove plants from their pots and transplant them.

Some gardeners observe that not all biodegradable pots are made equal. Those made from thicker materials can prevent plant roots from busting through and reaching the soil once planted in the ground. If you share this concern, tear the bottom of the pot before planting it in the ground.

If you decide to use plastic pots, look for thick-walled pots made of durable plastic. Flimsy plastic pots tend to break after just one use and consequently end up in the landfill after a single season. Check with landscapers and nurseries; many often have used pots they are willing to give away. Before reusing them, sanitize the pots in a 10 percent bleach solution and rinse well.

When you're ready to begin planting, fill your containers with potting mix. Make sure to leave ½ inch of space from the top to make watering your seedlings easier. Before planting, water the mix to moisten it and help it settle. Sow larger seeds deeper than tiny seeds, and keep in mind some seeds are so small that they sprout more easily when placed on the soil's surface and lightly covered with a pinch of potting mix.

Biodegradable pots made from peat, coir, or composted manure are a great way to reduce plastic waste while giving your plants a great start.

Creative gardeners can start seeds in just about anything, including these toilet-tissue cores with one end folded closed.

Aim to plant at least two seeds per pot or planting cell to guarantee at least one seed germinates. Place your pots in a warm, sunny location, water them when the potting mix begins to dry out, and wait patiently for the first tender sprout to emerge.

The Act of Planting

Growing your own transplants from seed requires attention and care, but there are many benefits, including a broader selection and more control over how your plants are grown from the start.

# SEEDLING CARE

There's a unique joy in patiently waiting for that first glimpse of green to unfurl from just beneath the soil surface. Some seeds sprout in a day or so, while others can take weeks, leaving you to wonder if it will even happen at all. But when it does, those vulnerable seedlings need your special attention to grow and thrive indoors. This is true whether you seed your own starts or purchase starts from your local nursery.

As a home gardener, you play a crucial role in providing the right conditions for seedling growth. Proper light, water, and temperatures are essential for their healthy development into robust plants. Since they are inside, the natural environment won't provide what they need, so it's up to you to take charge.

## *Soil Blocks*

Ambitious gardeners who want to avoid pots altogether use soil blocks. With the help of a blocker tool, potting mix is compressed into a sturdy, freestanding cube or cylinder. This approach saves time because there is no need to clean and sanitize used pots from last year. The open sides of the soil blocks promote healthy roots through air pruning, a process whereby roots naturally die off when they come into contact with air. While this may sound like a disadvantage, it actually prevents rootbound seedlings and encourages plants to develop a network of fibrous and fine roots that give them a leg up once planted in the ground.

Soil blocking can be a great experience regardless of your motivation, be it for healthier starts, reduced waste, or general curiosity. However, it requires some practice to get it right. The challenge lies in achieving the right consistency of potting mix so that your blocks hold together firmly and do not crumble apart. The key is to wet the potting mix before packing it into the blocker tool.

After you dampen your potting mix, place the blocker on a flat surface and scoop the moistened soil mix into the blocker chamber. Use your fingers to compact the mix as firmly as possible. When you're satisfied, flip the tool upside down to remove the blocks. Some tools require you to gently tap the blocks out, while others are engineered with a spring-loaded handle you squeeze to push them free. If they get stuck, gently pry any out with a butter knife.

Now that your blocks are ready, you can make a small hole in each one to plant your seeds and then lightly cover them with soil. Place your soil blocks in a 1020 tray for easy bottom-watering and transportation.

Soil blocking uses a soil-compression tool called a soil blocker to create cubes of potting soil for seed starting. It's a great way to reduce plastic usage and grow healthy seedlings.

142 American Horticultural Society | *Essential Guide to Organic Vegetable Gardening*

Your seedlings' nutritional needs are minimal at first, but fertilization might be necessary as they grow, primarily if you use a compost-free potting mix. Before your seedlings are ready for the great outdoors, they need to be hardened off, a process that acclimates them to your outdoor conditions to reduce shock from a sudden drop in temperature (see page 145).

## Give Them Light

Seedlings require 12 to 14 hours of sunlight to promote strong and healthy growth. However, providing adequate light for indoor plants can be difficult and is one of the main reasons why seedlings often fail. Relying on natural light from a south-facing window is one way to grow seedlings indoors, but this method can be affected by cloudy days and long shadows cast by nearby trees or structures. Moreover, modern windows are often equipped with films and filters that block the UV rays necessary for seedlings to develop properly. If you have grown indoor starts before, you might have noticed your young plants become stretched, thin, and weak as a result of these challenges.

If your seedlings are pining for more sunlight, supply them with a full-spectrum LED light. These lights use less energy than incandescent bulbs and don't get too hot, so you don't have to worry about leaving them on. Position the light 3 to 4 inches from the top of your seedlings and raise it as your plants grow taller. You can set your lights on a timer so you don't have to think about switching them on and off.

## Only the Strongest Survive

Earlier, we recommended seeding at least two seeds per pot to better your chances of success. Now that your seedlings are starting to grow, it's time to cull the weaker sprouts to prevent overcrowding and competition for resources. Start thinning your seedlings once plants develop their first set of true leaves, which are the next leaves to emerge after the cotyledons (the seed leaves).

Closely inspect each container or cell pack and identify the strongest, healthiest seedling. Remove weaker plants with scissors to avoid disturbing the roots of the one you want to keep. The aim is to have one plant per container. You can add culled seedlings to the compost pile. With proper thinning, the surviving seedlings will have plenty of room to develop a robust root system and lush top growth before you transplant them out into the garden.

A grow light setup is essential for providing your seedlings with the right intensity of light to support optimum growth.

When your seedlings develop their first true leaves, thin them so only the strongest seedling remains.

The Act of Planting   143

Watering is an essential task when growing seeds indoors. Watering can take place from the top, using a watering can, or from the bottom, by placing the pots or flats in a water-filled tray and letting them absorb the water from the bottom.

## *Water*

You can always water delicate seedlings with a gentle pour from a watering can or a fine mist from a spray bottle, but it is even better to water them from the bottom up. Bottom watering provides consistent moisture and reduces the risk of damping-off. Plus, it's a hands-off approach that saves time.

Try bottom watering your thirsty seedlings by placing them in a tray that can comfortably hold 1 inch of water. Let your pots sit in the water for an hour, and you'll see the water gently wick into the growing media through the pot's drainage holes. This technique helps moisten the potting mix without saturating it. Repeat once the potting mix dries out.

## *Sizing Up*

If you start your seedlings in cell flats or small pots, you'll need to move them to a larger container once they outgrow their current space. Otherwise, they may become rootbound and stunted. The size of the container you choose depends on how long your seedlings need to stay inside. As a general rule, the longer they stay indoors, the bigger the pot needs to be. For instance, if your seedlings need another few weeks to mature before they are ready to be planted outside, transplant them from a 2-inch pot to a 4-inch pot. The extra room gives them adequate space to stretch their roots until they are ready to be planted outside.

When you move your seedlings into bigger pots, it's also an excellent opportunity to give them the nutrients they need to grow. Start by filling your new containers with a potting mix that's doctored up with 50 percent compost. Once you've transferred your plants into the larger pots, water your newly up-potted seedlings with a diluted organic liquid fertilizer such as liquid kelp or fish emulsion. These fertilizers provide your seedlings with fast-acting nutrients they can absorb right away.

## *Hardening Off*

Seedlings grown indoors may struggle to adapt to their new outdoor surroundings. To make the transplanting process less stressful, harden them off slowly and let them adjust gradually to outdoor elements. If you plan to move your plants to the garden, start introducing them to outdoor temperatures about a week in advance. On sunny days, move the plants outside to experience the breeze and other outdoor elements. But make sure to bring them back inside before the temperature drops too low at night. Repeat this process every day for a week before planting them outside. This gradual transition helps plants adjust to their outdoor environment without experiencing stunted growth or getting damaged by windburn.

# TROUBLESHOOTING INDOOR SEEDLING CARE

| OBSERVATION | POTENTIAL CAUSE | POSSIBLE SOLUTION |
| --- | --- | --- |
| Nothing sprouted | Improper soil temperature | Use a heat mat to warm the soil. |
| | Under- or overwatering | Keep the soil consistently moist by bottom watering your starts. |
| Seedlings falling over/damping-off or yellow/brown leaves | Infected seeding equipment | Disinfect trays, pots, and other equipment. |
| | Poor air circulation | Increase airflow and strengthen seedlings' stems with a fan. |
| | Overhead watering | Water from the bottom. |
| Leggy/spindly seedlings | Insufficient light | Supplement your natural light with grow lights and keep lights 2 to 4 inches above seedlings. |
| Stunted growth | Lack of light | Set up supplemental grow lights. |
| | Lack of nutrients | Up-pot seedlings and refresh the potting mix with compost. Water plants with a diluted liquid fertilizer. |
| | Improper watering | Maintain consistent soil moisture. |
| Fungus gnats | Overwatering | Allow the soil to dry between waterings, and use sticky traps to reduce pest populations. |
| | Infested potting mix | Prevent future outbreaks by storing unused potting mix in an airtight container. |
| Seedlings not thriving | Too hot/cold | Maintain an optimal growing temperature (65°F to 75°F). |
| | Too much/little light | Provide 14 to 16 hours of light per day. |

It's frustrating to see your seedlings struggle. After all, you've put in a lot of work up to this point to give yourself a head start on the planting season. Use this chart as a guide to troubleshoot some of the most common issues with rearing seedlings indoors.

The Act of Planting **145**

When the seedlings are large enough to transplant outdoors, be sure the garden site is prepared and the seedlings have been properly hardened off.

## *Transplant into the Garden*

The moment is here! Your indoor seedlings have grown, and it's time to plant them in the ground. But before you're ready, prepare the planting area by following the tips outlined in chapter 6. Once you prep the soil, carefully remove your plants from their containers. Avoid yanking them forcefully because it can damage the roots and expose them to soilborne diseases once they are in the ground. Instead, gently squeeze the sides of the pot between your thumb and fingers to loosen the grip. If that doesn't work, you can use a butter knife or popsicle stick to loosen the soil around the edge of the pot. Of course, you can skip this step if you've planted your starts in biodegradable, plantable containers or soil blocks.

After removing your plants from their containers, carefully place them into a pre-dug hole. The hole should be approximately double the size of the previous container so the roots can spread out. In most cases, seedlings should be planted at the same soil level as in their container, because buried stems have the potential to rot and kill the plant. The exception to this rule is tomatoes, which are discussed in the sidebar on the facing page.

If the roots of your seedlings are tangled, gently massage them apart before planting them in the ground. For the best results, position the roots so they are trending downward, and firmly pack soil into empty spaces around the roots to eliminate any air pockets. Finally, give your transplants a thorough watering to help the soil settle into place and to provide your plants with the moisture they need to evade potential transplant shock. It may take a week or two before your plants fully adjust to their new surroundings, so don't expect much growth immediately.

The final consideration for a successful transplant is the weather. Wait for a calm, cool day, one that is overcast. Young plants set out in the blazing sun will struggle to adapt. If a cloudy day isn't on the horizon, and you want to set plants out, transplant them in the afternoon when the sun's intensity has diminished.

## *Trench Planting Tomatoes*

While most plants can perish when planted too deep, tomatoes are the exception to this rule. They have a unique trait that enables them to grow new roots from buried parts of their stem, leading to stronger, more productive plants. Take advantage of this by burying at least 6 inches of stem below ground.

Rather than dig a deep vertical hole, it's easier to dig a long horizontal trench 4 to 6 inches deep and the length of the plant's stem. When you're ready, remove any leaves along the bottom two-thirds of the plant and lay your seedling lengthwise along the bottom of the trench. Gently bend the top of the seedling toward the sky before securing its position by backfilling the trench. Aim to have at least 4 inches of stem with leaves intact above the soil line.

To trench-plant a tomato, dig a trench into the soil that is almost as long as the plant is tall.

Next, remove all the bottom leaves from the plant, leaving only a few remaining leaves at the top.

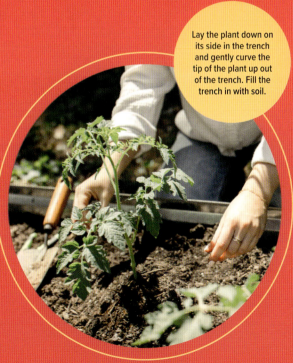

Lay the plant down on its side in the trench and gently curve the tip of the plant up out of the trench. Fill the trench in with soil.

The Act of Planting

The kale transplant at left is slightly pot-bound and is not yet ready for planting. The seedling at right has had its roots loosened and is ready to find a home in the garden.

### TRANSPLANTING CHECKLIST

○ The long-range forecast is frost-free and predicts at least a week of calm weather without heavy rain, snow, or wind.

○ The soil temperature is at least 60°F (this is more important for warm-season vegetables).

○ The outdoor temperature isn't too hot or too cold (65°F to 70°F is just right).

○ You have emergency cloches, mobile cold frames, or frost blankets on standby, just in case (see page 214 for more plant-protection ideas).

○ Your planting day will be overcast and calm.

Many factors contribute to successfully transplanting seedlings into the great outdoors. This checklist offers you some suggestions on how to nail it!

# TIMING *Is* EVERYTHING

**SO FAR, WE'VE COVERED** a lot about the act of planting seeds and starts. The final consideration we have yet to mention is timing, which can make or break your success. Seeds sown too early outdoors can be at risk of sudden death due to late-season frost. Even starting seeds indoors, which offers an advantage, can be detrimental if done too soon. If you keep the plants in a pot for too long, their quality will deteriorate unless you consistently give them more space. To help you navigate this crucial aspect, we've prepared a chart outlining the ideal indoor or outdoor planting times.

The act of planting, whether indoors under grow lights, outdoors into the soil, or with transplants purchased at a garden center, is one of the most satisfying parts of gardening. It does take some experimentation, especially when you're a new gardener, but after a season or two of growing, you'll gain confidence and skill. In the next chapter, we dive into ways to care for your vegetable plants as they grow and produce.

# TIMING QUICK-REFERENCE CHART

| CROP | START SEEDS INDOORS (NUMBER OF WEEKS PRIOR TO YOUR FROST-FREE DATE) | SAFE TIME TO TRANSPLANT STARTS OR DIRECT SOW OUTDOORS (RELATIVE TO YOUR FROST-FREE DATE) |
|---|---|---|
| Artichokes | 8 | On frost-free date |
| Beets* | 4 to 6 | 2 weeks before |
| Broccoli | 4 to 6 | 2 weeks before |
| Cabbage | 4 to 6 | 4 weeks before |
| Carrots* | 4 to 6 | 2 weeks before |
| Cauliflower | 4 to 6 | 2 weeks before |
| Celery | 10 to 12 | 1 week after |
| Collards | 4 to 6 | 4 weeks before |
| Corn* | 2 to 4 | 0 to 2 weeks after |
| Cucumbers | 3 to 4 | 1 to 2 weeks after |
| Eggplant | 8 to 10 | 2 to 3 weeks after |
| Kale | 4 to 6 | 4 weeks before |
| Kohlrabi* | 4 to 6 | 4 weeks before |
| Leeks | 8 to 10 | 2 weeks before |
| Lettuce | 4 to 5 | 3 to 4 weeks before |
| Melons | 3 to 4 | 2 weeks after |
| Okra* | 4 to 6 | 2 to 4 weeks after |
| Onions | 8 to 10 | 4 weeks before |
| Peas* | 3 to 4 | 6 to 8 weeks before |
| Peppers | 8 | 2 weeks after |
| Pumpkins | 3 to 4 | 2 weeks after |
| Spinach | 4 to 6 | 3 to 6 weeks before |
| Squash | 3 to 4 | 2 weeks after |
| Swiss chard | 4 to 6 | 2 weeks before |
| Tomatoes | 6 to 8 | 1 to 2 weeks after |
| * plants prefer to be seeded outdoors | | |

The Act of Planting

# USEFUL TOOLS *for* PLANTING

### PLASTIC POTS
are available in various shapes and sizes. For seeding, flats of interconnected cells are recommended, while larger individual plastic pots offer more space for starts to grow. Thicker plastic pots are durable and can be reused for many seasons, unlike thin ones that tend to break after a single use.

### 1020 TRAYS
are an adaptable solution for holding seeded pots, indoors or out. You can choose from trays with holes for outdoor drainage or ones with solid bottoms to prevent spills when watering indoors. Some trays come with a fitted **plastic dome** to create a tabletop greenhouse.

### BIODEGRADABLE POTS
made from materials like peat, coconut coir, or composted manure provide a plastic-free option for seedlings to sprout and grow in. To reduce root shock while planting, place these pots directly into the ground along with the seedling.

### SOIL BLOCKERS
are ideal for gardeners who want to be plastic-free. These metal seed-starting contraptions compress wet potting soil into blocks that are then seeded. They come in different sizes, depending on the crops you're seeding (learn more about soil blocking on page 142).

### HAND SEEDERS
make handling tiny seeds more manageable with a gentle tap. You can adjust the opening to control the number of seeds that come out, and the transparent cover allows you to see how many seeds remain.

### WALK-BEHIND SEEDERS
are perfect for large outdoor spaces. They create a furrow and deposit seeds as you walk down a row. Many have adjustable seed plates for different crops.

### HEAT MATS
placed beneath seeded pots or trays keep the soil warm to encourage quick germination. Add a **thermostat** to regulate the temperature evenly to prevent damaging your seeds or seedlings.

### GROW LIGHTS
promote healthy growth indoors and prevent weak and leggy seedlings. Full-spectrum LED bulbs are a safe and energy-efficient option.

### SPRAY BOTTLES
are useful for misting small, tender seedlings and moistening soil for potted plants.

### RIGHT-ANGLE TROWEL
is an ergonomic option for making transplant holes. Choose a trowel with a depth scale on the blade to quickly gauge transplanting depth.

### HORI HORI KNIFE
is a useful tool for making planting holes, cutting twine, slicing through thick roots, and more. One edge of the blade is serrated, while the other is not.

The Act of Planting

CHAPTER 8

# GARDEN *and* PLANT CARE

**TAKING CARE OF YOUR GARDEN** involves not only looking after your plants but also nurturing the soil. Soil building is a continuous process that is never truly complete. When you support the natural biological processes that enhance soil quality every season, you can increase your garden's overall resilience. Plants grown in resilient soil can tolerate and recover better from droughts, floods, heat waves, and pest invasions.

In this chapter, you'll learn to develop a soil maintenance plan depending on the type of soil you're working with. In addition to giving you tips and tricks for long-term soil protection, this chapter also explains the benefits of spreading mulch and offers weeding advice to make the most dreaded garden task more efficient. The chapter then transitions to plant care and covers fertilizing, plant support, and putting the garden to bed at the end of the season. It ends with a comprehensive garden to-do list meant to guide you through each season, no matter where you live.

the habitat of the soil-dwelling creatures you want to foster. It's as if a tornado sped through a crowded town, leaving nothing but destruction in its wake. The breakdown of soil structure can also lead to compaction and erosion issues that further degrade the soil.

Repeated tilling not only breaks down soil structure but also causes the living soil to become overly active by providing a sudden rush of oxygen underground. Saturating the soil with oxygen prompts microorganisms to consume organic matter faster than it can be replaced. This rapid decomposition quickly releases a flood of plant nutrients but also creates a feast or famine for the soil biome. Tilling, therefore, sacrifices the soil's long-term health for short-term gains and turns back the clock on all your soil-building efforts.

In some cases, tilling may be necessary. This is particularly true for soils that require extra effort when creating a new planting site or incorporating vast amounts of organic matter, soil amendments, or cover crops into the soil. However, in most cases, tilling should be used as a last resort.

## THE CASE *Against* TILLING

**ANNUAL SOIL TILLING,** once a mainstay in home gardening, has been reevaluated through the lens of the living soil, which is happier and healthier when left alone. While tilling is a quick way to cultivate a weed-free and fluffy planting bed, it upsets the soil's natural structure and

## An Alternative to Tilling

When you ditch the rototiller or plow, you start to restore the natural system of building soil—from the top down. A low-impact cultivation technique called broadforking is an easy-to-adopt alternative. A broadfork looks like a hefty pitchfork but has two long handles and a sturdy metal base. Extending from the tool's base are metal tines that, when driven into the soil, loosen it without turning it over. Broadforks work well for in-ground gardens but are also suitable for soil preparation within raised beds.

Many gardeners enjoy using a broadfork because it's easier than digging and turning the soil over with a shovel. It minimizes soil compaction compared to cultivating with a heavy machine, and it also prevents dormant seeds just under the surface from seeing the light of day, so weeding is less of a chore.

Broadforks are available in different weights and sizes, making it easy to find the perfect model for your needs. When choosing a broadfork, consider the size and material of the tool. You can choose between handles made of wood, steel, or lightweight fiberglass.

Depending on the type of garden you have, you should select the width of the tool and the number of tines that will work best for you. Wider bases cover more ground, but slimmed-down versions make quick work in tight spaces. The weight of the tool varies too. Some versions weigh upwards of 20 pounds, and these rugged tools are perfect for breaking hard-packed ground, whereas lighter models weighing only 10 pounds are perfect for managing established gardens.

Broadforks are handy tools for aerating and loosening soil without destroying the living organisms found there. It's also easier than turning the soil over and reduces the compaction that occurs when using a gas-powered tiller.

To use a broadfork, follow the steps below:

1. Drive the broadfork into the soil with the tips of the slightly curved tines pointing forward.

2. Step on the tool's base and support yourself with the two handles on either side of you. Use your body weight to push the tines deeper into the soil. A small jump can help the tool dig deeper if you are able to balance.

3. Step off the base, and with your feet firmly on the ground, push and pull the handles forward and back. Notice how the tines open up deep channels to loosen the soil.

4. Take a few steps back and repeat the process until you've covered your planting areas.

# WORKING *with* YOUR NATIVE SOIL

**A SUCCESSFUL START TO THE GROWING SEASON** requires preparing the soil to plant, which depends on the type of soil you have to work with. You can start by removing weeds, adding a good amount of organic matter, and aerating the soil. However, establishing a routine soil-maintenance plan helps you make the most of your soil's potential.

The foundation of a soil maintenance plan should prioritize garden practices that add or protect organic matter. But be mindful not to get carried away. You want to support the natural soil-building process without overwhelming it. Applying an excessive amount of organic matter can overload the capacity of living soil to decompose it, resulting in a nutrient buildup that can encourage pest and disease issues. Add up to 5 inches of compost for the first season or two to kick-start the soil-building process for new garden spaces, but as your garden matures, adjust compost applications based on your soil type.

It's important to understand that while adding organic matter to your soil can be helpful, it's not a cure-all solution. Large-scale drainage issues, drought conditions, or imbalanced soil pH can all impede the natural functions of the soil. Therefore, addressing these underlying issues alongside the regular addition of organic matter is essential to improving your soil quality over time.

Creating a practical soil plan for your garden starts with good record-keeping. Keep tabs on your improvements by testing your soil quality indicators each season. Look at your soil quality indicator report (see page 115). Do you notice any soil properties that need improvement? Working to correct any soil issues provides long-term benefits and creates a positive feedback loop over the years. With the right plan, you'll soon find preparing the soil each season easier and more practical.

## BREAKING UP CLAY

Clay soils are common in the southeastern states, from Pennsylvania to Louisiana. However, you may also have clay soils if you are gardening along a river floodplain, dried-up lake, or pond. Regardless of your location, working with clay soils can be a frustrating experience.

Clay soils are hard to dig and are susceptible to compaction. They also drain slowly. To mitigate these challenges, a gardener's best bet is to improve the soil structure with organic matter. Regular applications over the years improve and break up heavy clay soil. Lay down at least 3 inches of compost or aged and composted manure. Loosening the soil with a broadfork or pitchfork helps to mix it in.

## THE IMPACT OF GARDEN TASKS ON ORGANIC MATTER

| ADDS ORGANIC MATTER | PROTECTS ORGANIC MATTER | REMOVES ORGANIC MATTER | EXHAUSTS ORGANIC MATTER |
|---|---|---|---|
| Adding compost and manure | No-till cultivation | Soil erosion | Heavy, repetitive tillage |
| Planting cover crops | Using organic mulches | Over-fertilizing | Working wet soil (compaction) |
| The appropriate use of fertilizers and amendments | Keeping garden debris on site after harvest | Removing garden debris (weeds too!) | Leaving the soil surface bare |

Each season is another opportunity to maintain soil-building organic matter. It's easy to think of organic matter as something you add to the soil, but there are garden activities like tilling and weeding that deplete it too. Prioritize garden tasks that build and safeguard organic matter to counterbalance those that remove or exhaust it.

Garden and Plant Care **155**

It is a common misconception that adding coarse sand to clay soil improves its fine texture. However, this is not the case. Soil texture is intrinsic and cannot be altered by adding sand. In fact, adding sand to clay soil can be harmful, as it creates a cementlike mixture that is more difficult to work with than the original soil.

Clay soils are often poorly draining and compact easily. Regular additions of organic matter are the solution. Organic matter separates tightly packed clay particles and opens up channels for air and water movement.

Organic matter is also the answer for improving sandy soils. The organic matter binds together gritty sand particles and helps them aggregate more effectively. Good aggregation (i.e., soil structure) means greater moisture retention.

Many gardeners also use gypsum to improve heavy clay soils. While it does improve drainage and water percolation, gypsum is an expensive product that needs to be applied repeatedly to see a noticeable difference. Also, it only works in large amounts, and its overuse can lead to calcium buildup, which can negatively impact the living soil.

Instead, plant a fall cover crop each year to help loosen the soil over time. Choose a cover crop with long taproots that dig deep (see page 174 for a complete list of cover crops and their benefits). Finally, berm up in-ground beds to increase drainage, and create dedicated pathways to reduce compaction in your growing spaces.

Some clay soils are so compacted that tilling may offer the best solution despite the potential drawbacks. Tilling the soil can mix in large amounts of organic matter before the soil is workable by hand. But be careful not to till the soil when it's wet, as this can result in hard clumps that are difficult to manage when the soil dries.

## REHABILITATING SANDY SOIL

Sandy soils cover roughly 8 percent of the continental United States. They are typical in windy, coastal, and outwash plain areas and are extensive throughout the Gulf Coastal Plain region (including Florida, Georgia, and Texas) and certain areas of the Midwest (including Nebraska, Michigan, Wisconsin, and Minnesota). It's common to have mixed feelings about sandy soil. On one hand, it has adequate drainage and resists compaction. However, these benefits come with a price—low fertility and a vulnerability to drought conditions.

Unlike clay soils, which benefit from loosening up, improving sandy soil requires helping it bind together. By adding 3 to 4 inches of compost each season, you'll help soil particles clump together better. You don't need to worry about adding too much compost if you have sandy soil. This additional bulk helps prevent rapid water loss.

Tackle sandy soil's infertility with additional soil amendments that function as fertilizers. Composted manure and worm castings are good options (for a complete list of soil amendments, see page 124). Add small amounts of amendments throughout the growing season rather than all at once to avoid nutrient leaching, which is typical for this soil type.

For soils with a high pH, additions of pulverized lime may be necessary to raise the pH.

## MAINTAINING YOUR LOAM
Loam, beautiful loam! If you have it—well done. It's friable, moist, and nutrient-rich. It also provides an ideal habitat for plants and soil-dwelling organisms. Maintaining your rich loam soil guarantees an excellent harvest year after year. Even though loam may not need many improvements, adding compost is still a good idea.

Spread 1 to 2 inches of compost over your garden area at least once a year to support the living soil. If your loam leans toward clay on the texture triangle (see page 101), use a broadfork to help aerate it before planting. If your loam soil is on the sandier side, consider adding a manure-based compost to replenish any nutrients that might be lacking.

## FLUSHING OUT THE SALT
Saline soils are often found in regions with coastal or arid climates, where rainfall is infrequent and evaporation rates are high. Salinization may also result from drainage problems that occur over time, particularly when you irrigate with unfiltered groundwater, which typically contains a higher concentration of salts.

The good news is most salts dissolve quickly in water. Adding gypsum is one tactic to remove them. Gypsum works to displace molecules of salt stuck to soil particles. Once salts are free, they readily dissolve in the water between soil aggregates. The next significant rain or deep watering session will flush the dissolved salts from the soil. This approach only works if underlying drainage issues are corrected; otherwise the soluble salts will not be able to flush away.

If you're managing salty soil, avoid using manure as an amendment. Manure contains soluble salts that build up over time with regular use. Although some of these salts provide helpful nutrients, they also add to your existing soil-salinity problems, potentially hindering plant growth.

## STABILIZING SOIL PH
Certain soil types—such as those found in evergreen forests, peat bogs, or regions with a lot of rain—tend to be acidic. When soil is too acidic, it interferes with plants' ability to absorb certain nutrients and makes it easier for toxic elements to move through the soil. Alkaline soils are on the other side of the pH scale and are common in the western United States and on prairie lands. Alkaline soil can affect the availability of certain nutrients (such as iron), hinder plant growth, and impact the essential functions of living soil.

If you're working to stabilize your soil pH, adding lime (for acidic soil) or elemental sulfur (for alkaline soil) once or twice a year can be helpful. The amount you need and how frequently you should apply it will depend on the buffering capacity of your soil, which is its ability to resist a change in pH. Soils with high clay and organic matter levels have a higher buffering capacity, requiring more product to adjust the pH level. However, they also require less frequent applications. A simple soil test can provide information about your soil's buffering capacity and recommend how much lime or sulfur to apply based on the test results (see page 161 for how to take a soil test).

# WEEDING

Weeding is a crucial, but often unwelcome, gardening chore. Removing weeds while they are young is key for long-term success.

**A WEED IS ANY PLANT** that is unwelcome or out of place, and weeding is a crucial garden venture few of us enjoy. No matter how much you yank and pull, the weeds never stop growing. The worst weeds proliferate and invade the garden, competing with crops for nutrients, sunlight, and water. The added foliage can also impede air circulation and provide a good hiding place for pests.

The harsh reality is you'll never have a completely weed-free garden. Birds bring in seeds from other yards, runner weeds creep in and take over from unkempt corners, and any soil disturbance can bring dormant seeds to light. Identifying the common weeds you struggle with provides a clue for the best way to root them out.

If most of your weeds are annuals, wait for a hot and sunny day and use a long-handled wire hoe or your favorite weeding tool. Tools that cut weeds off at their base and minimize soil disturbance yield the best results and prevent future weeds from sprouting. Perennial weeds, in comparison, are much harder to eradicate. They easily pop through cardboard weed barriers and are challenging to smother with mulches. Their extensive root system stores enough energy to quickly grow back even after you yank out their green leaves. Dig them up entirely with a trowel, shovel, or weeding fork. The sooner you get to a weed, the simpler the task. Removing a seedling takes much less effort than dealing with a well-established mature weed.

Although it's tempting to ignore the bed of weeds and go straight for a ripe melon, there is no way to avoid them. However, there are some tricks you can use to be more efficient, such as mulching to keep new weeds from sprouting or sheet mulching (see page 120) to tackle overgrown areas that are too daunting to weed by hand. Use the following tips to tackle weeds all season long.

- **Mind your edges.** Garden edges are the transition between the cultivated garden and the weeds and grasses that try to elbow their way in. Regularly patrolling garden edges for weeds can stop them before they take hold. Preventing weeds from creeping in with stone, metal, or plastic barriers can help to stop them in their tracks. Or try edging the garden perimeter with a half-moon edger to create crisp boundaries that prevent weeds for at least a few months.

- **Grow them out.** Before you plant for the season, try growing weeds first. Prepare your soil as you would typically before planting. Water your beds thoroughly and wait. After a few days, you can easily uproot sprouted weeds with a hoe or smother them with a tarp. This approach works well for gardens with an established seed bank from the previous season or those that need rehabilitation after a few years of abandonment.

- **Hit them *where* it counts.** If you have limited time or can't imagine tackling all your weeding in one day, hit weeds where it matters the most—the flower. Weeds such as the field thistle can produce up to 5,000 featherlike seeds that are easily spread by the wind. Snipping off the flowers before they can go to seed will save you hours of weeding next season.

- **Hit them *when* it counts.** Lightly scratching any bare soil with a hoe after each rain will disturb weed seeds starting to germinate before they take root; this is much easier than pulling established weed plants.

- **Water where it matters.** Limit your water resources to only those plants you wish to grow to prevent weeds from getting out of hand. Installing a drip irrigation system that targets your crops is much more effective at controlling weed growth than an oscillating sprinkler head that pours water over the entire garden.

# MULCHING

**NOT ONLY IS BUILDING SOIL** a priority each year but so is protecting the topsoil you work so hard to create. While compost is the champion of soil building, mulch is the second-best thing. Spreading a layer of mulch locks in moisture, blocks weeds, and prevents fertile topsoil from washing away.

Organic mulches such as straw or shredded leaves have several advantages over synthetic mulches like plastic or polyester fabrics. They not only act as a soil protector but also break down eventually and feed the soil. On the other hand, synthetic mulches effectively suppress weeds but tend to smother the soil's below-ground ecosystem. They also tend to deteriorate and litter the ground when buried or forgotten over time.

Mulching is among the most helpful practices for gardeners. Done properly, it adds organic matter to the soil, reduces weeds, stabilizes soil temperatures, and locks in soil moisture.

Whether using straw, shredded leaves, or untreated grass clippings, freshly mulched beds are a beautiful sight for gardeners. It means less work weeding and watering.

## *Are Dyed Mulches Safe for the Garden?*

The good news is there is no evidence that commercial mulch dyes contain toxins that leach into the ground. Instead, most dyes used to color mulch are carbon-based or made from iron oxides that are safe for the garden. But this doesn't mean commercial dyed bark mulch is a gardener's best friend.

The real worry about dyed commercial mulch is the source. Commercial mulches are rarely made from fresh bark chips but instead from recycled wood. On the surface, this is great! Recycling organic materials is a good idea. The problem: Recycled wood may come from construction projects, demolitions, or used shipping pallets, so it could contain unknown chemicals. Some research is required to uncover the source of the wood used to make dyed mulch—it probably won't be obvious on the product label. If you don't like taking risks or doing homework, use all-natural arborist wood chips instead.

Garden and Plant Care  159

Organic mulch is best applied after you've prepped the soil in the spring and removed any weeds. Early-season mulch keeps new weeds from cropping up, and any that do are weak and easy to pull out. Mulch also keeps the soil damp during the hottest times of the year and insulates the soil during the darkest days of winter.

Lay down an even layer of mulch by placing small mulch piles every 2 feet across your garden bed. Use a rake to smooth them out, aiming for a layer 2 to 4 inches thick. If you are mulching around established plants, give them room to breathe. Mulch stacked against their bases can lead to disease and pest issues.

There is a slight problem with mulch worth pointing out. Dense layers can harbor garden pests like snails and slugs that hide from the afternoon sun and emerge during the cooler nights to feast on vulnerable leaves and shoots. Mulch can also rob the soil of moisture in dry, arid climates, where a thick mat of material can prevent light rains from permeating the soil. In soggy regions, mulch can prevent the soil from drying and promote soilborne diseases like root rots. However, the soil-building benefits are far too great to ditch mulch. You can mitigate potential setbacks by choosing the right material for your garden.

# GARDEN MULCH OPTIONS

| TYPE | PROS | CONS |
|---|---|---|
| Straw/hay | • Decomposes slowly<br>• Provides insulation | • May contain weed seeds or pesticide residues<br>• Lightweight; may blow away easily |
| Wood chips | • Long-lasting<br>• Helps retain soil moisture<br>• Can often be sourced for free from arborists | • May form a thick layer, inhibiting water penetration<br>• Can attract termites or carpenter ants<br>• Decomposition can deplete nitrogen on soil surface. Never incorporate wood-based mulches into garden soil; leave on the surface. |
| Bark mulch | • Improves soil structure<br>• Enhances water retention | • Some varieties may float during heavy rain<br>• Can contain harmful toxins from recycled construction wood (see page 159)<br>• Decomposition can deplete nitrogen on soil surface. Never incorporate wood-based mulches into garden soil; leave on the surface. |
| Leaf matter | • Readily available and free<br>• Enriches the soil with nutrients<br>• Insulates soil<br>• Supports microbial activity | • May mat down and form a barrier that prevents water infiltration<br>• Can be unsightly if not shredded |
| Pine straw | • Lightweight, but stays in place | • Decomposes relatively quickly<br>• May need frequent replenishing<br>• Pine needles may be harvested for mulch in ways that negatively impact piney woods<br>• Can be flammable |
| Compost | • Enriches soil with nutrients<br>• Improves soil structure<br>• Supports beneficial microorganisms<br>• Retains moisture | • May contain weed seeds<br>• Can be expensive if you don't make your own |

Remember that the effectiveness and suitability of each mulch will vary depending on your gardening environment and personal preferences.

# ASSESSING *Plant* NUTRIENTS

Signs of nutrient deficiencies can be challenging to discern, but nitrogen deficiency is among the easiest to diagnose, thanks to yellowing between the leaf veins (known as interveinal chlorosis). Signs of other nutrient deficiencies are far less clear.

Plants tell you if the soil is lacking: Symptoms of deficiency such as wilted and discolored leaves or stunted growth provide clues as to what your soil is missing. But don't be too quick to blame the soil; an aphid infestation could just as easily trigger a wilted, misshapen leaf. The many signs of water stress, pest pressure, and disease can be tricky to differentiate.

A simple soil test provides the necessary information to make sound and practical decisions about your soil nutrients. Laboratory tests reveal the specific nutrient composition of the soil as well as other helpful metrics like soil pH and the percentage of organic matter present. If fertilizer is required according to soil test results, reach for organic fertilizers made from natural materials. Not only do they add essential plant nutrients, but they often increase soil organic matter too.

## HOW TO TAKE A SOIL TEST

To submit a soil test, you must first provide a soil sample. Collect random samples by walking in a zig-zag design throughout your garden area. With every few steps, reach down and gather a trowelful of soil. If you are sampling over turf, remove grass and dig down at least ½ inch before taking your sample. Once you have taken multiple samples, mix them together in a bucket. Many send-away lab tests provide a cardboard sample box or a bag to fill or other specific instructions to follow before mailing it off.

### LIVING SOIL CAN PROVIDE ALL OUR PLANTS NEED.

Naturally poor soils or intensely planted gardens may require added nutrients to give plants the boost they need to grow *that* much bigger and *that* much juicier. Many gardeners are familiar with the trifecta of nutrients—nitrogen (N), phosphorus (P), and potassium (K)—the primary micronutrients commonly seen on the front label of every fertilizer. While nitrogen is arguably the most important nutrient to manage, plants rely on many different nutrients to grow and prosper, including carbon, hydrogen, and oxygen (which they access from water and the atmosphere), and nitrogen, phosphorus, potassium, sulfur, calcium, iron, magnesium, boron, manganese, silicon, nickel, chlorine, copper, zinc, and molybdenum (which they access from the soil).

Take a soil test in the fall to ensure you get the results back quickly and have time to incorporate any necessary amendments or organic fertilizers before spring planting.

Garden and Plant Care   **161**

It's best to take soil tests in the fall before planting next year's garden to give the soil enough time to break down and incorporate any organic matter, soil amendments, or fertilizers applied. Otherwise, you may not get an accurate snapshot; plus it helps you beat the spring rush of samples sent to the lab. If you have a large garden, break it into a few sections for testing, especially if you notice different soil textures or growth disparities throughout your space.

## READING YOUR SOIL TEST RESULTS

Once the results are in, now what? The most basic soil test reveals the nutrient composition of your soil, which is reported in a range from very low to very high for each nutrient tested. A very low or low result likely reveals a deficiency in the soil. In such a case, you'll want to add a fertilizer to correct the shortage. If your report reads out high to very high nutrient concentrations, avoid adding fertilizers or amendments that will introduce more of the same.

# *The* NUTRIENTS

## NITROGEN

Nitrogen is the primary nutrient that enables plants to photosynthesize and produce food, encouraging plants to push out new growth. The living soil also requires this precious nutrient to build plant bodies and proteins. The absence of nitrogen in the soil is a primary reason for stunted growth and lack of microbial activity.

But there is such a thing as too much nitrogen. Excess nitrogen encourages plants to grow too quickly, so they become leggy, weak, and prone to toppling over. The extra energy put into growing new leaves and stems means plants won't bother with blooms and fruits. High concentrations of nitrogen also alter the soil community to favor more bacteria. As a result, fungal populations decline, and with them, so do all the symbiotic plant benefits they provide.

**Nitrogen is responsible for lush green growth. Too much of it, however, results in weak, leggy growth and fewer fruits and flowers.**

Phosphorus is needed for strong roots, flowers, and fruits. It is particularly important for good root crop production.

Nailing down the amount of nitrogen needed to create a lush garden without overdoing it is challenging, even with a lab test, because nitrogen is always on the move. Soil's ability to cling on to nutrients works like a magnet. Soil generally has a negative charge, and most nutrients carry a positive charge. Nitrogen is the exception, and since it can't readily attach to soil particles, it is incredibly mobile and quickly flushed from the soil. The quicker your soil drains, the faster nitrogen disappears.

As a result, lab tests do not provide an accurate nitrogen reading, because they only measure the mobile nitrogen. Instead, your focus should shift to the amount of nitrogen stored in organic matter and slowly released over time through decomposition. While measuring nitrogen can be complicated and inconsistent, gardeners can provide a consistent supply by regularly adding organic matter or periodic doses of nitrogen-rich fertilizers, eliminating the concern of unreliable results.

If signs of nitrogen deficiency crop up during the growing season, you can replenish nitrogen levels with incremental applications of alfalfa meal, soybean meal, or bone meal. Avoid overloading the soil with nitrogen before you sow seeds, because it will likely be washed away before your plants will benefit. Moreover, nitrogen leaching creates harmful environmental impacts and contributes to algal blooms in our lakes and rivers.

## PHOSPHORUS

Phosphorus is responsible for developing strong roots and setting flowers and fruits. It is also essential for initiating new growth and is particularly important for young plants and seedlings. Phosphorus is naturally released through the weathering of soil minerals and the decomposition of organic matter.

A soil test provides reliable phosphorus readings and recommends specific garden application rates. However, the trouble with phosphorus is it can cling so tightly to soil particles that plants can't access it. Consequently, soils with high levels of phosphorus may still produce deficient plants. Navigate this situation by adding bone meal, fish meal, or rock phosphate, especially in the early season. Plants can easily absorb the nutrient through their roots if it is available in the soil nearby.

Unlike nitrogen, adding too much phosphorus only poses a small risk to plant health, especially in the vegetable garden. Most annual vegetable crops require large amounts of phosphorus to grow and reproduce within one

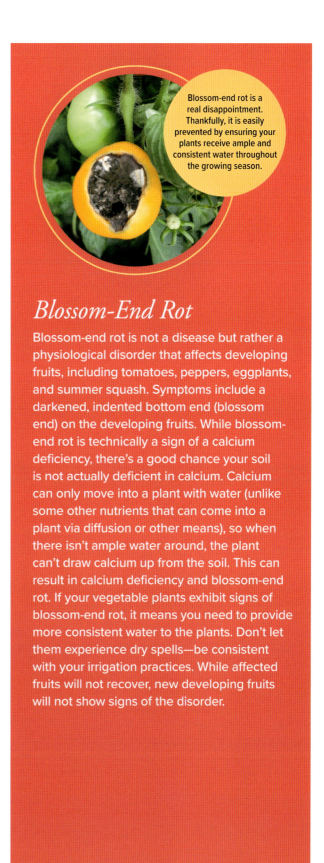

Blossom-end rot is a real disappointment. Thankfully, it is easily prevented by ensuring your plants receive ample and consistent water throughout the growing season.

## *Blossom-End Rot*

Blossom-end rot is not a disease but rather a physiological disorder that affects developing fruits, including tomatoes, peppers, eggplants, and summer squash. Symptoms include a darkened, indented bottom end (blossom end) on the developing fruits. While blossom-end rot is technically a sign of a calcium deficiency, there's a good chance your soil is not actually deficient in calcium. Calcium can only move into a plant with water (unlike some other nutrients that can come into a plant via diffusion or other means), so when there isn't ample water around, the plant can't draw calcium up from the soil. This can result in calcium deficiency and blossom-end rot. If your vegetable plants exhibit signs of blossom-end rot, it means you need to provide more consistent water to the plants. Don't let them experience dry spells—be consistent with your irrigation practices. While affected fruits will not recover, new developing fruits will not show signs of the disorder.

## Is There a Difference Between a Soil Amendment and a Soil Fertilizer?

For simplicity's sake, the difference is mainly due to semantics. In general, soil amendments are bulky materials meant to enhance the soil by providing organic matter intended to feed the living soil. Fertilizers, on the other hand, are added to provide vital plant nutrients. The distinction is slight because most soil amendments are also organic fertilizers.

Legally speaking, the distinction is important. Fertilizer companies are required by law to include the minimum guaranteed nutrient composition on their label. The three numbers on every bag represent the minimum percentage of nitrogen, phosphorus, and potassium, which allows you to accurately calculate how much of a specific nutrient you add to the soil.

Soil amendments such as compost and manure provide plenty of plant nutrition—in some cases, all of it. However, they are not sold as fertilizers. The precise nutrient content of these amendments is usually unknown and can vary significantly depending on the source of the feedstocks used or animal waste collected. Compost or manure-based products legally sold as fertilizers are tested and amended with additional ingredients to meet the minimum guarantee mentioned on the label.

Potassium regulates all plant functions related to water, including vigor and hardiness, making it essential for plump, tasty fruits.

season. Certain perennial crops—such as asparagus or select herbs—on the other hand, can suffer if phosphorus concentrations top the charts. They don't use as much of this nutrient, so it can accumulate in the soil with regular applications. If the lower leaves of your perennial crops start to curl and develop spots, or if new leaves grow thin and needlelike with burnt tips, avoid further phosphorus applications.

## POTASSIUM

Potassium (sometimes called potash) regulates all plant functions related to water and is, therefore, incredibly important. Some of these functions include nutrient absorption and transportation throughout the plant; the production of fruits, flowers, and seeds; and even the plumpness and taste of vegetables and fruits. Potassium also acts as an immunity booster—plants with ample access to this nutrient can better withstand stress from pests, disease, and overfertilization.

Potassium has a positive charge, so it is easily attracted to the negative pull of soil particles. This attraction helps potassium stick around and accumulate in the soil. But potassium, unlike phosphorus, doesn't cling too tightly, making it more readily available for plant use. Luckily, potassium is often plentiful in soils with adequate organic matter.

You can rely on your soil test results to monitor your potassium levels. You only need a boost if your soil analyses indicate low concentrations. To maintain potassium levels, add potassium-rich fertilizers like kelp meal, langbeinite (a naturally mined crystalline material), potassium sulfate, and compost.

## OTHER IMPORTANT PLANT NUTRIENTS AND POTENTIAL SIGNS THAT THEY ARE LACKING

| PLANT NUTRIENT | WHAT IT DOES | SIGNS OF DEFICIENCY |
|---|---|---|
| Calcium | Vital for building strong plant cells and increasing disease resistance | Blossom-end rot (see page 163) |
| Magnesium | The central element in chlorophyll molecules and disease-fighting enzyme formation | Increased susceptibility to disease, premature leaf drop, poor fruit development |
| Sulfur | Required to metabolize nitrogen and promote protein synthesis | Delayed maturity, stunted growth, yellowing young leaves |
| Iron | Essential for chlorophyll synthesis, energy transfer, and nitrogen fixation | Yellowing between veins (interveinal chlorosis), stunted growth |
| Manganese | Activates enzymes involved in producing chlorophyll and metabolizing nitrogen | Interveinal chlorosis, mottled leaves |
| Zinc | Involved with enzyme activity and the creation of growth hormones | Stunted growth, distorted leaves, chlorosis |
| Copper | Essential for enzyme activation, cellular energy production, and lignin formation | Wilting, dieback, twisted or distorted leaves |
| Molybdenum | Required to metabolize nitrogen and promote enzyme activity | Yellowing of older leaves, reduced growth |
| Boron | Affects cell division, membrane structure, and sugar transport | Brittle or distorted young leaves, dieback |
| Chlorine | Required in photosynthesis and osmosis | Wilting, reduced growth, leaf tip burn |
| Nickel | Required to metabolize nitrogen | Stunted growth, abnormal leaf development |

Plants need smaller doses of the listed nutrients in addition to nitrogen, phosphorus, and potassium. The living soil recycles nutrients plants depend on through the decomposition of organic matter, and soil with plenty of it may not be lacking. If you identify a deficiency, apply an appropriate fertilizer. Monitor your nutrient levels and make adjustments according to your soil test results or plant behavior.

Garden and Plant Care 165

# APPLYING FERTILIZERS

**THERE IS A SIGNIFICANT** difference between organic and synthetic fertilizers. Synthetic fertilizers deliver a fast flood of nutrients readily dissolved in water and instantaneously accessible to plants. Conversely, many organic fertilizers rely on microbes to digest the product before nutrients are available. This process can take months, so the immediate reward of synthetic fertilizers is hard to resist; however, their continued use in the garden can damage soil health.

Many synthetic fertilizers deliver nutrients as salts, and the residues left behind can acidify the soil, pushing beneficial decomposers away from your crops. The mobility of synthetic nutrients can also contaminate groundwater and harm wildlife downstream. Instead, organic fertilizers promote a more sustainable approach, as they enable the gradual accumulation of nutrients through the actions of living soil. This process keeps the nutrients around for a longer period, either held in the bodies of soil organisms or attracted to the negative charge of spongy organic matter and adhesive clays.

How available these nutrients are for plant use depends on the activity of soil organisms, which is influenced by your soil conditions. Warm and moist soils promote a rapid breakdown of organic fertilizers, while dry or cold soils take much longer. If you need immediate nutrition, look to organic liquid fertilizers, such as fish emulsions, that do not need to be broken down by soil microbes before they are effective. For this reason, liquid fertilizers are a good choice for container gardens with limited soil ecosystems. You can apply them directly to the soil or spray them onto plant leaves.

It is important to note that fertilizers are only required if there is a nutrient deficiency in the soil. If you've identified a deficiency based on a soil test or specific indicator of plant stress, choose a fertilizer that will deliver what you need. Consider the release time of those nutrients too. In general, powdered forms release nutrients more quickly than pelleted forms. Always follow the package instructions for appropriate application rates. The following fertilizing techniques offer a variety of approaches to use when applying organic fertilizers to the garden.

- **Broadcasting** is a method commonly used to fertilize large areas quickly. It is a great way to fertilize at the beginning of the season before planting. First, fill a bucket with your preferred fertilizer and toss it onto the ground, one handful at a time. It may take some practice to apply the fertilizer evenly, but try your best to avoid over- or underfeeding sections of the garden. Once you have added enough fertilizer, lightly rake the broadcasted area to incorporate it into the top inch or so of the soil.

- **Banding** applies fertilizer where nutrients are needed the most: near plant roots. This method works exceptionally well with newly seeded plants. However, it's crucial to note that using a high concentration of fertilizer can harm young roots. To apply fertilizers in bands, start by using a shovel or trowel to dig a small trench that is at least 3 inches deep. Next, lay the fertilizer evenly within the trench and cover it with soil. Keep at least 2 inches of soil between any fertilizer and planted seeds. Alternatively, if you are transplanting young starts, plant them at least 4 inches away from a fertilizer band to prevent burning your tender plant roots.

Broadcasting is the best way to distribute granular fertilizers across a broad area.

- **Side-dressing** is frequently used for established perennial or mid-season annual plants, mainly if you cultivate in sandy soils that lose nutrients after each rain or watering. You can also side-dress soil amendments such as compost and manure throughout the growing season. Spread the fertilizer evenly around the base of a plant and gently mix it into the soil. Brush off any that falls onto plant leaves to prevent damage.

- **Foliar feeding** adds liquid fertilizer directly to plant leaves, where it is immediately absorbed, with no breakdown required. Foliar feeding is a great way to correct nutrient deficiencies quickly during the growing season, should they arise. Evenly spray plant leaves with the fertilizer mix using a spray bottle or hand-held applicator. Make sure to follow the package directions to avoid causing harm.

*Side-dressing* is the term used for distributing fertilizers around the base of an existing plant.

## ORGANIC PLANT FERTILIZERS

| FERTILIZER | N | P | K | NOTES |
|---|---|---|---|---|
| Alfalfa meal | 3 | 2 | 1 | • Contains its own beneficial microbes<br>• Slightly basic, which can increase the soil pH if used in large quantities |
| Blood meal | 15 | 1 | 1 | • Use as directed, as the high nitrogen value can be damaging to young plants<br>• An excellent choice for heavy feeders |
| Bone meal | 3–6 | 20 | 0 | • An excellent source of calcium<br>• Promotes root growth and flower production |
| Feather meal | 12 | 0 | 0 | • A great alternative to blood meal |
| Fish emulsion | 4–5 | 2–4 | 1–2 | • This liquid readily provides plant-available nutrients for instant results |
| Fish meal | 9 | 7 | 0 | • An excellent source of trace minerals |
| Cotton seed meal | 6 | 2 | 1 | • A balanced source of NPK<br>• Slightly acidic, which can alter the soil pH if used in large quantities |
| Rock phosphate | 0 | 33 | 0 | • An excellent source of calcium |
| Kelp meal | 1–2 | 1 | 2 | • A great source of trace minerals<br>• Promotes root growth and overall plant health |
| Crab meal | 4 | 3 | 0 | • Contains chitin, which can stimulate the production of chemicals that boost natural plant immunity |

These organic materials represent popular organic fertilizers. You can use them individually to correct a specific nutrient deficiency or blend them for a balanced mix of nitrogen, potassium, and phosphorus. Note: The provided NPK values are a guide but will vary between individual products. Refer to the product label for lab-certified values.

Garden and Plant Care

# GROWING VERTICALLY

Vertical growing offers so many benefits, including saving space, increasing airflow, and simplifying the harvest.

When growing large-fruited crops vertically, support the fruits with slings made from bags, netting, or cloth.

Cages for tomatoes, peppers, and tomatillos help support the plants and keep ripening fruits off the ground.

**VINING PLANTS SUCH AS** peas, beans, tomatoes, cucumbers, and melons prefer additional support in the garden. Training sprawling plants to go vertical using stakes, trellises, or cages is a great way to save space and pack in more plants. Vertical growing also protects soft-fleshed produce by keeping it off the ground where insects could otherwise feast on it. Additionally, helping your plants to climb increases airflow—as they sway in the breeze, the likelihood of mold and mildew is reduced.

Some plants demand support and climb up whatever they encounter. Twining bean vines quickly wrap around fences, and tendril-bearing plants—such as peas and cucumbers—like to grab on to neighboring plants to pull themselves skyward. Support your plants and keep them contained by making a string trellis from natural twine you can easily remove and toss into the compost heap at the end of the season. Other options for trellising include chicken wire, cattle panels, or fabric netting secured to a wall or durable frame.

If you plan to grow melons or winter squash on a trellis, the weight of hanging fruits can be problematic. Weighted fruits may break off at the stem or cause the entire plant to crash down. Use a makeshift "hammock" made from cloth, netting, or nylon material to prevent this. Surround hanging fruits with the hammock and tie the loose ends to the trellis for the best results.

Other plants, such as vining tomatoes, do not come ready-made with adaptations to climb on their own. Instead, gardeners secure the long vines and branches to staked supports to get them off the ground. This also works well to discourage top-heavy vegetables like peppers, eggplant, and broccoli from toppling over and uprooting themselves. You can use just about anything for a stake—bamboo, wood, heavy wire, and metal poles are standard materials. Keep in mind the heft of the plant you wish to support when choosing a stake. Indeterminate tomatoes, for example, become heavy once they set clusters of fruits. They need a stake that supports all their weight. At a minimum, use a 2- by 2-inch wooden stake driven into the ground at least 6 inches, or use a metal pole that won't bend under the weight of the soon-to-be harvest.

In most cases, you'll need to secure plants to the stake with a soft cloth strap or specialty garden tape. To keep the cloth from rubbing and damaging the plant, fasten your plant tie to the stake tightly so it doesn't slip before loosely looping the material around a branch. Make your loop big enough to allow plenty of room for branches and stems to grow thicker throughout the season.

Vegetable cages (sturdy wire cylinders or rectangles with an open top) can also be used in place of a stake or trellis. Whichever support you choose, install it directly after you seed or transplant your starts to avoid root damage later in the growing season. Explore your creativity and play around with different options until you find what works best for your specific crops and garden space.

# WATERING

**CROPS NEED THE RIGHT AMOUNT OF WATER** to flourish; too much or too little impacts your harvest. There is no guarantee when the rain will come, and you may need to rely on supplemental water at some point. How much water your garden requires depends on the crops you grow, the regional climate, and the soil type. In any case, bringing water to the right place at the right time requires careful planning.

So, what is the right amount of water? Perfectly moist soil has the right balance of air and water in the spaces between the soil particles that plants and microorganisms prefer (called the pore space). Many gardeners suggest giving plants at least an inch of water weekly. However, this guidance is misleading because it oversimplifies the water requirements for specific soil types and climates. So rather than worrying about how much water you add from above, pay attention to the moisture content below ground.

How long your soil stays moist is governed by the soil's water-holding capacity, which you can increase with regular applications of compost. An increase of 1 percent in soil organic matter can soak up an additional 20,000 gallons per acre. Therefore, each heap of compost you add allows your soil to absorb water that would otherwise wash away.

Of course, your soil can also be too wet, in which case plant roots and soil organisms struggle for air. Issues with overwatering are prevalent in soils with poor structure or those with underlying drainage issues. Plants grown in raised beds or containers can also experience the impacts of soggy soil if they are overly irrigated or grown in lackluster soil from the get-go. Allowing the soil to dry out between watering sessions can help prevent waterlogging.

Just because the surface of your soil is dry doesn't necessarily mean the root zone is parched as well. Measure your specific soil moisture with a soil moisture meter, a long, slender probe inserted into the soil at the base of a plant. Using this tool provides a reading from low to high so you can adjust your watering schedule accordingly. Otherwise, you can use your finger, stuck at least 2 inches into the ground, to gauge whether it's time to water or not.

There are many ways to water the garden; what works best for you depends on your location, garden size, regional weather patterns, and personal preferences. Would you rather spend a blissful morning hand-watering plants or spend time on other projects thanks to your hands-off automated sprinkler or drip system? Each approach has advantages and disadvantages, so contemplate what works well for your space.

## HOW LONG TO WATER

Gardeners are often unsure of how long to water their plants. This depends on the method of irrigation you choose and how much water it distributes in a given timeframe. It also depends on how dry the soil is when you start watering. Some overhead sprinklers need to run for 1 hour, others for only 30 minutes, in order to distribute ample water for your plants. The same goes for drip irrigation systems. Some take hours to deliver enough water, while others provide ample hydration after only 45 minutes of run time. The best way to tell when to turn off the hose or irrigation system is to use the trowel test. Whether you're

Knowing when and how long to water your vegetable garden can be tricky.

watering by hand, by sprinkler, or by irrigation system, after every 10 to 15 minutes of watering time, dig down into the soil using a garden trowel to see how deeply the water has penetrated into the soil. The goal should be a deep, thorough, penetrating watering that wets the soil down to a depth of several inches, or down to where there is already moisture present. Once you've performed the trowel test with a particular sprinkler or hose nozzle, you'll get to know how long it needs to run in order to provide enough moisture to reach the proper depth. Make note of this in your garden journal so you'll know for next time.

It's best to avoid shallow, frequent irrigation, because this promotes shallow root growth. If all of the moisture is at the soil's surface, roots have no need to grow deeply and become more self-sufficient. Deep, less frequent watering is always best.

How mature the plants are, how quickly the soil drains, whether there is mulch in place, and many other factors play into how much water to add to any given bed.

## WATERING OPTIONS FOR YOUR GARDEN

| WATERING METHOD | ADVANTAGES | DISADVANTAGES |
|---|---|---|
| Hand watering | • Precise control over water placement<br>• Suitable for small gardens or container plants<br>• Minimizes wasted water | • Time-consuming<br>• No potential for automation<br>• Labor-intensive<br>• Potential for inconsistent watering |
| Soaker hose | • Even water distribution on flat ground<br>• Targets root zones<br>• Minimizes wasted water<br>• Easy to install | • Initial start-up cost<br>• May deteriorate over time<br>• Uneven watering on sloped land |
| Drip irrigation | • Efficient water usage<br>• Reduces weed growth<br>• Provides consistent and controlled watering<br>• Easily automated | • Initial set-up cost<br>• Steep installation learning curve<br>• Requires maintenance<br>• May clog over time |
| Overhead sprinkler system | • Covers large areas<br>• Can be automated for convenience<br>• Inexpensive<br>• Easy to move around<br>• Adjustable spray patterns | • Water is wasted due to evaporation<br>• Can spread foliar diseases<br>• Uneven water distribution<br>• Creates a potential for overwatering<br>• Unpredictable water coverage in windy conditions |
| Rain barrel | • Environmentally friendly<br>• Reduces water bills<br>• Provides natural and untreated water | • Limited water storage capacity<br>• Can be difficult to distribute the collected water<br>• Dependent on rainfall<br>• Requires a proper setup for efficient collection<br>• Not practical in arid regions |

Consider the initial start-up cost, installation requirements, and suitability as you decide how to water your garden. You can also build and expand irrigation systems as your garden grows or your preferences change.

# Recognizing the Signs of Water Stress

During times of water scarcity, plants limit the volume of water they send to their leaves and roots to conserve a sufficient flow of water within their stems. Conserving water in this way is crucial for maintaining their life-supporting nutrient delivery system. Consequently, plants often adjust by wilting or dropping leaves and killing off roots.

Wilted leaves also occur when plants are overwatered. Soggy soil conditions with limited oxygen encourage root rot to set in, damaging plants' ability to absorb water and nutrients. This causes plant leaves to turn limp and weak before they drop off.

It can be challenging to tell if a fallen leaf is the result of over- or underwatering. Look at the leaves still attached to your plant. If leaves appear wilted and crispy, your plants likely need more water. If the leaves are limp but not crunchy, look around for clues such as a moldy smell or mushy plant stems that can indicate overly soggy soil.

One of the first signs of water stress is wilting. But plants can also wilt from overwatering. It's important to always check the soil itself prior to watering.

## COMMON SIGNS OF STRESS

| UNDERWATERING | OVERWATERING |
| --- | --- |
| Wilted or dropping leaves | Mushy stems |
| Dry, crispy leaves | Limp leaves (not crispy) |
| Curled or yellowing leaves | Yellowing or browning leaves |
| Grayish hue to leaves | Rotten odor |
| Stunted leaf and root growth | Signs of fungus gnats |

The signs of water stress can look similar to other pest and disease issues. Plenty of gardeners have rushed to water the garden at the first sign of leaf wilt only to realize later they had a spider mite infestation. Avoid jumping to conclusions and thoroughly examine damaged plants before responding. Of course, if you live in a sweltering climate, heat and water stress could be common problems to address.

# PUTTING *the* VEGETABLE GARDEN TO BED

At the end of the growing season, the goal should be to protect your soil through the dormant season.

**AT THE END OF THE GROWING SEASON,** gardeners often clear that year's plants to make way for next season's crops. Removing old stalks and dead leaves can prevent gray mold or blight spores from accumulating in the soil. Carting off garden debris also eliminates places for overwintering pests to hide. Take, for example, the European corn borer—this formidable foe burrows into thick stalks to spend the winter protected from wind, snow, and rain.

Tidying the garden does indeed help manage certain pests and prevent disease. However, a resilient garden that results from quality soil and plenty of diversity will provide natural checks and balances. From this perspective, garden debris harbors not only plant pests but also the beneficial insects that keep those pests in check. Instead of making a clean sweep at the end of the growing season, putting the garden to bed should be less about preventing future issues and more about supporting the benefits you wish to encourage.

You also want to protect the living soil and prepare the ground for the potentially harsh conditions the offseason brings. Whether it's extreme cold, torrential rains, or strong winds, covering your soil at the end of the season will ensure your fertile ground is there when you're ready to get back at it. You can cover the soil with a thick layer of mulch or plant a cover crop to hold the soil in place (see page 174).

## CHOP-AND-DROP

If you have a busy life, the chop-and-drop method is for you. By leaving the garden a little "messy," you'll provide a habitat for the beneficial bugs you want to protect and add organic matter to feed the living soil by composting in place.

For this method, put your garden to bed by chopping plants where they stand and dropping the debris to the ground. This method works well for gardeners who don't feel like tending to a compost pile or grabbing a wheelbarrow to haul off debris. Typically, you'll want to chop and drop after you're done with your last harvest. But you can do it on a small scale throughout the growing season too.

Clean up old annuals with a sharp weeding knife by slicing the stems at the base of the soil instead of pulling out the entire plant, roots and all. Doing so minimizes soil disturbance, and the remaining roots add extra organic matter deep underground as they decompose. Plus, leaving roots in the ground helps prevent fertile topsoil from washing away during heavy rains.

Some crops like corn, broccoli, and tomatoes have thick roots and stalks that are hard to cut down and, if they remain in place, are difficult to plant through the following season. Remove larger annuals with thick stems by cutting a 2-inch circle around the base of the stalk with a weeding knife to sever the horizontal roots holding it in place. It should break free with a good yank and leave many of the small feeder roots behind. The following season, you can loosen the soil with a broadfork to break up the remaining root mass if it is difficult to dig.

If you have long vining plants or thick woody stalks and stems, chop them into pieces before you drop them to the ground. Dealing with smaller pieces will help manage the debris and allow it to decompose more quickly. It helps to have a good set of pruners or a small hand saw to complete the task.

Some critics of this method complain about prolific self-sowing the following season. Seeds will sprout if you let your crops go to seed before chopping day. Luckily, leaving seed heads intact keeps birds well-fed through the winter. If any small plants sprout in the spring, remove them with a quick pass of the hoe. Additionally, some crops like lettuce, arugula, basil, and cilantro are great when they self-seed—you'll reap the benefits of an early harvest with little effort as soon as the weather warms up.

Chop-and-drop involves cutting leftover crops into pieces at the end of the growing season and letting them compost in place through the winter.

## SOW A COVER CROP

A cover crop is any plant grown to cover the ground and feed the soil. Some gardeners call cover crops "green manure" because of their benefits. While any plant can technically be called a cover crop, particular plants are popular for their specific benefits. For example, legume crops such as field peas or clover naturally add nitrogen to the soil as they grow. Certain grasses, such as winter rye, have extensive roots that fan out to add plenty of organic matter underground and hold soil in place.

The trouble with cover crops is that most vegetables have difficulty taking hold when planted in a sea of dense cover crops such as buckwheat. Therefore, gardeners often remove or manage cover crops before the planting season begins. The removal process may seem daunting, especially if you plan to ditch the tiller, because discs and plows are the easiest way to incorporate the plants into the soil.

Thankfully, plants naturally die off for a few reasons, and you can use that to your advantage. Annual plants die back after their life cycle is complete or if winter temperatures are low enough to winter-kill. *Any* plants, however, can be knocked back when starved of light or water with a tarp, including cover crops.

Choosing the right cover crop for your garden can benefit soil-building without added headaches. With the proper planning, you can wait for cover crops to complete their life cycle (some gardeners step in to mow them down or knock back the plants, called "rolling and crimping," just before they go to seed), wait for winter temperatures to kill the crop, or use a durable tarp to smother plants early in the season.

Cover crops such as this clover are another way to help preserve soil during the offseason.

## POPULAR COVER CROPS AND THEIR BENEFITS

| CROP TYPE | WINTER KILL TEMPERATURE (°F) | PLANT HEIGHT (INCHES) | BEST USED FOR |
|---|---|---|---|
| Buckwheat | 30 | 24 | Feeding beneficial insects |
| Winter rye | −40 | 72 | Creating in situ mulch |
| Forage radish (oilseed radish) | 20 | 18 | Breaking up compacted soil |
| Field pea | 15 | 48 | Adding nitrogen |
| Berseem clover | 20 | 24 | A winterkill crop for warmer regions |
| Oats | 10 | 48 | Weed prevention, erosion control |

Choosing the right crop depends on your soil-building goals. Any cover crop will feed and sustain soil life, but some bring additional benefits, such as breaking up soil compaction or suppressing weeds. Consider these options to get you started.

# How to Sow a Fall Cover Crop

Be ready to plant a fall cover crop after your season's harvest. You don't have to wait for all your annual vegetable crops to call it quits either. Instead, plant patches of annual ryegrass, oats, or clover as each vegetable crop stops being productive. Staggered planting guarantees you'll be able to plant the majority of your cover crop before it gets too late in the season. This way, you can feel comfortable waiting until the last minute before chopping down your tomato vines. At least the majority of the cover crop got planted, right? Soon, your garden will look like a patchwork of green, and you can mulch over any small missed spots.

Aim to plant your cover crop between late August and mid-October. After late fall, cover crops may germinate too slowly to beat the worst of winter, except for those areas that never see a frost. Even if your late-planted cover crop germinates, it may not grow enough through the winter to produce the benefits you seek. If you miss your window, you're better off mulching the garden instead.

Transplants can be planted directly through mowed cover-crop debris 2 to 3 weeks after the cut takes place.

To plant a cover crop, smooth out the intended area with a rake and remove large debris that could impact germination. If you have a lot of annual vegetables to remove, remember to snap them off at the base, leaving the roots in place, and cart off debris to the compost heap. Broadcast cover crop seeds according to the seed packet instructions.

It can be challenging to distribute tiny seeds evenly, so don't fret if you have a few spots that end up overseeded. Once you're done broadcasting, gently rake over the seeds. You can take this opportunity to spread out dense clusters before watering them in.

Now, sit back and watch your cover crop grow. In the spring, mow the plants down, fold the plants over at their base just after they come into flower (but before they set seed), or smother them with a tarp. You can remove the debris before planting or cover the flattened crops with a hefty heap of compost before you plant. Wait 2 to 3 weeks to plant after cutting down or crimping your cover crops.

Mustard is a good fall cover crop for home gardens. It is planted late in the season and cut down when it is in flower the following spring.

Garden and Plant Care  175

# SEASONAL *Garden* TO-DOS: PRESEASON

**THE FOLLOWING SECTION** highlights important garden tasks to remember throughout the season, divvied up into preseason, early-season, mid-season, late-season, and offseason categories so you can manage your tasks according to your climate. Early season for cold-climate gardeners would be early spring, and the offseason would be in the cold winter months, but for hot-climate gardeners that don't experience frosts, the early season may be in the fall, when temperatures are cool enough to start planting, and the offseason may be in the heat of the summer.

Before the growing season begins, repair any damage to beds and garden structures, including cold frames, trellises, and the like.

**PRESEASON IS ARGUABLY** the most important. It sets the tone for the rest of the growing season. Build momentum as the weather conditions allow and start to prepare the soil. It's also time to put your offseason planning to work and make big adjustments to your garden layout or infrastructure before plants enter the ground.

○ **Inspect for damage.** Inspect your garden for damage that needs to be dealt with before you plant. Inspect garden features such as stone walls, support trellises, or raised beds that can be damaged by snow or ice. Heavy offseason rain or winds can erode soil in temperate climates, and inspecting for damage can pinpoint areas with chronic drainage issues.

○ **Search for critter clues.** Look for new burrows, damaged branches, or eaten buds to see if there have been new visitors to the garden. Taking care of unwanted animals now will prevent the potential for significant damage later. If you notice deer have moved in, it might be time to build a fence.

○ **Clean up.** Add winterkill cover crops to the compost heap, or cover them with a few inches of finished compost. If you garden in cool, wet regions, remove fall mulch to encourage the soil to warm more quickly in preparation for planting.

○ **Start seeds indoors.** Start warm-season annuals indoors to get a head start, especially if you live in an area with a growing season of less than 100 days. Use the help of a heat mat or artificial light to increase your success.

Gather and prepare seed-starting equipment.

○ **Freshen up container soil.** Containers don't readily support the living soil (unless your container is really big!) and need a refresh each season to replace plant nutrients. Replacing or amending your container soil with fertilizer will help support potted plants through the growing season (for tips on recycling/reusing potting soil, go to page 135).

○ **Aerate.** Garden soils can settle over the offseason due to wind and rain. Loosen the soil with a broadfork (for complete use instructions, see page 154) or sturdy pitchfork. Avoid heavy tilling whenever possible to preserve the living soil.

○ **Feed the soil with organic matter.** Early-season applications provide the living soil with the fuel it needs to flourish. For new gardeners working to improve the native soil, add as much as 5 inches of compost if you can. You won't need as much for established gardens, and mixing won't be required. In that case, add a 2-inch layer of compost onto your growing area and let the living soil mix it in for you. Now is a good time to add soil-building amendments too.

Garden and Plant Care

# SEASONAL *Garden* TO-DOS: EARLY SEASON

Start weeding early and often. Weeds are easiest to remove when they are young.

**THE EARLY SEASON** can trigger different emotions based on the kind of gardener you are. Some people feel hopeful and excited when they can finally start working on their garden. Meanwhile, others feel panicked and anxious, considering it a race against the clock. Regardless of your emotions, it's time to dive in!

○ **Weed.** Weeds are easier to manage when small and tender. Spend the time now to hand-pull, hoe, or spray organic herbicides on any unwanted weeds before planting. Edging the garden early in the season is also an efficient way to keep creeping weeds out.

○ **Direct sow seeds.** Mind the weather while planting. Unexpected frosts can harm or even kill your seedlings with little notice. Keeping track of your garden's last frost will help you track a trend over time, which is likely to change as the climate shifts.

○ **Transplant.** Start to harden off warm-season annuals planted indoors for a week or two. Cool-season crops like salad greens and those that can handle chilly nights can be planted right away in the ground, raised bed, or container. For tender crops like tomatoes, melons, cucumbers, and peppers, wait until nighttime temperatures are in the 50s before setting them out.

○ **Mulch.** Use organic mulch to prevent weeds from growing while the weather warms. Using early-season mulch in colder climates can hinder soil temperatures from warming up, so it may be appropriate to skip this preseason task and wait until after planting.

○ **Water.** Young plants and sprouting seeds rely on frequent watering because of their shallow root structures that don't dive deep. Immediately water new plants or sown seeds, and pay close attention to your soil moisture, especially when it's hot or windy. If you intend to use an irrigation system, set it up while plants are young to avoid future damage.

○ **Fertilize.** New seedlings need a steady supply of phosphorus to get off to a good start. If your soil lacks this critical nutrient, consider banding in some phosphorus-rich granular amendments (for a complete list of organic fertilizers, see page 167).

○ **Protect plants.** An unexpected cold snap may settle in during early-season growth in cold climates. Shield young plants from freezing temperatures with a protective, lightweight cloth, or use a cold frame. If you garden in a hot region, protect young plants from the scorching heat with a shade cloth.

Add mulch early in the season, as soon as possible after planting.

Protect young plants from surprise frosts with cloches or row cover.

Garden and Plant Care  **179**

# SEASONAL *Garden* TO-DOS: MID-SEASON

Mid-season is prime time for harvesting spring-planted crops such as shell peas.

**THE INITIAL PLANTING PREPARATIONS** slowly give way to garden upkeep. By this time, your garden is likely filling in and starting to set flowers and fruits. But it might be the point of the year when you begin to notice problems too. Consider knocking off these mid-season tasks to keep your garden thriving.

- **Harvest early-season plants.** Quick-to-grow crops like arugula, spinach, radishes, peas, lettuce, and green onions may be ready to harvest. After you pick your crops, seed a second round for a continuous yield.

- **Fertilize plants.** Not all plants need an added boost during the growing season, especially if you work to cultivate living soil. However, heavy feeders like peppers, tomatoes, squash, melons, corn, cucumbers, broccoli, and cabbage could use some coaxing during mid-season to maximize their output. A balanced organic fertilizer (5-5-5) will encourage plants to send out new shoots and blooms.

- **Keep on top of weeds.** It never ends for the diligent gardener. Wind and birds have a terrible habit of dropping seeds, causing weeds to grow even in the best-mulched places. Keep at it the best you can. If you get overwhelmed, focus on the weeds about to go to seed. Preventing seeds from mixing into your soil this year will do wonders for next year's endeavor.

- **Add seeds.** Now is the time to plant for your late-season harvest. Sow another round of carrot, beet, broccoli, cauliflower, and cabbage seeds that will mature before the first frost or summer heatwave, depending on where you garden.

- **Transplant.** Plant any remaining seedlings you started a few months ago. If you didn't bother to grow your own starts, check out your local garden center. They often discount warm-season annuals like cucumbers and summer squash when it's too late to direct sow these crops. Take advantage of any deals and add more plants to your garden if you have the extra space.

- **Water.** Increase your watering routine if you notice signs of plant stress (see page 171). Avoid overhead watering if you live in a hot and humid climate. Excess moisture on plant leaves can encourage mold and mildew.

- **Provide support.** Support top-heavy and trailing crops like tomatoes, beans, cucumbers, melons, peppers, and eggplant by using a trellis, cage, or stake to keep them from falling over or spreading out of bounds.

- **Encourage pollination.** To attract pollinators, you can fill any space with nectar-rich flowers such as zinnias, sunflowers, marigolds, and cosmos. Deadhead flowers to encourage new blooms so pollinators stick around. If you choose to grow under fabric or plastic row cover, fewer insects may buzz around. Take matters into your own hands and gather pollen using a small paintbrush. Gently brush the collected pollen onto a new flower of the same crop and repeat.

- **Scout for pests.** Scan your garden for unhealthy-looking plants and identify any issues like dead areas, wilted or discolored leaves, unusual growth, or lack of fruits. Turn over the leaves to identify the culprit or use a hand lens to inspect plant buds and stems for small pests like spider mites. Choose the best defensive action if you detect a pest (see pest controls on page 200).

- **Manage disease.** It's important to remove infected plants as soon as you notice them to prevent diseases from spreading if there is a persistent issue. Thin out plants and increase airflow to reduce disease outbreaks in the garden.

- **Record notes.** As the gardening season progresses, note any problems you see. Maybe you planted your tomatoes too close or realized ten kale plants are nine too many. Keep track of insights and observations to avoid repeating mistakes next year. But don't forget to recognize your successes too. They will inspire next season's gardening goals.

Install trellises for vining crops such as pole beans early in the season. As they grow, train the vines to grasp the structure and climb.

Create a mixed garden by adding lots of flowering plants. They'll lure in pollinators and other beneficial insects.

Garden and Plant Care

# SEASONAL *Garden* TO-DOS:
# LATE SEASON

Plant garlic cloves in the autumn for harvest the following summer.

**YOU MAY BE EXHAUSTED** and ready for a break at this point of the year. Find the time to sneak in a late cover crop or plant a few rows of garlic before it's too late. Enjoy the last of your harvest and relish a job well done while ticking off the last tasks on your to-do list.

○ **Plant bulbs.** Garlic cloves and onion sets can be planted late in the season. If you live in a cold climate, choose hardneck garlic (see page 245) and long-day onion varieties (see page 249) and protect them with a dense layer of straw or leaves. Warm-climate gardeners can choose softneck garlic or elephant garlic. You'll want them to take root before the ground freezes.

○ **Weeding.** Don't give up now! Removing late-season weeds will set you up nicely for next year. Focus on those last weeds about to go to seed. If you have the energy, tackle that neglected corner that has gotten out of control.

○ **Water.** If the temperature is dropping in your region, don't be fooled by cooler temps; plants still need water in arid climates. Wean plants away from weekly waterings in preparation for the end of the season.

If you don't plan on growing a cover crop, insulate and protect the soil with a coarse mulch, such as straw or shredded leaves.

○ **Mulch.** Cover the soil with mulch before the offseason to prevent downpours and winds from eroding the fertile topsoil you cared for all season. Use a coarse mulch like straw to protect the soil from compaction.

○ **Save seeds.** Many crops have started to go to seed or are ripe enough for the seeds to be harvested and saved. Collect seeds from the plants that grew the best or withstood adverse conditions like true champions. Those are the genes you want to preserve for next year.

○ **Gather a soil sample.** Testing your soil every other season allows you to keep tabs on how your soil-building activities progress over time. Sending off your sample in the fall helps you avoid the long wait times that occur in the early-season race to get planting.

○ **Sow a cover crop.** Choose a cover crop based on your goals. Plant forage radish to break up hard clay soils, berseem clover for an easy winterkill even in mild winters, or winter rye to build mulch cover in situ.

○ **Chop-and-drop.** While there is an argument for keeping a tidy garden, chop and drop garden debris to provide more habitat and food for the good guys while adding soil-building organic matter without the need to haul in compost.

Save seeds from favorite flowers, herbs, and vegetables.

Garden and Plant Care

# SEASONAL *Garden* TO-DOS:
# OFFSEASON

Bring frost-sensitive plants that are still producing indoors if you can. A windowsill garden of herbs is perfect for flavoring winter dishes.

**AFTER A BUSY GROWING SEASON,** it is finally time to press pause. Depending on your location, this means it is either too hot or too cold to garden outside successfully. This break gives the gardener time to reflect and reboot. Cherish this time to sort seeds, thumb through seed catalogs, and make plans for next year.

- **Bring sensitive plants indoors.** In cold climates, bring your perennial herbs inside for the winter so you can enjoy fresh seasonings year-round. Dig up sensitive plants and pot them for the transition indoors.

- **Go over your garden journal.** Find a relaxing day to go over your garden journal. Highlight your successes and reflect on those things that went wrong. Plan next season's crop layout, highlight specific crop varieties you'll grow again, and daydream about future garden projects.

- **Share seeds.** If you saved seeds throughout the season and have more than you need, share them with friends or neighbors. Attend a local seed swap and pick up a few new vegetable varieties to try out next year.

Sharpen tools during the winter months to ready them for the coming growing season.

○ **Clean and sharpen tools.** Extend the longevity of your tools by removing rust and sharpening any blades. Sterilizing your cultivation and harvest tools curbs the spread of disease. Sand and oil any wooden handles to remove splinters and to prevent cracking.

Maintaining your vegetable garden is essential for long-term success. Staying on top of chores—even those you don't find enjoyable—keeps things from getting overwhelming while ensuring the garden stays productive. In the next chapter, we'll discuss the many ways gardeners can protect their plants from various threats, including insect pests, weather extremes, animals, and more.

# GARDEN *Care* TOOLS

**PERENNIAL SHOVELS**
are handy because their small profile makes them suitable for digging holes in tight spaces.

**POTATO FORKS**
are like pitchforks, but they have curved tines instead of straight tines, giving you more leverage when pulling tough-to-rid perennial weeds and grasses.

**WEEDING KNIVES/HORI HORIS**
can relieve some of the angst associated with removing unwanted plants. The serrated side slices through tough debris, and the pointed tip makes removing taproots a cinch.

**LONG-HANDLED WIRE HOES**
work best for weeding small seedlings without disturbing the soil. The long handle keeps you upright and protects your lower back.

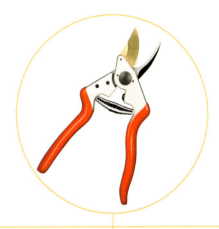

### BROAD FORKS
can help loosen soil before planting your crop. The sturdy metal tines punch through the soil effortlessly, creating gaps for air and water to percolate.

### HAND PRUNERS
are useful for harvesting crops and removing dead or diseased plant parts. Pruners come in many shapes, but it is best to find one that fits the size of your hand well.

### WHEELBARROWS
are essential for carting around mulch, bringing garden debris to the compost, and applying soil amendments. Two-wheeled barrows make hauling heavy loads more manageable and prevent the whole load from tipping over.

### SOIL MOISTURE METERS
eliminate guesswork about whether or not it's time to water the garden. Its long probe senses underground soil moisture at the root zone. Some meters have a digital readout, while others point to a numbered scale that ranges from dry to wet.

Garden and Plant Care

CHAPTER 9

# PLANT PROTECTION

**PLANTS HAVE THEIR OWN NATURAL DEFENSES** against harsh conditions, yet gardeners often need to provide additional protection from pests, diseases, and seasonal weather. While nurturing the soil is the best way to keep plants healthy, it may not always be enough to prevent all plant hazards. Gardeners can prevent potential threats by scouting for pests and diseases, spacing crops appropriately, and providing the right amount of water and nutrients.

Experienced gardeners learn from past observations and develop their own regional rituals to encourage a successful harvest. After a few seasons, plant protection can become second nature. For instance, a gardener may mark a specific week on their calendar as a reminder to drape a protective row cover over their arugula before a swarm of flea beetles arrives. Similarly, in northern locations, one may use the region's last frost date as guidance to protect new seedlings from cold temperatures.

This chapter explores the various prevention and controls you can use to protect your plants by managing pest, disease, and weather-related issues. You'll learn how to identify common pests and diseases and how to use organic controls to mitigate them. The chapter wraps up with guidance on how to help your plants withstand adverse weather conditions. By the end of this chapter, you'll feel confident you can handle whatever comes your way.

# DEALING *with* PESTS

Leaf-chewing pests such as this imported cabbage worm challenge gardeners, but employing preventive techniques like covering plants with row covers goes a long way toward minimizing their damage.

Some pests feed only on a small group of host plants, while others have a wider range. Mexican bean beetles and their larvae (shown here) skeletonize the leaves of many different types of bean plants.

**THE BEST ORGANIC PEST DEFENSE** is noticing problems before they spin out of control. Looking for pests is a great excuse to stroll through the garden each week. Why not admire the flowers or harvest a few carrots as you search for unwanted insects? If you notice five aphids on your basil, squish them or brush them off. Problem solved. If left unaddressed, female aphids can quickly reproduce, as their offspring emerge already carrying the next generation. Once an infestation takes hold, it requires a lot more effort to quash.

You don't always have to see pests to identify the culprit. Do you see holes in the leaves, signs of webbing, or splits in the stems? These symptoms can clue you in to what type of pest you might be up against. Suckers (bugs with piercing mouth parts), such as aphids and stink bugs, tap into leaf tissue by punching tiny holes through the leaf's protective layer. Defoliating pests, such as caterpillars and beetles, are known to devour leaves and stems. Signs of feeding can appear as small holes, while at other times, entire leaves are gobbled up, leaving nothing but the veins. There are also underground pests, such as borers and root maggots, that gnaw on roots and tunnel through root crops, causing severe harm before you even notice them.

Be on the lookout for signs of large pests such as rabbits, moles, and deer too. These critters can be particularly devastating in the garden. Do you see burrows, large chunks of missing lettuce, or complete crop destruction overnight? Mammals could be to blame.

Once you've identified pests, decide how much damage you can tolerate. Do you need picture-perfect arugula, or can you accept a few holes? Learning to live with less-than-perfect yet equally delicious produce can ease your pest woes.

If you decide to take action, always opt for preventive measures first. In case you require a more potent solution, it's best to choose organic controls and apply them during the pest's most vulnerable stage.

Once you take action, observe whether it worked. Wait a day and see if there are dead bugs, smaller colonies, or any more damage to your plants. There's no sense in using controls that aren't effective, and it's wise to document what works well or what might work better next time.

# Common Garden Pests

Preventing infestations and minimizing damage starts with correctly identifying the pests you see. Not all bugs are awful after all; some are essential, such as pollinators and those that prey on nuisance bugs. Each pest profile below identifies susceptible plants and explains how to recognize pests. There are also suggestions to prevent damage and, when needed, apply effective organic controls to fight back. For profiles about the good guys, see page 197.

Aphids on a tomato leaf

Cabbage looper on Chinese cabbage

Carrot rust fly damage

## *Aphid*

**Identifying features:** Small, soft-bodied, pear-shaped insect. Colors range between white, gray, green, yellow, brown, black, or red. They excrete honeydew, a sugary substance, to attract ants for protection.
**Type:** Sucker
**Host plants:** Aphids are not picky. You can find them on most crops, but asparagus, beans, lettuce, and those crops in the cabbage family (broccoli, cabbage, cauliflower, kale, radishes) are some of their favorites.
**Damage:** Excess honeydew will form gray sooty mold on plant surfaces. Leaves can curl and be discolored. New growth may appear stunted.
**Prevention:** They prefer tender new growth and hang on plant stems close to or under leaves. Squish them or blast them off with a hose.
**Controls:** Apply diatomaceous earth, horticultural oil, neem products, or insecticidal soaps.

## *Cabbage Looper*

**Identifying features:** Adult moths have speckled gray wings with unique white patterns; they lay eggs under leaves. The real pest problem emerges as a smooth, pale-green caterpillar that moves similarly to an inchworm.
**Type:** Defoliator
**Host plants:** Arugula, cabbage, broccoli, Brussels sprouts, kale, kohlrabi, radishes, lettuce, peas, and spinach.
**Damage:** Large holes on the undersides of leaves. Larger caterpillars may bore into the heads of cabbage or broccoli. Unmistakable green frass (insect feces) is a sure sign they are active.
**Prevention:** Pick off caterpillars and crush any small yellow-white domed eggs deposited underneath leaves. Use a row cover to prevent moths from laying eggs in the first place.
**Controls:** *Bacillus thuringiensis* works well on small caterpillars, as do spinosad and insecticidal soap products.

## *Carrot Rust Fly*

**Identifying features:** Adults are black-bodied winged insects with orange heads and legs. The larvae—which appear as slender, cream-colored maggots—are the real danger.
**Type:** Root pest
**Host plants:** Carrots, celery, dill, fennel, and parsnips.
**Damage:** Larvae tunnel through plant roots and leave behind rust-colored frass. Severe infestations may cause plant wilt or death due to stress.
**Prevention:** Adult flies are attracted by the scent of host plants. Plant susceptible crops in early summer (cold regions) and late winter (mild regions) when flies are inactive. Use a fabric cover to prevent adults from laying eggs after planting. Adults do not fly higher than crop foliage, so a 3-foot fabric fence around your crops can keep them out.
**Controls:** Chemical controls are ineffective for controlling larvae, which live safely underground. Beneficial insects like ground beetles and parasitic wasps are effective biological controls.

Plant Protection 191

Flea beetles and their damage on an eggplant leaf

## Flea Beetle

**Identifying features:** Small, shiny black insects that quickly hop around like fleas.
**Type:** Sucker
**Host plants:** Lettuce, spinach, arugula, tomatoes, peppers, potatoes, cabbage, and kale.
**Damage:** Numerous tiny pinholes are scattered across the leaves. Seedlings are easily stunted and damaged by heavy feeding.
**Prevention:** Cover plants with a protective fabric. Plant a trap crop to redirect beetles away from the plants that matter most.
**Controls:** They are notoriously difficult to control because they move so quickly. Diatomaceous earth and spinosad products can be effective, but prevention of this pest averts the most damage.

Wireworm damage on potatoes

## Wireworm

**Identifying features:** Adults are harmless, large black beetles easily identified by a distinct clicking sound. The destructive wormlike larvae are light brown to yellow and shiny, with segmented and slender bodies.
**Type:** Root pest
**Host plants:** Any root crop, especially carrots and potatoes, but they also feed on young lettuce, bean, onion, melon, and cucumber roots.
**Damage:** Root crops display round holes. Mature plants can appear stunted or wilted, and seedlings can easily succumb to wireworm tunneling through the base of the stem.
**Prevention:** Larvae are numerous in a new garden space previously covered in sod. It may take a season or two before numbers naturally dwindle.
**Controls:** Beneficial nematodes can keep populations in check. Before planting, dust transplanted seedlings with diatomaceous earth to protect the roots.

A slug feeding on a turnip leaf

## Slug

**Identifying features:** Soft-bodied pest with a protective layer of slimy mucus. They are the most active at night or on rainy, cool days.
**Type:** Defoliator
**Host plants:** Slugs are not shy and prey on most plants. Some favorites include lettuce, basil, beans, and kale.
**Damage:** Chew marks appear as long, irregularly shaped holes, and an unmistakable slime trail is left in their wake.
**Prevention:** Hand-pick off plants and eradicate any dark, cool, damp places to hide.
**Controls:** Dust troubled areas with diatomaceous earth or use an organic, iron-based bait.

A striped cucumber beetle on a cucumber leaf

## Cucumber Beetle

**Identifying features:** Adult beetles are bright yellow with black heads and have either black stripes or black spots on their wings. They have long segmented antennae and six spindly legs that move quickly to cover a lot of ground. They emerge from the soil early in the season to lay eggs and feed.
**Type:** Defoliator and root pest
**Host plants:** Despite their name, cucumber beetles are attracted to a range of crops, including asparagus, beans, beets, corn, potatoes, tomatoes, and, yes, cucumbers.
**Damage:** Both the adults and their larvae can inflict severe damage on plants. Adults chew their way through leaves and flowers, leaving large, irregular-shaped holes and stunted plants. As they chew, the beetles can also transmit bacterial wilt and cucumber mosaic virus, which can lead to plant death. Young larvae feast on plant roots and gnaw on any fruits that touch the ground.
**Prevention:** To protect young seedlings from feeding, cover them with a floating row cover. You can also wait to plant the beetles' preferred crops until after their peak season, which lasts up to 4 weeks in the spring as soon as temperatures reach 55°F.
**Controls:** Beneficial nematodes, neem, pyrethrin, and spinosad products can control this pest.

Squash bug nymphs and adults congregate on a zucchini plant and fruit

A squash vine borer larva inside of a squash stem

Mexican bean beetle larvae on a bean leaf

## Squash Bugs

**Identifying features:** Adult squash bugs have a flat, gray body angled toward the head, similar to a stink bug. Their orange-and-brown-striped abdomens make them easily identifiable. They lay oblong reddish-brown eggs that hatch into sap-sucking nymphs that emerge pale gray and turn gray as they mature.
**Type:** Sucker
**Host plants:** Adult squash bugs live true to their name and are attracted to winter squash and pumpkins. You may also find them crawling on cucumbers, melons, and summer squash.
**Damage:** Tiny nymphs pierce plant tissue with their sharp jaws to feed on sap. Heavy feeding causes wilted, yellowing leaves that turn brown. They also transmit cucurbit yellow vine disease, which spreads from plant to plant as they feed.
**Prevention:** Look for eggs laid on the undersides of leaves between plant veins. Squish any you see to prevent an infestation. It's best to plant vulnerable crops early in the season to allow for growth and increased resilience before pests arrive.
**Controls:** Neem and pyrethrin products are effective when applied as soon as the first eggs are detected, with a follow-up application in 1 to 2 weeks.

## Squash Vine Borers

**Identifying features:** Adult vine borers have black bodies with red markings on the abdomen and legs. They flaunt iridescent metallic front wings and transparent posterior wings that allow them to hover like a wasp. They are most active during the day and lay brown eggs. When the cream-colored larvae hatch, they quickly grow up to 1 inch long. Larvae, protected by brown cocoons, overwinter in the first 2 inches of soil.
**Type:** Borer
**Host plants:** These pests are attracted to all crops in the cumber family (melons, cucumbers, pumpkins, and squash), but they inflict the most damage on pumpkin, winter squash, and summer squash cultivars.
**Damage:** Female moths lay eggs at the base of a plant, and after the larvae emerge, they burrow into plant stems for protection. As they tunnel through the plant's stem, they disrupt the flow of water, which results in immediate wilting and plant death.
**Prevention:** Monitor adult moth populations with yellow sticky traps. Once you see a few of them, cover your crop with a floating row cover. This will help prevent the moth from laying eggs on your plants. If you spot any damaged plants, cut into the affected stem to kill the larvae to prevent them from overwintering.
**Controls:** Apply *Bacillus thuringiensis* or spinosad products as soon as eggs hatch but before larvae bore through plant stems.

## Mexican Bean Beetle

**Identifying features:** Many people mistake these copper-toned beetles for their beneficial cousin, the ladybug. Although the two species belong to the same family, you can easily differentiate between them by examining the back of the beetle. If you notice eight black dots on each wing, then you're dealing with a pest. Adult beetles can lay 40 to 60 bright-yellow eggs in clusters on the undersides of leaves.
**Type:** Defoliator
**Host plants:** They prefer crops in the bean family, such as green beans, lima beans, scarlet runner beans, and soybeans. A few may also be attracted to cabbage and kale plants.
**Damage:** Young beetles feed on the undersides of leaves as they mature. Heavy feeding results in skeletonized leaves that turn brown. Adults cause the most damage to your harvest by feeding on flowers, bean pods, and stems, which will lower your yield.
**Prevention:** If you struggle with this pest year after year, consider removing beans from your crop list for a year to reduce the pest's population.
**Controls:** Beetles can fly large distances and are challenging to control as a result. Planting an early trap crop of beans can attract a significant number of beetles, making them easier to treat with organic controls like neem, pyrethrins, or spinosad products.

Timely pest management is key to keeping pest outbreaks in control. Regularly patrol your garden looking for signs of issues before they get out of hand. Growing a diverse, resilient garden is important for deterring pests.

This yellow sticky card is being used to attract and trap spinach leaf miners and aphids.

## PREVENTION

Some of the most effective pest solutions are preventive, and you may already practice them in your garden if you've been growing for a few seasons. Many organic gardeners encourage biodiversity and plant various herbs, vegetables, and flowers to attract pollinators. This practice increases populations of beneficial insects and soilborne organisms that control pests naturally. Likewise, maintaining healthy soil helps plants tolerate pest pressure and more readily recover from any damage inflicted.

However, it's possible that what has worked in the past may be changing. Researchers expect pest ranges to expand as the climate warms, and pest behaviors and life cycles will shift as a result. Experts have already observed that increasing temperatures can disrupt natural biological pest controls by causing a mismatch between pests and their natural predators. For example, research has shown that when temperatures rise, aphid development speeds up, and they reach their population peak earlier in the season before ladybug populations have a chance to accumulate. This lack of synchronization between predator and prey disrupts the biological control beneficial insects provide and leads to more crop damage.

With the acceleration of insect development due to warmer conditions, we are now also facing multiple pest generations per growing season. This shift in pest behavior may lead to the appearance of unwanted bugs earlier or later in the season than we are accustomed to. To effectively manage these changes, we need to adapt our gardening practices. This means incorporating preventive practices, biological controls, and the careful use of product controls when necessary.

Timely pest management is key to effective control. For instance, certain plants attract the same pests every season, and being aware of this can give you a head start in your pest-control efforts. If you know what to expect, you can choose pest-resistant crop varieties if they are available. Beyond that, physical barriers and traps are other effective options, but they need to be used at the right time and place to be truly beneficial.

## *Pest Traps*

Pest traps can work as a deterrent or attractant, depending on the type used and the timing of placement. For the best results, it's important to carefully place traps at the right height, since most flying insects hover over plant foliage and attack from above. If you position your traps just above the height of your crop foliage and raise them as your plants grow, you'll provide the most protection. Set out a few traps to identify those insects that visit your garden, or hang numerous traps to mass-capture bugs and prevent crop damage.

**Sticky traps,** with their bright blue or yellow colors and strong adhesive coating, are a time-saving solution for pest monitoring. Bugs attracted to these vibrant colors unwittingly fly into danger and get caught. By checking these traps just a few times a week, you can easily keep track of what's buzzing in and out of your garden without spending excessive time searching. If you spot a few cabbage moths caught in your trap, it's a clear sign to cover your broccoli and prevent any further attempts at egg-laying. Yellow sticky traps are best for trapping whiteflies, spinach leaf miners, fungus gnats, winged aphids, and thrips. Blue sticky traps are best for trapping western flower thrips and a few other thrips species.

**Trap cropping** involves strategically placing certain plants to act as decoys and attract insects away from the crops you want to protect. For instance, some farmers plant 'Blue Hubbard' squash along the perimeter of their pumpkin fields early on to lure squash bugs away from their main crop. Squash bugs are drawn to the 'Blue Hubbard' plants because they find them more appetizing, and the insects are easily picked off or treated with organic controls, leaving the cash crop unharmed.

**Pheromone traps** attract pests by taking advantage of their biology. Insects use pheromones—natural scents and chemicals—to communicate and attract mates. These scents are specific to individual pests and are highly effective in attracting a single type of bug while keeping beneficial insects safe.

To attract pests, lures scented with synthetic versions of these chemicals are placed in a bottle, bag, or water pan. However, these lures are so powerful you should keep them away from your garden or crops to avoid attracting the pest you want to control. When setting up pheromone traps, consider the route a pest must take to reach the trap. If it involves flying over your garden, you'll want to adjust the location of the trap accordingly.

## *A Gardener's Best Friend*

The best way to prevent pests from damaging your plants is to create a physical barrier between them. One way to do this is by using a lightweight fabric called a floating row cover. These covers are made of woven textiles and allow light and moisture to pass through while keeping insects off of your crops.

Floating row covers are so lightweight that you can drape them over your plants without weighing them down. Simply drape the fabric over your plants and secure the ends with mounds of soil, stones, or sandbags to keep them in place.

Another popular option is to build mini-hoops to support the fabric and allow for better air circulation and space.

Floating row covers are a great tool to protect your plants from chewing insects. They also offer additional benefits, such as shielding plants from the sun, preventing damage from frost, and slowing soil-moisture evaporation.

However, as with many things, there are also downsides to consider. The wrapped plants may not look as natural or beautiful as you'd like. Plus, you need to remember to pull back the row covers to give pollinators access to pollinate your crops.

Mini hoop tunnels keep row cover up off of plants to improve air circulation.

Plant Protection

## BIOLOGICAL CONTROLS

Most insects aren't what you would consider a pest, and encouraging beneficial bugs to stick around is a smart pest-prevention strategy. For instance, predatory insects like ladybugs have a voracious appetite and can consume large numbers of insects per day. There are also parasitic bugs like *Trichogramma* wasps. They have evolved to feed their young by laying eggs on unsuspecting insects; when the eggs hatch, the young survive by consuming the host.

This tobacco hornworm has been parasitized by a beneficial wasp. The small, white, ricelike sacks on its back are the cocoons of another generation of pupating parasitic wasps. It has already stopped feeding on the tomato plant and will soon die.

Beneficial insects, including these adult green lacewings, can be purchased from insectaries and released into the garden, though there is no guarantee they will stick around.

You can encourage beneficial insects to stay around by providing them with a mixed habitat of perennials, annuals, flowers, and herbs. Diverse gardens function more like a self-sustaining ecosystem, one that provides food, shelter, and room for beneficial insects and birds. When you work to cultivate complexity, it helps manage and prevent problems before they take hold.

Interplanting herbs and flowers with your vegetable crops creates a welcoming environment where nectar-rich blooms encourage pollinators to buzz around. Multiple tiers of low-growing and towering crops provide shade and resources for predatory and parasitic insects to thrive. You can also plant permanent insectaries along the border of your garden beds—fill them with perennial flowers and grasses to provide an environment where beneficial insects can overwinter.

Suppose you need help attracting beneficial insects. In that case, you can get them by mail order from several commercial insectaries. But before you order, do your research and only purchase predatory insects native to your area (avoid Chinese praying mantids, for example, or non-native ladybugs). Purchase beneficials reared in an insectary, not those that were wild-collected. Ask questions. Beneficial insects usually arrive as eggs attached to paper strips or as tiny larvae, but sometimes adult insects can be purchased too (lacewings, for example). If you're anticipating an order arrival, make sure you are home, because these living creatures will not survive the sweltering heat or the frigid cold if left outside in poor conditions.

Once they arrive, you can set out beneficial insect eggs, adults, or larvae on a cool morning to prevent stress. Disperse them evenly throughout the garden as best you can. If you are setting out insect eggs, protect them from heavy rains that will wash them away. Some gardeners place the paper tabs of eggs in an upside-down paper cup to serve as an umbrella. Simply fasten the cup to a sturdy plant, fence post, or pole. Ensure you have a hospitable environment with lots of prey and nectar for them to eat, or they will leave for fairer grounds as soon as they hatch.

Birds are also a huge benefit when it comes to controlling pests. Experts estimate bird species across the globe consume upwards of 400 to 500 million metric tons of insects a year and have a significant impact on pest control. Almost all birds feed insects to their young, so having birds live and nest near the garden is beneficial.

# *Beneficial Insects*

Learn about the beneficial insects patrolling your garden. Each profile here describes their unique appearance, their role in naturally fighting pests, and their preferred habitat.

A convergent ladybug

## *Ladybug*
**Predator**

Ladybugs, also known as lady beetles, are easily identified by their domelike shape that splits along a centerline to reveal wings. There are around 450 species of ladybugs in the United States (both native and non-native) that come in a variety of colors. Ladybug larvae have an alligator-like appearance until they pupate, and both adult and larval ladybugs have unique mouthparts they use to feed on prey.

**Habitat:** To keep them around, plant nectar- and pollen-rich flowers like cosmos or dill, which provide them with a continued source of food even after they have eaten all your unwanted pests. It is also important to give them shelter to overwinter—this can be under rocks, nestled in plant debris, or inside hollow plant stems. The non-native Asian harlequin ladybug is the species that overwinters in your home.

**Controls:** These insects are famous for devouring aphids, but they also consume a wide range of soft-bodied insects and even pest eggs.

## *Lacewing*
**Predator**

Lacewings are insects with green or brown bodies and large eyes. They have long wings that cover most of their body and display intricate weblike patterns. Both adult lacewings and their alligator-like larvae are known for being voracious eaters, much like ladybugs.

**Habitat:** Lacewings thrive in diverse garden landscapes with a variety of crops and flowers. Lacewing pupae safely overwinter in undisturbed soil.

**Controls:** These insects are known for their insatiable appetite; they prey on a wide range of soft-bodied insects such as mealy bugs, thrips, spider mites, scales, aphids, and whiteflies.

A brown lacewing larva with an aphid

## *Beneficial Nematodes*
**Parasite**

Microscopic soilborne nematodes can be beneficial or detrimental to plant health, depending on the species. Beneficial nematode species prey on soil pests by entering their bodies through their mouths or any small opening they can find. Once inside, they release a specific type of bacteria that infects the pests, killing them within a few days.

**Habitat:** Nematodes prefer moist soil rich in organic matter—their abundance and activity decline in dry, compact, or heavy clay soils.

**Controls:** Nematodes seek out many different soil-dwelling pests, such as grubs and the larvae of beetles, wireworms, and weevils.

## *Predatory Mite*
**Predator**

Predatory mites aren't insects at all but members of the arachnid family. They are extremely small, pear-shaped creatures with eight legs.

**Habitat:** Natural areas around the garden can serve as habitat for predatory mite populations that are dispersed by wind to new garden locations.

**Controls:** Predatory mites prey on every life stage of pest mites—such as the two-spotted spider mite, rust mite, or bulb mite—as well as immature thrips, whiteflies, and scale insects.

## *Parasitic Wasp*
**Parasite**

They are no threat to humans, and many don't even carry stingers. There are hundreds of species of parasitic wasps. They have slender bodies, and females display stingerlike appendages (ovipositors) meant to lay eggs inside an unsuspecting host. When the eggs hatch, the young eat their host alive.

**Habitat:** While the larvae feed on insects, the adult wasps require nectar or pollen to survive. They are particularly attracted to flowering plants in the daisy and mint families.

**Controls:** The parasitic wasp's voracious larvae happily feed on aphids, beetles, caterpillars, thrips, and whiteflies.

A parasitic wasp about to insert eggs into aphids

Plant Protection 197

# ORGANIC *Product* CONTROLS

Organic gardeners can still use spray products; they just have to be derived from natural sources.

**DESPITE YOUR HARD WORK** in taking preventive measures, pest populations can sometimes increase rapidly. Gardeners may need to resort to organic product controls to treat persistent pests or new bugs in the area. Because organic pesticides rely on natural ingredients instead of potent neurotoxins or chemicals, most don't work instantly. Many kill pests slowly by interrupting feeding patterns or by causing fatal dehydration. For this reason, they may not handle huge pest explosions as quickly as their synthetic counterparts.

It is important to remember that just because a pesticide is organic, it doesn't mean you can use it without consideration. Some organic pesticides can be harmful to non-target species, such as the bees that pollinate your raspberries. Moreover, they can lead to an imbalance in the synergistic relationship between plant roots and soil organisms, and these organisms can be harmed if products are used excessively.

If you decide to use any of the pest-control products discussed in this section, it's important to use them in a way that minimizes exposure to humans, pets, and beneficial insects. Once you have successfully eliminated the pests, it's important to return to your preventive measures to keep them from coming back. It's also worth noting that using the same product repeatedly year after year can cause pests to become tolerant to it. To avoid this, switch up your pest-control products periodically.

For pesticide products purchased as a concentrate, follow the label instructions to ensure you are using the product effectively and safely. Additionally, store all organic pesticide sprays and concentrates in their original containers, in a dark and dry location, and at temperatures between 40°F and 100°F.

If you are unsure whether a particular pesticide is appropriate for use in organic vegetable gardens, look for the OMRI (Organic Materials Review Institute) seal of approval on the product's label.

## *Neem*

Neem oil is a natural extract obtained from the neem tree (*Azadirachta indica*). The active ingredient in the oil, azadirachtin, helps to reduce pest populations gradually by limiting the appetite and reproduction of a wide range of insects. Although it may not provide instant results, it works effectively in preventing the growth of insect populations. Generally, neem products come in a concentrated form that you mix with warm water before spraying on plants.

**Controls:** Neem is preventive and works best on young bugs before they get out of hand. Spray neem to control aphids, caterpillars, whiteflies, spider mites, and beetles.

**Best practice:** Start using neem to control pest populations as soon as they are noticed—a weekly application will help prevent them from getting out of control. Apply neem to both sides of the leaves, and avoid applying it in full sun. Direct sunlight can burn oil-covered leaves. You can store neem concentrate for up to 2 years. If you have mixed up too much for a single application, spray any excess on plants that are at high risk of powdery mildew—neem also works to control this fungal disease.

**Caution:** Watch out for honeybees, and do not apply neem for 24 hours if you expect them to visit the garden. You can keep them off treated plants by covering them with a row cover.

## *Insecticidal Soap*

Soap sprays kill insects that are hit directly, but the products lose their potency once they dry. There are a lot of homemade soap concoctions shared throughout the gardening world you can mix, but we don't recommend it. Detergents and dish soaps can be harsh and damage

Diatomaceous earth sprinkled into collars placed around the bases of broccoli plants keeps slugs and pill bugs at bay.

Bt is an effective control for caterpillars such as this cross-striped cabbage worm.

plant foliage if your ratios are off, plus these concoctions are not regulated or tested for safety. Instead, purchase commercial insecticidal soap products designed and labeled precisely for pest control.

**Controls:** The fatty acids in insecticidal soaps damage the protective coating of soft-bodied pests like aphids and caterpillars, causing them to dehydrate and die quickly.

**Best practice:** Thoroughly wet both sides of the leaves and spray targeted pests directly if you can see them. Repeat applications every 5 to 7 days as new pests hatch and form colonies. If you have hard water at home and purchase a concentrate, use bottled water to make sprays because the minerals in hard water reduce the effectiveness of insecticidal soap. Mix only as much concentrate as you need for the day, and keep spray bottles out of the sun. Direct sunlight will degrade the quality of your soap spray and make it less effective.

**Caution:** Soaps work on a wide range of insects, including beneficial insects. Avoid spraying plant parts and flowers where beneficial insects may reside. Spraying in the early morning or evening, when pollinators are not as active, can minimize the potential harm to them.

## *Diatomaceous Earth (DE)*
Diatomaceous earth is made from the pulverized fossils of tiny sea creatures called diatoms. This product looks like baking flour, but on the microscopic level, it resembles shards of broken glass that slash and slice an insect's protective outer layer. When insects pass through the dusty white powder, they suffer fatal dehydration.

**Controls:** This product is excellent for killing slugs, pill bugs, and wireworms.

**Best practice:** You can use DE to kill leaf-eating pests by dusting the leaves of your plants. You can also create a barrier of white powder at the base of your plants to stop slugs. DE works best when the climate is dry, since rain makes the powder clump together and lose some of its sharp edges. In case of rain, reapply DE to your plants once they have dried. It is important to store your DE in an airtight container to keep it dry. When properly stored, DE can last indefinitely.

**Caution:** DE is a fine powder you do not want to inhale. Wear gloves and a protective mask when possible. You can also seek out food-grade DE, which is the safest for both humans and animals.

## *Bacillus thuringiensis (Bt)*
*Bacillus thuringiensis* is a soil bacterium that naturally kills the leaf-eating larvae (caterpillars) of moths and butterflies by rupturing their guts as they feed on treated leaves. Since Bt only works on the larvae that eat treated leaves, it's safe to use around pollinators and predatory beneficial insects.

**Controls:** Bt is effective against all caterpillars that feed on plant leaves. However, it is not effective on adult butterflies or moths, and it does not impact the eggs laid by these insects.

**Best practice:** To control caterpillars, apply Bt to the areas of the plant where you know these pests feed. It is recommended to use Bt every 10 days until the pests are no longer a problem. Direct sunlight degrades Bt after a

# ORGANIC PESTICIDES

| PRODUCT | CONTROLS | NOTES |
|---|---|---|
| *Bacillus thuringiensis* (Bt) | Beet armyworms, cabbage loopers, cabbage worms, corn earworms, cutworms, diamondback moth caterpillars, tomato fruit worms, tomato hornworms | It works best on young pests just after they hatch and start to feed. |
| Beneficial nematodes | Asparagus beetles, carrot weevils, caterpillars, Colorado potato beetle larvae, corn earworms, cucumber beetle larvae, cutworms, flea beetle larvae, fly larvae, leaf miners, Japanese beetle grubs, root maggots, thrips, wireworms | Not all nematode species manage the same pest. Match the correct pest to the correct species for the best result, or purchase a mixture for all-purpose control. |
| Diatomaceous earth | All beetles, caterpillars, mites, slugs, and snails | DE works best to manage soft-fleshed bugs. It is less effective on bugs with hard exoskeletons. It's also less effective once the powder is wet. |
| Horticultural oil | Soft-bodied pests such as aphids, insect eggs, scale | Mineral- or vegetable oil–based versions are available. These products are only effective on contact. |
| Insecticidal soap | Soft-bodied pests, bean and potato beetle larvae, earwigs, grasshoppers, leaf hoppers, squash vine borers, thrips | Repeated use is okay as pests do not develop a resistance to this product. |
| Kaolin clay | All beetles, caterpillars, mites, slugs, snails, and worms | Clay can also be used to prevent sunburn on fruits and leaves. |
| Neem | Asparagus beetles, beet armyworms, cabbage loopers, cabbage worms, Colorado potato beetles, corn earworms, cutworms, diamondback moth caterpillars, flea beetles, fly larvae, leaf miners, harlequin bugs, squash bugs, thrips, tomato fruit worms, tomato hornworms, whiteflies | Works on contact and as a systemic insecticide, so its effectiveness increases over time and with repeated use. |
| Pyrethrins | Aphids, asparagus beetles, bean beetles, beet armyworms, cabbage loopers, cabbage worms, Colorado potato beetles, corn earworms, cucumber beetles, cutworms, diamondback moth caterpillars, flea beetles, fly larvae, leaf miners, harlequin bugs, spider mites, squash bugs, thrips, tomato fruit worms, tomato hornworms, whiteflies | The active ingredient is extremely toxic to all insects and aquatic creatures. Use with caution and as a last resort. |
| Slug and snail bait | Slugs and snails | Follow the slime trails to uncover and treat these pests' favorite hideouts. Choose baits based on the active ingredient iron phosphate, rather than less pet-friendly formulations based on metaldehyde. |
| Spinosad | Asparagus beetles, bean beetles, beet armyworms, cabbage loopers, cabbage worms, Colorado potato beetles, corn earworms, cucumber beetles, diamondback moth caterpillars, flea beetles, leaf miners, harlequin bugs, pill bugs, spider mites, squash bugs, thrips, tomato fruit worms, tomato hornworms | Resistance to these products can become an issue with repeated use. To reduce the likelihood of resistance, alternate between spinosad and neem products. |

There is a range of organic pest-control products to choose from, depending on your needs. Always read the label instructions before using any product.

200   American Horticultural Society | *Essential Guide to Organic Vegetable Gardening*

few hours, so it's important to apply it late in the day. This way, it will work to kill pests during their nightly feeding. Keep in mind that powdered Bt products can last up to 5 years, while liquid Bt products last up to 2 years.

**Caution:** It has no impact on directly sprayed pests, so bees and other pollinators won't be affected.

## *Spinosad*

Spinosad, a type of bacteria called *Saccharopolyspora spinosa,* produces a potent neurotoxin lethal to insects. The toxin has an exciting effect on infected insects, making them overstimulated and unable to continue feeding. The insects that come into contact with spinosad or ingest spinosad-treated leaves typically die within a few days. Unlike Bt, spinosad kills insects via both contact and ingestion.

**Controls:** Spinosad works to control all types of caterpillars and some species of beetles that eat leaf tissue.

**Best practice:** Thoroughly apply spinosad to dry leaves by wetting both sides and targeting places where insects may be hiding. Like Bt, spinosad breaks down in the direct sun, so using it during the late hours of the day will provide the greatest impact. Be careful around beneficial insects like honeybees—spinosad can hurt them if they come into contact with treated leaves within 24 hours. Under good storage conditions, spinosad products last about 3 years.

**Caution:** Since spinosad kills on contact, it is not safe to use around pollinators or beneficial insects. It is also toxic to aquatic creatures and should never be sprayed near bodies of water.

# CRITTER CONTROL

So far, we've covered small garden pests, but it's the large creatures such as moles, voles, chipmunks, rabbits, deer, and raccoons that can cause the most heartache. They always seem to know precisely when it's time to harvest, often beating you to the punch. It's disheartening to head out into the garden to harvest lunch only to find that a rabbit has already enjoyed a feast without you.

As with insect control, identifying the animal before taking action is crucial. Once you know what you're up against, you can confidently use the proper control to keep animals from devouring your crops. Effective defenses keep pests out of the garden, and you can choose to scare pest animals, block them out, or physically remove them from your area.

Proper fencing is the most effective way to keep animals out of the garden.

## *Fencing*

Protecting your garden from curious critters with a fence is incredibly effective. Fences work by preventing animals from jumping over or by shielding your vegetables from view.

If you're concerned about big animals like deer, elk, or moose, it's important to have a fence that's at least 7 feet tall (the taller, the better). Fences made of solid wood or plastic panels provide the best protection. However, they can come with a considerable price tag, so plastic deer netting or electric fencing are alternatives that still offer reliable protection for many seasons.

It's possible you don't want a tall fence at all. After all, installing one can be a big undertaking, one that takes time and resources. So here's a trick that can keep large animals out of your garden. These creatures struggle to determine the distance between two objects, which can be used to your advantage. Instead of building one tall fence, you can opt for two shorter ones made from any material you want, spaced no more than 4 feet apart. This makes it difficult for animals such as deer to jump over both fences in one go. The small space between each fence is enough to outsmart even the most nimble deer, as they may be able to jump high but not far.

Sometimes, you don't need an entire fence to protect your garden. If you notice a few crops are being eaten or damaged, use chicken-wire cages or barriers to protect only the crops you need to. In a pinch, use floating row covers to hide your crop from view, but they won't do much if a curious animal decides to look underneath.

Plant Protection 201

Live traps are an option for capturing nuisance animals, but you need to check with your local authorities regarding regulations and restrictions around their use.

Gardeners often face the problem of digging rodents, which can be quite a headache even if they have a sturdy fence around their garden. If you are dealing with gophers, moles, or other digging animals, consider installing chicken wire or metal hardware-cloth fencing at least 3 feet vertically under the ground from the base of an existing fence. This is a huge undertaking, so first, determine if you're up to the task. Alternatively, if you garden in raised beds, install wire-mesh bottoms before filling them with soil, which is a more manageable way to deter these annoying creatures.

## *Repellents*
Organic repellents contain ingredients that irritate or repel animals, discouraging them from lingering around. Some of these repellents include black pepper, garlic, cinnamon, and other spices that make the plants unpalatable to animals like rabbits, chipmunks, and deer. Others contain ingredients like putrid eggs or other foul-smelling items. On the other hand, some repellents mimic the smell of predator urine or blood to frighten animals away.

These repellents are available in sprays or in pellets that can be scattered around your garden. Applying them around the garden's boundaries can serve as the first line of defense against any critters that might try to invade your vegetable patch. These products offer long-lasting effects in dry weather conditions. However, a heavy rain can wash away the scent or flavor, so you'll have to reapply for them to work.

## *Mechanical Deterrents*
Mechanical deterrents are used as a scare tactic to prevent animals from entering the garden. Flashy materials like mylar ribbons, shiny CDs, or holographic tape can be strung from trees or fences to scare birds that may eat your planted seeds before they sprout.

You can also set up decoy animals resembling birds of prey or common predators such as foxes to deter rodents and smaller creatures. There are even audio repellents you stick in the ground that emit a high-pitched sound to ward off tunneling animals like voles. The effectiveness of these products depends on many factors, so a willingness to experiment is a must.

A new riff on the traditional scarecrow has also hit the market. Inflatable human-sized effigies that flap and wave in the wind are popular among gardeners, especially those with chickens or ducks to protect. These devices are akin to those eye-catching air dancers you see promoting a car wash or store grand opening.

However, one thing to note is animals are intelligent. They can quickly become desensitized to your efforts once they learn the threat isn't real. Switch up your deterrent techniques. Move the decoy around the garden, switch to a different pitch of audio deterrent, or try automatic tactics like a flood light or a motion-activated sprinkler to deliver a sharp burst of water to shock the interloper.

## *Live Traps*
Live traps are a humane way to remove animals from the vegetable garden after you have exhausted all the critter controls listed above. However, you may learn that your local municipality or state game commission does not permit trapping and releasing nuisance animals to a new location. While it may seem harmless and an excellent solution to your pest woes, releasing an animal into a new environment can have unexpected consequences.

For one, the animal may be sick, which can spread disease to a new population of animals. Relocation is also very disorienting to a creature that suddenly finds itself in a new environment and doesn't know where to look for food and water. You may also be separating a mother from her babies during certain times of the year. Always check with your local game commission to learn what to do with trapped nuisance animals.

If you are able to trap animals in your area, never use poison as bait. While poison is an incredibly effective means of dealing with stubborn pest problems, it puts other animals at risk that may see the slowly dying creature as an easy meal. When raptors, owls, coyotes, or even cats and dogs consume a poisoned animal, they become poisoned too.

# PLANT DISEASE

**DEALING WITH PLANT DISEASES** can be challenging, as their symptoms can often be mistaken for those caused by pests or environmental conditions such as heat and drought. Furthermore, plants under stress due to these factors are more susceptible to diseases, as their natural defenses are weakened. To make matters worse, some pests can spread diseases, making the situation even more complex.

Plant disease is caused by living pathogens that can spread from one plant to another via wind, rain, or biting insects. While previous chapters have highlighted the beneficial fungi and bacteria that help plants grow, it's equally important to acknowledge the harmful pathogens that cause infections and blights. Some pathogens target specific plant families, while others are more opportunistic and attack whatever they can.

## KNOW THE PATHOGEN

Have you ever noticed patchy designs on the leaves of your cucumber plants, or an open canker with an unknown liquid oozing out from the base of your pepper plant? These are signs of plant diseases caused by one of three main types of pathogens—bacteria, fungi, or viruses. Identifying the type of pathogen making your plant sick is crucial in finding a potential solution, if one exists.

**Bacterial infections** are challenging to treat because once a pathogen takes hold, plants have few natural defenses to fight back. Bacteria will infect plants by passing through a tear, a wound, or a tiny leaf pore called a stoma. Once inside, bacteria can break down plant tissue or meddle with water and nutrient transport and cause the characteristic wilting of leaves seen in most bacterial infections. However, scabs, spots, and cankers are other common signs.

**Viruses** do the same and enter through an opening in the plant's tissue to access the inner portion of plant cells. Once they breach a plant's defenses, they quickly multiply, using the plant's own genetic machinery to replicate proteins and robbing the plant of its ability to function normally. No organic controls exist for viral infections, and your only defense is to control the feeding insects that can transmit the virus in the first place. Worst of all, a virus is capable of infecting reproductive tissue and developing seeds, so the disease is passed on to the next generation of plants.

Preventing diseases is easier than managing them after they take hold. Adopt practices that limit the risk of disease from the start.

Viruses such as cucumber mosaic virus are impossible to eradicate. Removing the plant from the garden and properly disposing of it is the only remedy.

Plant Protection    203

**Fungal infections** cause a wide range of plant diseases. Unlike other types of infections, fungi do not need to rely on plant wounds or tears to negatively impact plants or to spread. They have a unique adaptation known as *appressoria,* which are specialized cells that develop on the tip of their hyphae (fungal "roots"). These cells help fungi to forcefully enter plants by grabbing on to them and exerting immense pressure to punch through their tissue. Once they make their way inside, they begin to digest plant tissue, causing a fungal infection to set in.

It can be difficult to know whether the disease symptoms expressed by plants are due to bacteria, viruses, or fungi because they can all look alike. Concerned gardeners can identify specific pathogens by sending a tissue sample to the local Extension office or university pathology lab for testing. Always call ahead to see if they offer the specific testing services you need. If they don't, they may be able to suggest a better option. Some land-grant universities offer free plant pathology testing.

Whether they are fungal or bacterial in nature, blights and other infections spread readily under the proper conditions.

## COMMON SYMPTOMS AND SIGNS OF DISEASE

| BACTERIAL | FUNGAL | VIRAL |
|---|---|---|
| Brown leaf spots | Fuzzy growth or powder residue | Puckered leaves |
| Blemishes on fruits and vegetables | Brown or yellow rust spots | Twisted or curled leaves |
| Oozing ulcers (some smell bad) | Wilted leaves | Purple leaf veins |
| Dead areas on leaves | Stunted growth | Bronze or chalky leaves |
| Waterlogged tissue | Waterlogged tissue | Abnormal growth |
| Leaf wilt or drop | Rotting fruits and seeds | Reduced yield |
| Sudden death | Seedling death | Ringed lesions |
| Dead corky tissue on stems | Visible mushrooms or fungal structures | Sunken blemishes |

# DISEASE PREVENTION

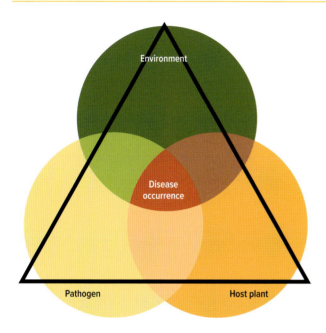

**THE DISEASE TRIANGLE** is a helpful tool for understanding the transmission of plant diseases. It has three sides, each representing a crucial factor that must be present for an infection to occur. The first side represents the presence of a disease-causing agent, such as bacterial cells, fungal spores, or a virus. The second side represents a host plant that is susceptible to that specific disease. Finally, the third side describes the proper environmental conditions that must be present for the disease to take hold.

As a gardener, you are not just a passive observer in the fight against plant diseases. You have the ability to actively disrupt disease transmission by breaking one or more of the links in the disease triangle. By understanding plant infections from this perspective, you can take a proactive stance to prevent the transmission of diseases to a plant host, especially under favorable conditions.

For example, if you plant winter squash in an area where powdery mildew spores are abundant and mid-season conditions are hot and humid, all three links in the disease triangle are present, and you'll likely see the disease take hold and spread. Alternatively, suppose the humidity holds off, and you water the garden in a way that reduces wet foliage. In that case, the conditions for mildew to prosper are not provided, and the disease will remain dormant.

Gardeners have a range of practical tools and techniques at their disposal to prevent disease transmission in their gardens. Start by selecting disease-resistant plant varieties and removing disease-spreading weeds. You can also prevent the conditions that favor disease development by improving air circulation and adopting careful watering practices. Additionally, minimize disease spread by sterilizing tools, controlling disease-spreading pests, and promptly removing infected plants. Let's explore some solutions in more detail.

## SEEK OUT DISEASE-RESISTANT CROPS

Diseases can only spread if they can infect a plant host. You can prevent disease transmission by selecting plant varieties resistant to disease. Popular crops like tomatoes, wheat, corn, and squash have been extensively researched and hybridized to possess disease-resistant traits. Likewise, there are heirloom varieties that offer disease resistance too. The 'Tigerella' tomato, for example, is resistant to late blight, and 'Provider' green beans are resistant to mosaic virus and powdery mildew.

Seed companies have developed a comprehensive coding system to show which seed varieties are resistant to specific pathogens. For instance, if you see the initials "BR" while ordering seeds, it indicates the crop is resistant to black rot disease. "PM" denotes resistance to powdery mildew. These codes come in handy when choosing from a wide variety of seed options, and most seed catalogs use these codes to make shopping easier. However, it is crucial to note that diseases can evolve and may eventually overcome a crop's natural resistance over time. Thankfully, there are a number of other approaches you can rely on to stop the spread of disease.

## CROP ROTATION

Crop rotation is a widely used farming practice that helps maintain crop health. It involves planting different crops in different locations each year. This helps prevent plant infections caused by a buildup of pathogens in the soil from the previous season's planting. By rotating crops, you effectively break the cycle of infection.

Crop rotation is one way to help manage diseases. These two images show the same garden bed in two successive seasons. In year 1, it housed lettuce and kale. In year 2, the garden was planted with cauliflower and peas. Perhaps in year 3, it will host tomatoes and peppers. Note the different plant families cycling through each year.

Growing vining crops up trellises and spacing seeds and plants at the proper distance are useful strategies for reducing fungal issues.

If you have a small garden, rotating the location of your crops may not be possible. Instead, planting susceptible crops in containers might be a better option. This is especially true if you notice your plants have been infected with fusarium wilt, as the spores can overwinter and infect your crop the following year. By planting crops in containers and keeping them away from the infected area, you can prevent disease transmission. Eventually, without a viable host, the pathogen will disappear.

## YET ANOTHER REASON TO WEED

Weeds not only occupy space in your garden and compete with crops for nutrients and light, but they can also carry and spread diseases. As many weeds are closely related to favorite vegetable crops, they are the ideal host for the same pathogens that can impact your crops. Insects that feed on infected weeds will quickly spread the disease to your vegetables once they take a bite.

Take lamb's-quarter (*Chenopodium album*), for example. Gardeners may choose to spare this edible weed and harvest its tasty spinachlike leaves. Unfortunately, lamb's-quarter is an alternate host for several types of mosaic virus, which can spread to neighboring pepper, tomato, cucumber, and squash plants via leaf-biting insects.

To avoid the spread of disease, it is best to keep weeds to a minimum. However, if you enjoy cultivating edible weeds, don't stop now. Instead, focus on removing those weeds that serve as alternate hosts as soon as they start to show signs of infection.

Take the time to draw a detailed crop map in your garden journal. This will help you track what you planted and where, ensuring you are organized and prepared for the next planting season. Some gardeners create a garden layout worksheet that they can copy and fill out each year. This becomes an invaluable resource, jogging your memory about any disease issues and the location of troublesome crops you should move around to avoid another infection.

## GIVE PLANTS ROOM TO BREATHE

It can be tempting to pack in as many plants as possible to maximize your harvest potential, especially if you don't have much room. But in doing so, you create the environmental conditions that promote disease and connect all three links in the disease triangle.

Instead, give your plants space to breathe to eliminate the stagnant conditions pathogens love. Adequate space between your plants allows a nice breeze to pass through the garden, wicking away excess moisture and dispersing clouds of fungal spores before they have a chance to settle into the soil. Most seed packets come with recommended plant spacing you can use as a guideline.

Gardeners who opt for intensive planting techniques can stagger plant heights throughout their garden in order to reap the benefits of good air circulation while still maximizing their harvest. Planting in different layers offers more air movement around each plant.

You can also improve air circulation by trimming large plants as they reach maturity. It's common for gardeners to regularly pinch back and trim the lower leaves of tomatoes, for example, to remove the wall of vegetation that can lead to stagnant air. Vining crops like cucumbers and squash can also be trimmed back to keep them contained so they don't overcrowd their neighbors. By doing this, you can get away with tighter plantings too.

## KEEP IT DRY

Extended periods of rainy weather can create the perfect conditions for the proliferation and transmission of plant disease. Disease-causing pathogens require moisture in order to attach themselves to leaves and infect plant tissues. In addition, wet conditions can enable the spread of diseases from plant to plant through contaminated droplets that fall or splash up from the ground during a storm.

Although you cannot control the weather, you can take steps to keep your plants dry when you water your garden. The best way to prevent damp conditions is to water your plants at the base instead of showering them from above. Drip irrigation setups are one way to limit the amount of water that contacts plant leaves. This practical setup provides a slow and steady drip of water that enters the soil without ever touching your plants.

Wet foliage promotes the establishment of fungal diseases, particularly on tomatoes and cucurbits. Water at the base of the plant whenever possible to keep foliage dry.

Removing infected foliage and throwing it in the garbage (not the compost pile) can help stifle the disease's spread.

For gardeners who prefer watering by hand, use a wand attachment that allows you to target the soil instead of a broad fan of water that may shower the foliage. Alternatively, if you have a sprinkler set up for overhead watering, water your plants in the morning so their leaves can dry out quickly during the heat of the day.

## STERILIZE TO STOP THE SPREAD

Garden tools can often spread disease because they can carry pathogens from one plant to another. Luckily, you can control this mode of transmission by disinfecting your tools between uses. But before you do, remove any dirt and debris so that the disinfectant can reach all surfaces.

Plant Protection 207

# Common Diseases

It is important to learn how to identify the signs and symptoms of common vegetable diseases. Each disease profile includes information on the mode of transmission and prevention and control measures that can be taken to disrupt the disease cycle.

## Soft Rot

### Bacteria

This soil bacteria infiltrates plants through injured roots, where it quickly multiplies. The bacteria release specific enzymes that chew away plant tissues, resulting in decay. Infected plants can spread the disease to neighboring plants through contact with the slimy ooze they produce.

**Host plants:** No crops are safe from the effects of this disease.

**Damage:** Infected areas ooze and are soft and watery. Impacted plants will continue to rot after harvest and emit a foul odor.

**Prevention:** Avoid planting in very wet soil and overwatering your crops. It is highly recommended that sensitive crops be harvested in dry weather.

**Controls:** There is no cure for this bacterial disease, and plants should be removed as soon as possible. Do not compost infected plants.

## Bacterial Wilt

### Bacteria

Two bacteria strains are responsible for bacterial wilt. *Erwinia tracheiphilia* infects crops in the cucumber family, while *Ralstonia solanacearum* infects crops in the nightshade family. *E. tracheiphilia* lives in the guts of cucumber beetles, which feed on infected plants and can quickly spread the bacteria to healthy plants. On the other hand, *R. solanacearum* is a soilborne bacteria that infects nightshades from the ground up. It thrives in warm soils and easily contaminates root-damaged plants.

**Host plants:** Cucumbers, squash, pumpkins, melons, tomatoes, peppers, eggplant, and potatoes.

**Damage:** Once an infection takes hold, the plant's ability to transport nutrients and water is stifled, resulting in a swift and unavoidable death. You can identify the signs of infection by observing wilted leaves and stems, brown spots on fruits, rotting roots, and brown streaks within the stem tissue. The plant may suddenly die.

**Prevention:** Cover susceptible crops in the cucumber family with a floating row cover to stop beetles from feeding.

**Controls:** There are no organic controls.

## Fusarium Wilt

### Fungi

Fusarium wilt spores live in the soil and on infected plant debris for a very long time, making this one disease you want to avoid as much as possible. The fungi infect healthy plants by entering through wounded plant roots. Once it takes hold, the disease can infect reproductive tissue and transfer the disease to seeds that are produced.

**Host plants:** This wide-reaching disease impacts many crops.

**Damage:** Once the fungi have entered a plant's vascular system, the flow of water is restricted. You may notice wilted leaves that do not improve after you water your crops. Infected young seedlings turn yellow, wilt, and die within a few days. If you suspect fusarium wilt, look to see if plants have long, dark streaks of brown vascular tissue in the stem or roots.

**Prevention:** Due to the ability of this disease to linger, you can solarize your soil to potentially kill the pathogen hidden underground. Cleaning and sanitizing all tools after working with infected crops is mandatory. You may also find disease-resistant versions of your favorite crops.

**Controls:** There are no organic fungicides on the market that can control the spread of this disease.

## Mosaic Virus

### Virus

Multiple strains of this virus exist in the soil. Weeds and perennial plants can harbor the virus, so the disease can reappear year after year. Insects that feed on infected weeds pass the disease to crops as they feed.

**Host plants:** Tomatoes, peppers, celery, cucumbers, squash, garlic, peas, beans, and spinach are commonly impacted by this virus.

**Damage:** Common symptoms include distorted leaves that show yellow-mottled patterns. Infected plants are almost always stunted and produce undersized fruits, if any at all.

**Prevention:** Look for disease-resistant varieties when possible. Control sucking insects that can transmit the disease from plant to plant as they feed.

**Controls:** There is no cure once a plant is infected. Remove all infected plants as soon as possible.

## Tomato Spotted Wilt

### Virus

This virus lives in the sap of plants and is spread by sucking pests called thrips. Once thrips feed on infected plants, they easily transfer the disease to healthy plants.

**Host plants:** Despite this disease's name, it can impact a range of crops, including beans, cucumbers, eggplant, lettuce, peppers, potatoes, spinach, and, of course, tomatoes.

**Damage:** Dark-brown or yellow leaf spots, distorted leaves, tip dieback, leaf bronzing, and stunted plants are common signs of infection.

**Prevention:** Look for disease-resistant varieties when possible. This disease also thrives in greenhouse settings, so thoroughly inspect seedlings for signs of thrips before bringing them home.

**Controls:** This disease can't be controlled. Remove any infected plants as soon as possible, and do not add them to the compost.

208  American Horticultural Society  |  *Essential Guide to Organic Vegetable Gardening*

Although bleach might seem like a good option, it can be corrosive and cause your metal tools to rust more easily. Instead, use rubbing alcohol, hand sanitizer, or a spray disinfectant to safely clean tools such as pruners, trowels, and rakes.

## GET RID OF INFECTED FOLIAGE

Remove infected foliage as soon as possible! But keep in mind that removing infected foliage can stir up fungal spores and exacerbate the issue by rubbing plants together. Still, infected foliage (and in some cases, an entire infected plant) has got to go, and you can minimize your risk with a few tips. Although it can be difficult to let go of a plant you have been nurturing for months, the sacrifice is well worth it.

First, wait for a calm day with no breeze whenever possible. The lack of wind will lower the potential of spreading disease to healthy plants. Second, grab a plastic trash bag on your way to the garden. You can safely remove individual diseased leaves by gently sliding the bag over the leaves before cutting them off. If the entire plant needs to go, carefully place the bag over the plant before uprooting it with a shovel. For smaller branches or stems, clip them out and place them in a sandwich bag that you quickly seal before moving on. Lastly, remember to sanitize any tools you use in the process to prevent new infections later on.

## ORGANIC DISEASE-CONTROL PRODUCTS

You've done your best to prevent disease, but you've noticed the signs, and it's already here. The unfortunate reality is that most crop diseases are not curable, and once a plant is infected, there isn't much you can do aside from removing it from the garden. That said, there are a few products you can use to control or suppress disease, and gardeners should have them on hand in case the unavoidable happens.

Before you resort to using a disease-control product, it's crucial to accurately identify the disease. This will help you choose the right control method, as not all controls work on all diseases. For instance, using a fungicide to control a bacterial wilt won't yield much success. Once you've

Organic disease-management products are best used early in the infection cycle. Be sure to choose the appropriate product for the pathogen.

pinpointed the disease, follow the product's instructions to the letter. This will not only protect you but also enhance the product's effectiveness. When you're ready to use organic disease controls, always wear protective clothing and avoid inhaling any mist.

### *Biofungicides*

Biofungicides make use of the good microorganisms naturally found in soil. Some of these microorganisms attack fungal or bacterial pathogens, while others produce beneficial antibiotics that curb harmful disease symptoms. Some microorganisms can even prompt a plant's immune system to kick in and fight back. Most products come as a liquid spray, but you can also find soil inoculants that contain these beneficial bacteria to introduce a front line of pathogen prevention. The most commonly used microorganisms in effective biofungicides include species of the following bacteria: *Bacillus, Streptomyces, Pseudomonas,* and *Serratia.*

**Controls:** Alternaria leaf spot, anthracnose, bacterial blight, bacterial leaf spot, damping-off, downy mildew, early blight, gray mold, late blight, potato scab, powdery mildew, rust, and white mold.
**Best practice:** Different species of bacteria are more effective on some pathogens compared to others. Read the label information to see if the active bacterial species in the mix will fight the disease you are trying to prevent or

Biofungicides are useful controls for diseases like this powdery mildew.

Early blight on potatoes is managed by copper-based fungicides, which are best used at the first signs of disease or as a preventative.

Sulfur-based products prevent fungal spores from becoming active. They are a good choice for managing septoria leaf spot on tomatoes, along with other fungal pathogens.

treat. Thankfully, some strains are effective for a range of bacterial or fungal diseases. Apply these products weekly to prevent disease, especially in wet, muggy, and humid conditions.
**Caution:** Biofungicides have highly specific hosts and do not harm beneficial insects.

## *Copper Products*

Copper products are available as liquids or powders, depending on your disease-control needs. Copper works to denature and destroy pathogen cells before they can attack plants. Thick liquid products quickly coat plant leaves for lasting protection, while powdered options can be used to dust entire crops.

**Controls:** Alternaria leaf spot, anthracnose, bacterial blight, bacterial leaf spot, bacterial soft rot, downy mildew, early blight, gray mold, powdery mildew, rust, and white mold.
**Best practice:** Apply copper products at the first signs of disease. Use less product for young plants and seedlings, but layer it on thick for older plants.
**Caution:** Repeated use of copper products can cause this heavy metal to accumulate in soils. Soil with too much copper can impact the livelihood of soil organisms and cause toxicity in plants. Copper products are also toxic to aquatic animals, so avoid applying them near bodies of water or storm drains.

## *Horticultural Oils*

The application of horticultural oils creates a protective barrier that helps prevent fungal spores from attaching to the surface of a leaf, shoot, or stem.

**Controls:** Alternaria leaf spot, Cercospora leaf spot, and powdery mildew.

**Best practice:** Never mix horticultural oils with sulfur products—this creates compounds that damage plant tissue. If you do use sulfur products, wait a few weeks before applying horticultural oils.
**Caution:** A fresh coat of oil will intensify the sun's rays, so reserve use for cool or cloudy days to avoid the risk of burning plant leaves.

## *Sulfur Products*

Sulfur compounds work by direct contact to prevent fungal spores from breaking dormancy and becoming active. Sulfur vapors can also indirectly control fungal spores, which allows sulfur fungicides to work from a distance.

**Controls:** Alternaria leaf spot, black rot, potato scab, powdery mildew, rust, and Septoria leaf spot.
**Best practice:** Do not use sulfur products within 2 weeks of horticultural oil applications. The resulting mix creates harmful compounds that damage leaf tissue. Sulfur products work best when they are applied once a week.
**Caution:** Sulfur products are toxic to aquatic species, so avoid using them near waterways.

## *Neem Oil*

Neem products are most notable for knocking back pest populations, but the active ingredient, azadirachtin, is also very effective against some diseases.

**Controls:** Anthracnose, powdery mildew, rust, and scab.
**Best practice:** Neem works best as a preventative. It should be sprayed once a week to prevent a disease from taking hold. You can also use neem products to stop the spread of disease.
**Caution:** Neem is toxic to all pollinators. Do not spray on open flowers in areas where they are active.

# WEATHER PROTECTION

A simple covering of shade cloth is enough to protect cool-weather-loving crops from soaring temperatures.

Leaving hoop tunnel frames in place allows the gardener to quickly cover the bed with plastic or row cover should a potentially destructive weather event, such as a frost or hailstorm, be on the horizon.

**GARDENERS HAVE A LOT TO WORRY ABOUT,** including pests, diseases, and, most importantly, the weather. While you can take plenty of preventive actions to control pest and disease outbreaks, you cannot prevent bad weather. Instead, gardeners are forced to predict and react to the forecast as best they can to protect their plants and harvest.

Understanding the impact of climate change on gardening is crucial. One visible trend across the country is a rise in average summertime temperatures. Researchers have found that summers have warmed by an average of 2.4°F nationwide. Certain locations, particularly in the southern and western regions of the United States, are now experiencing summers with at least 2 additional weeks of above-normal temperatures.

Soaring temperatures are a significant concern for gardeners who may notice leaf cupping, sunburnt leaves and fruits, and blossom drops, conditions that can affect all but a few sun-loving vegetables such as squash, pumpkins, zucchini, and cucumbers. Extreme heat can lead to bolting. This can also affect the taste of vegetables, often making them bitter and tough. While bolted plants are still edible, the quality of your harvest will suffer.

Sudden drops in temperature are also problematic for plants. Prolonged freezing conditions are enough to kill most annual vegetables, making it crucial for gardeners to keep track of their season's first and last frost dates. However, these traditional dates are also changing, adding to the unpredictability of spring planting. Even plants that can withstand the cold may develop issues like buttoning, a common problem with broccoli and cauliflower. This results in premature florets that never grow into the large heads you might expect. Cold temperatures can also cause leaf burn and a quick death to all but the hardiest cold-weather crops such as kale, Brussels sprouts, and spinach.

Alongside managing extreme temperatures, gardeners have to grapple with fluctuations in their water resources. For instance, regions like the Southern Plains can witness a sudden shift between a catastrophic flood and a historic drought within the same season, leaving gardeners to struggle with a feast or famine of water resources. This imbalance can lead to fruit cracking, in which water-hungry plants take advantage of the long-awaited rain. When plants consume excessive amounts of water, the inner tissues expand rapidly, while the outer skin fails to keep up, resulting in tears in the fruit. This problem becomes more prevalent as the crops mature.

Gardeners also face the challenge of coping with the increasing frequency and intensity of storms due to climate change. Researchers have reported that storms are becoming more frequent or intense nationwide. The Northern Great Plains are experiencing more large-sized hail, the Southeast is grappling with intensifying hurricanes, and the Northeast has seen unprecedented floods over the past decade. As a gardener, you may have to adapt to

Floating row cover offers a surprising amount of frost protection. The two lettuce plants closest to the front edge of this bed were not covered by the row cover and are covered in frost, while the plants in the back of the bed were fully protected and remain frost-free.

Cold frames protect plants in the colder months, allowing gardeners to get a head start in the spring and extend the harvest in the fall.

these new norms when it comes to protecting your plants, no matter where you are located.

Although you cannot control the weather, you can take steps to minimize crop damage. Whether you are dealing with extreme heat, bitter cold, heavy rain, strong winds, or hail, you can protect your plants by being vigilant and monitoring the weather forecast in your area.

## SURVIVING THE COLD

Gardeners should know that unexpected frost is possible, even if your region's frost date has passed, especially during early- and late-season gardening. Frost can cause damage or even kill vulnerable plants. Therefore, gardeners need to keep an eye on the weather and be prepared to protect their plants at a moment's notice.

One of the quickest and easiest ways to protect your plants from frost is to use a floating row cover. This can insulate plants and keep them a few degrees above the ambient temperature. These covers are available in different thicknesses, depending on the level of protection you need, and they can also serve as an insect barrier (see page 195).

A cloche or bell-shaped covering can be a great choice if you have smaller plants or seedlings that require protection. You can either buy these devices or create them at home using an old plastic jug or glass jar. However, it's important to remove the covering during the day to allow ventilation for your plants.

For more elaborate frost protection, construct mini hoop houses using wire or plastic tubing bent over a garden bed or raised bed. These structures can support heavier cloth or plastic sheets and can be installed quickly during fringe seasons when temperatures fluctuate. You can also cover mini hoop houses with a shade cloth or insect netting to protect your plants from heat and bugs later in the season.

If you're looking for a more permanent solution, consider building a cold frame. These boxlike structures are bottomless, and you can make them out of wood, hay bales, or concrete blocks. They have a transparent lid of windows or polycarbonate panels you open or close to adjust the heat. Cold frames help warm the interior and protect plants from frost. For the best results, make sure your cold frame faces south to maximize the amount of light that enters and heats the structure.

## BEATING THE HEAT

Shade cloth is a great way to protect plants that are sensitive to heat—such as lettuce, broccoli, cabbage, and kale—from the harsh sunlight. You can cover the entire garden with a large shade cloth suspended from support poles, or you can choose specific planting beds or rows to cover using mini hoop tunnels. Shade cloth is particularly helpful in hot climates where protecting vegetable plants from extreme heat and sun is essential during certain parts of the year.

If you don't want to rig up shade cloth, you can use the shade created by towering plants, such as corn or a wall of beans, to protect delicate plants from the sun's direct

Hail can cause a lot of damage in a vegetable garden. Thankfully most plants will outgrow the damage with time.

heat. For example, plant a row of lettuce in the shade cast by your pole beans to prevent the lettuce from bolting. Alternatively, if you experience heat waves during the summer, it's worth researching heat-resistant or slow-to-bolt vegetable varieties.

Certain fruits, such as peppers and tomatoes, are susceptible to sunburn, particularly if you regularly prune the plants. If this issue persists, consider reducing the amount of foliage you trim. This allows additional leaves to provide shade for the ripening fruits and protect them from the sun. However, it's important to keep in mind that this strategy may increase the risk of disease if there isn't sufficient circulation, and you'll need to decide if the potential benefits outweigh the risks.

## DEALING WITH DROUGHT

During hot weather, droughtlike conditions are more likely, which can cause your plants to wither if they do not have access to additional water. If you can provide plants with irrigation, it is best to water them in the early morning or at dusk when the sun is less intense. This allows more water to percolate into the soil instead of evaporating in the hot, dry air.

In drought conditions, mulch will be your best friend. Applying a thick layer of mulch lowers the soil temperature and prevents the sun from baking the soil dry. If you rely on both mulch and overhead watering, remember, you will need to use more water than usual to infiltrate the thick layer of mulch to reach the soil. Alternatively, you can use drip irrigation placed below the mulch mat to ensure water reaches the roots. Ensure the mulch does not block or plug the emitters by inspecting them regularly.

## BRACING FOR STORMS

Extreme storms can pose a significant challenge for gardeners because they can cause substantial damage to crops in a short period. Unfortunately, you can't prevent hail, heavy rain, and high winds. You are at the mercy of Mother Nature, so all you can do is hope for the best and prepare for the worst.

To protect your plants from heavy rain, focus on flood-prevention tactics. Place your garden on higher ground whenever possible, and make sure you've corrected any drainage issues ahead of time. In dire situations, you can use flood barriers or permanent bermed perimeters to prevent water from flowing into your garden.

If you are expecting high winds, move potted plants to a safe location where they won't topple over. Secure tall plants with stakes and check that any trellised plants are firmly attached to their supports, especially if they have heavy fruits. It is recommended that loose branches or stems be reinforced with extra twine to help them brace for impact. In areas with frequent high winds, consider creating a windbreak to reduce the impact. Fences, hedgerows, and other barriers are all effective, but make sure not to position them too close to your garden, as they can cast shade and affect plant growth.

If you've ever experienced a hailstorm, then you know how devastating it can be when balls of ice tear through leaves and break the sturdy stems of your plants. The damage caused can be crippling. To protect your plants, grow them under the sturdy cover of a greenhouse or hail netting. However, if you don't have access to these options, use temporary covers. Place anchored-down pots and pans, trash cans, or any other sturdy object over your crop to provide some protection.

Whether the culprit is a mammalian pest, a leaf-munching insect, a deep freeze, or scalding summer sun, protecting vegetable plants is critical for cultivating a productive garden. In the next chapter, we'll dive into the most fun part of food gardening—the harvest.

## Level Up Your Crop Protection

Gardeners use permanent greenhouses or semipermanent high tunnels to prolong their growing season beyond their climate's natural limits by safeguarding their crops from severe weather conditions. These transparent structures—generally made from plastic sheeting, glass, or polycarbonate panels—allow sunlight to pass through while trapping heat. This natural warmth protects plants from chilly temperatures without supplemental heat, although that is always an option. These sturdy structures also safeguard crops from wind, rain, and snow, keeping them protected despite the harsh weather conditions outside.

Whether you're in a mild or cooler climate, these structures are a game changer. In milder regions, they enable year-round growth of cool-weather crops. In chilly areas, they're a must-have for ripening crops such as tomatoes and peppers before the first frost. Plus, they're perfect for giving warm-season crops a head start no matter where you live.

If you intend to build a greenhouse or high tunnel, it's important to plan and construct it properly. You'll need a level spot with plenty of unobstructed sunlight.

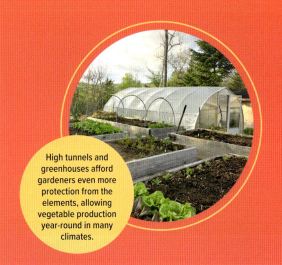

High tunnels and greenhouses afford gardeners even more protection from the elements, allowing vegetable production year-round in many climates.

**HUMANE ANIMAL TRAPS** are caged structures with a door that closes once an animal triggers the bait. Animals are not harmed during capture, and once in the cage, they can safely be transported away from the garden. Always check your local regulations before releasing any animals.

**PHEROMONE TRAPS** use scented lures to attract and capture male insects so you can detect them early. Checking the traps regularly will help you identify the arrival of a particular bug so you can take the necessary preventive measures before an infestation occurs.

# PLANT-PROTECTION TOOLS

### FLOATING ROW COVERS
are lightweight, breathable fabrics that you can drape over your crops to protect them from pests, sunscald, or a sudden cold front that passes through.

### INSECT NETTING
is a meshlike preventive crop cover made from polyester or other UV-resistant materials that keep pests from coming into contact with crops. Options are available that keep out even the tiniest pests, such as whiteflies, aphids, or thrips.

### HOOP STRUCTURES
made from bent plastic tubing or metal wire can be used as supports to secure insect netting, shade cloth, or floating row covers over your plants. You can make your own or purchase kits from your local garden center.

### STICKY TRAPS
are cardboard or plastic cards covered in sticky glue meant to lure and trap insects that land on the surface. They are great for monitoring and controlling pests in the garden or greenhouse.

### HOLOGRAPHIC TAPE
is a shiny, reflective material used to keep birds away from ripening fruits and vegetables. Strips of tape can be cut to length and hung from trees, vines, or other garden structures to provide both visual and audio deterrents as they flap in the wind.

### ELECTRIC FENCING
is often used to contain livestock animals, but it is also handy to keep larger pests such as deer, elk, and moose out of the garden. Compared to other types of fencing materials such as wood or vinyl panels, electric fences are affordable, easy to install, and temporary.

Plant Protection 215

CHAPTER 10

# HARVESTING

**WHILE IT IS TRUE THAT** gardening is a journey, it's always nice to finally arrive at what many consider the destination. You've researched, planned, and built a vegetable garden to be proud of. Enjoying the harvest is a great reward.

Just as the earlier steps in your garden plan were full of *ifs* and *sometimes,* the harvest is much the same. At this stage, you will learn when your vegetables and herbs are ready for harvest, which harvest techniques you should use, and what to do with the produce after harvest. This chapter breaks down each of these topics to make this final step enjoyable.

## HARVEST *Time*

**THE YEAR'S FIRST HARVEST** of a homegrown salad or a sun-ripened tomato is a celebration-worthy moment. After all the eager anticipation it took to get to this point, you may be tempted to rush it. The reward is in the patience. Delay your harvest until the vegetables are just ripe enough.

Most vegetables are at their best when harvested at the peak of ripeness. This is one of the reasons homegrown vegetables taste better than store-bought vegetables; their flavor is allowed to develop while still being nourished by the plant. Vegetables that are shipped long distances and then sit on a grocery-store shelf before purchase are not harvested at the peak of ripeness. They're harvested when they're stable enough for transport and then are forced to ripen when they reach their destination. It's not hard to tell the difference between a vine-ripened tomato and one that reddens up in storage after harvest. Biochemical changes happen in the vegetable as soon as it's harvested. Vegetables eaten soon after harvest will naturally have different flavors than those shipped across the country or around the world.

Because every vegetable is different, the time to harvest each is different. Pay attention to the details to make the best determination of your harvest window.

## DAYS TO MATURITY

The time to start thinking about the harvest is when you plant your crop. As you read the seed packet to look at the recommended spacing and depth of seeding, look also at the *days to maturity*. Remembering back to long- and short-season varieties (see page 58), you know each vegetable—and each variety of each vegetable—has its own estimated days to maturity. This number is the seed producer's best projection of how long it will take for the vegetable to be ready to harvest under ideal conditions. When you plant your transplants or seeds into the garden, note the date you expect to be able to start harvesting that herb or vegetable. (This is when your garden notebook or calendar comes in handy.) This will remind you to pay closer attention to the crop around that time.

The date marked on your calendar is an ideal. Whether your vegetables will be ready to harvest on that date depends on their growing conditions. Vegetables may take longer to mature when:

- Warm-season crops experience cool, wet weather.
- Cool-season crops are growing during too-cold or too-hot weather.
- There's a lack of sunshine.
- Tomatoes and peppers experience temperatures hotter than 85°F during the day and 70°F at night. They'll drop their blooms or abort their immature fruits, meaning no mature fruits will develop during that period (this is a physiological disorder known as blossom drop).
- The plants don't have the nutrients they need to develop their leaves, their roots, or their fruit.
- The garden gets too much water.
- The garden doesn't get enough water.

This list is long, and it illustrates just how important it is to be adaptable in your garden plan. Nothing in gardening is for certain. Nature is always in charge.

## SIGNALING HARVEST

In addition to paying attention to your crops' targeted days to maturity, there are other signals that vegetables and herbs offer to help you determine the right time to harvest. These same signals are what tell garden-poaching wildlife it's time to act. Much to any gardener's chagrin, the largest, most perfect-looking tomato will disappear when that tomato is just right.

Signs of harvest readiness on watermelons include a bright yellow spot on the bottom and a brown tendril opposite the fruit's stem.

The easiest way to tell when a beet is ready for harvest is by checking the size of its "shoulders" to estimate the size of the root.

Beginning gardeners tend to make the mistake of leaving vegetables on the plant until they're past their prime. The thinking might be that if your okra is almost thumb-sized today, it'll be the perfect size tomorrow—then tomorrow comes and you find the okra has doubled in size and is now woody and inedible. In time, you will get to know how vegetables behave in your garden and will improve your produce-picking skills.

The Ready to Harvest chart on page 224 offers specific harvest-readiness indicators for common types of produce. Often, you can use your senses to determine when a vegetable may be at its prime. Examples of these signals include:

- **Scent.** Think about the smell that fills the kitchen when you cut into a fresh cantaloupe. A cantaloupe that's ready to slip from the vine will have that same fragrance.
- **Color.** A watermelon develops a distinct yellow spot where it sits on the ground when it's ready to eat.
- **Sheen.** Eggplant skin turns glossy when the fruit is ripe.
- **Size.** Green beans fill out their pod just right—not too big, not too small—when they're tender and ready for cooking.
- **Density.** Cabbage will fill out and feel firm like a volleyball when its leaves have grown into a mature, fully formed head.

## ROOT VEGETABLES

Visual and tactile cues are helpful for most vegetables, but when a portion of the vegetable is buried in the ground, these details are largely hidden. Determining the maturity of carrots, radishes, turnips, beets, and other root vegetables requires another way of thinking.

To start, pay attention to your root vegetable's estimated days to maturity. Pull one or two around that time as a test. Harvest the rest if you're happy with the size, or retest 3 to 5 days later.

Sometimes you can tell a root vegetable's size by its "shoulders" visible at soil level. Of course, if you buried the seed a bit deeper than ideal, you might not be able to see the shoulders. Still, look for clues at the soil surface about how large a root vegetable might be. Compare one with another to pull the largest for your test harvest.

The root vegetable's greens are not generally useful in determining harvest readiness. It's possible to have awesome carrot tops with spindly carrot roots. Appreciate root vegetables' greens for their own usefulness, though. You can harvest up to one-third of the greens throughout the season without harming root growth.

## Oops: The Early or Late Harvest

It's easy to miss the ideal window for harvesting vegetables. A vacation in the summer, a week of late nights at work, or bad weather can keep even the most attentive gardener away at an inopportune time. Sometimes you have to make the choice: Harvest just before a vegetable is ripe or leave it on the plant a little longer than ideal. Sometimes you don't make this choice consciously but accidentally by harvesting too early or too late.

### FRUITING PLANTS
Fruiting plants are tricky. Some can be harvested before they are fully mature and will continue ripening afterward. Getting their timing right is less critical. Other fruits stop maturing at harvest, so you need to pay more attention to their harvest window. There are also fruits that can be eaten at any stage of maturity, so their harvest time is up to your preference.

The longer you leave the fruit on the plant, the more you're tempting wildlife to move in and enjoy it before you. There's nothing quite like a vine-ripened, homegrown tomato—a belief that's shared by people and raccoons alike.

### PODS
Okra, beans, and peas have a short harvest window. It's better to err on the side of picking too early than to leave them for too long. While they will not continue ripening after harvest, once they reach a certain size on the plant, they become tough and woody.

### LEAFY GREENS AND HERBS
Leafy greens and herbs usually have a long harvest window. You can eat them at any stage, so there's no harm in picking them too early. In the case of head lettuce or cabbage, it is best to let them fill out their heads fully before harvest—they won't fill out after being cut. You do want to be sure you get to these vegetables and herbs before they bolt.

### ROOT VEGETABLES
Root vegetables are forgiving in their harvest time, for the most part, but they don't continue maturing after being taken from the ground. Those with leafy greens can be left in the garden for months, even through mild winters. Salad radishes are the exception here. They have a short season, and as annuals, they'll bolt faster than their biennial counterparts.

Garlic can be harvested at any time, from before it starts forming a head (known as green garlic) to full head formation. If you're planning to cure and store your garlic for later use, harvest when it's fully mature.

Potatoes can be harvested at two stages: new (before they form tougher skins) and mature (with the tougher skins already formed). Exposure to sunlight will cause potatoes to form green spots on their skin; these spots are toxic but can be cut off before cooking. Make sure there is sufficient soil hilled up over the developing tubers to mitigate greening. Other than that, it's best to wait until potatoes are the size and maturity you want before digging them.

Fruiting plants, such as tomatoes and cucumbers, are best harvested when the fruits are fully ripe but not overripe.

# HARVEST STYLES

Whole-head harvesting is perfect for crops such as this bok choy.

Leaf lettuces can be harvested as take-what-you-need crops by only harvesting the outermost leaves, leaving the rest of the foliage intact for a future harvest.

Cut-and-come-again harvests are those made repeatedly from the same plant, typically a green. Most or all of the leaves are removed, but the growing point remains intact to regrow and produce subsequent harvests.

**LOOKING AT VEGETABLE PLANTS** side by side, it's obvious different vegetables require different harvest tools and techniques. Garden shears won't do much good for getting carrots out of the ground, while pulling by hand will not help you harvest a pumpkin. The tools and techniques vary according to the variety of vegetable and stage of maturity as well. A head of lettuce requires a sharp knife, whereas individual lettuce leaves can be plucked by hand (or harvested with a small pair of garden snips). The frequency of harvest and intended use of the produce also come into play. Here, read about the various harvest styles and the tools they require. See the Harvest Styles chart on page 222 for how to harvest common crops.

## WHOLE HEAD

Harvesting a whole head of a leafy vegetable is a straightforward task. Most often, you'll look for the place where the head meets the stem and cut the head off with a sharp knife.

Head lettuce and cabbage are common whole-head vegetables. These are formed as individual leaves grow in tight formation. These vegetables are ready for harvest when they're firm. Squeeze them, and they'll have little give—especially a mature cabbage head. Harvest below the head with some of the wrapper leaves still attached to prevent accidentally nicking the head itself.

Artichoke, broccoli, and cauliflower require a more nuanced approach to harvest. You want to let the head fully develop, but if you let the flowers open, you've waited a day too long. You're looking for a tight, full head.

## TAKE WHAT YOU NEED

Most leafy greens and herbs can be harvested using a take-what-you-need approach. This allows you to extend the harvest from a single plant, rather than having to devote a lot of space to planting many of the same type of plant.

Harvesting only what you need works especially well with plants that grow in a rosette pattern: branching plants with a growth point at the stem. As you harvest only the outermost leaves, the newer leaves closer to the middle continue growing. The plant puts its energy into producing more new leaves as you remove the older leaves.

Depending on what you're harvesting, you may be able to pinch off the stems with your fingers, or you could use harvest snips or scissors. More succulent vegetables, like bok choy and celery, might need a sharp knife for the cleanest harvest. Be careful to avoid cutting the leaves you want to stay attached to the plant.

Besides leafy greens and herbs, you can take what you need from potatoes too. It's possible to carefully dig a few new potatoes from around the edges of the mound and leave the rest of the potatoes in place to fully mature. This is a nice option for small gardens or any garden where you haven't dedicated much space to growing potatoes.

## CUT AND COME AGAIN

Similar to harvesting only what you need, cut-and-come-again crops extend the harvest over time from a single planting. Crops that can be harvested in a cut-and-come-again style are typically leafy greens and herbs that grow as a rosette with a central growth point. When you cut some or all of the leaves above that growth point—but not the growth point itself—the plant will regrow. Think about mowing grass—a perennial plant, though not edible. Mowing cuts the grass above its growth point, and then the grass grows back to be cut again (and again). With the popularity of cut-and-come-again harvest among greens growers, specific varieties have been developed just for this method.

Some plants that typically produce heads can also be harvested using the cut-and-come-again style. Often broccoli and cabbage will produce smaller side-shoot heads after the central head has been harvested. Use a sharp, clean knife for harvest. Plant hygiene is especially important, as you want to keep these plants healthy so they'll continue producing.

Cut-and-come-again leafy greens and herbs are often direct-seeded into the garden in a tight growing pattern. This requires ignoring the spacing information on the seed packet and planting only 2 to 3 inches apart. This makes it easier to harvest, and it also chokes out weeds from growing in between the plants. To harvest leafy greens and herbs, grasp a handful of leaves at the top, then cut straight across the lower part of the leaves, about 2 inches above the ground. Harvest carefully, as once you cut the center of the rosette, the plant is finished producing.

To harvest vegetables that grow as a head, harvest as usual, where the head meets the stem, and the plant will regrow the smaller heads itself.

Root vegetables, such as these parsnips and carrots, are pulled or dug from the ground when they reach the ideal size.

All types of peas should be snipped from the plant with your thumb and forefinger or a pair of harvest snips.

Cut-and-come-again harvest style works a few times for each planting. Cool weather and consistent moisture may extend the cut-and-come-again life span of these crops. When you notice the plants are slow to grow back, don't have their typical vibrant color, or have a bitter taste, they're finished producing.

## DIGGING ROOT VEGETABLES

With the exception of potatoes, sweet potatoes, and a few other crops, root vegetables primarily grow as individuals. (Read about how to harvest potatoes in the take-what-you-need style on the facing page.) You can harvest what you need in terms of root-vegetable greens—beet greens and turnip greens are sought-after vegetables on their own— but the roots themselves are a one-and-done harvest.

The deeper the vegetable grows, the more care you must use in harvesting it. You may be able to pluck shallow-rooted root vegetables—radishes, beets, and turnips— straight from the ground, but it's easy to snap a carrot or

Harvesting  **221**

## HARVEST STYLES

| WHOLE-HEAD HARVEST | TAKE WHAT YOU NEED | CUT AND COME AGAIN | DIGGING ROOT VEGETABLES | INDIVIDUAL HARVEST |
|---|---|---|---|---|
| Artichokes | Arugula | Arugula | Beets | Asparagus |
| Arugula | Basil | Bok choy | Carrots | Beans |
| Bok choy | Bok choy | Broccoli | Garlic | Corn |
| Broccoli | Brussels sprouts | Cabbage | Leeks | Cucumbers |
| Cabbage | Celery | Chives | Onions | Eggplant |
| Cauliflower | Chives | Cilantro | Parsnips | Melons |
| Celery | Cilantro | Dill | Potatoes | Okra |
| Cilantro | Collard greens | Kale | Radishes | Peas |
| Dill | Dill | Lettuce | Turnips | Peppers |
| Kohlrabi | Kale | Mint | | Pumpkins |
| Lettuce | Lavender | Mustard greens | | Summer squash |
| Parsley | Lemongrass | Parsley | | Tomatoes |
| Spinach | Lettuce | Spinach | | Winter squash |
| | Mint | Swiss chard | | |
| | Oregano | | | |
| | Parsley | | | |
| | Potatoes | | | |
| | Rhubarb | | | |
| | Rosemary | | | |
| | Sage | | | |
| | Spinach | | | |
| | Swiss chard | | | |
| | Thyme | | | |

lose a garlic head as you're pulling it. For deeper-rooted crops, loosen the soil around the roots with a digging fork. The deeper the root, the deeper you'll need to dig. Be careful to not spear a vegetable in the process. You can eat the damaged and broken vegetables right away, but they won't store well.

Grasp the vegetable by its greens and pull straight up. Knock off the soil back into the garden to keep as many nutrients and soil organisms as possible.

Potatoes stand alone in their harvesting needs, as potatoes are actually a thickening of the plant's underground stems—essentially tubers growing off the many roots of the potato plant. Potato tubers sometimes stray away from the plant, making it more possible to accidentally spear one while you're digging. Potatoes bruise surprisingly easily, so handle them with care after harvest.

## PODS, INDIVIDUAL VEGETABLES, AND FRUITING VEGETABLES

Vegetables that grow as individuals, pods, and fruits above ground have their own harvest styles.

**Asparagus:** Cut the emerging spears with a knife or shears just above soil level for a period of 6 weeks in the spring.

**Beans, corn, peas, tomatoes:** Hold the plant with one hand and the vegetable with the other. Snap the vegetable off the vine while holding the plant still.

**Cucumbers, eggplant, okra, peppers:** Harvest by cutting the fruits from the vine using harvesting snips.

**Melons:** Ripe cantaloupes slip right off the vine into your hand. Cut ripe watermelon from the vine using harvesting snips.

**Pumpkins, summer squash, winter squash:** Use garden shears to cut the fruit from the vine. Leave a 2- to 3-inch stem on pumpkins and winter squash for curing (see page 228).

## *Harvest Tips*

No matter what you're harvesting or how you're harvesting it, there are some best practices every gardener can use. These include:

**Harvest in the morning.** The ideal harvest time is just after the dew dries, before the sun's heat sets in. This is especially true for cool-season crops that wilt in the sun and heat. Overnight, vegetables rehydrate with moisture they transpire throughout the day. Starches formed throughout the day are converted to sugars in the evening.

**Cut down on the wind.** Wind pulls moisture from plants. The effect is more severe for harvested produce, because that head of broccoli can't replenish with moisture from other parts of the plant after it's been cut. Try to harvest when it's not so breezy.

**Bring the harvest inside as soon as possible.** Many vegetables need to be taken out of direct sunlight and into a cool place immediately after harvest.

**Use the proper harvest technique.** It's tempting to try to pull the okra pod off the plant because you forgot to bring your harvest shears to the garden, but your hand-pulling is likely to damage the plant, the pod, or both.

**Harvest when dry.** Harvesting from wet plants can encourage fungal and disease transfer between plants. Vegetables and herbs that degrade with moisture will not store well if harvested when wet.

**Harvest regularly.** Check your garden every day in peak season. With a regular harvest, your garden will produce at its best. You may be surprised at how fast some vegetables grow when given the right conditions. Removing fruits and leaves when they're ripe encourages the plant to continue making more. (The exception here is with plants that produce only one vegetable per planting. Once you harvest a kohlrabi or a carrot, that plant is finished producing.)

**Harvest with clean hands and tools.** From a food-safety perspective, little is more important than starting with clean surfaces. Wash your hands and sanitize your tools and surfaces to reduce the chance that you might spread harmful microbes between your plants and your food.

Harvesting **223**

# READY TO HARVEST

This chart offers characteristics to help you understand when your vegetables and herbs are ripe for the picking and how to harvest them come that time. The days to maturity suggested here are the estimated days from planting outdoors to the time of harvest. Some crops will be put into the garden as seedlings, so they'll need time to germinate and grow before transplanting. See the chart on page 149 for a calendar of when to start seeds for your transplants based on your climate.

| VEGETABLE/ HERB | DAYS TO MATURITY | HARVEST READINESS | HARVEST STAGES (BABY OR MATURE) | LIFE SPAN |
|---|---|---|---|---|
| Artichokes | 75–90 | Buds are 2"–4" in diameter | M | 5 years |
| Arugula | 20–40 | Leaves are 4"+ | B, M | Bolts in hot weather |
| Asparagus | 730 | Stalks are 6"–10" tall, the diameter of a pencil | M | Produces for 15+ years |
| Basil | 60–80 | Plants have 8+ leaves | B, M | Produces until flowering; remove flowers for growth until frost |
| Beans | 50–70 | Pick just as pods begin filling out; pods should snap easily when bent in two | M | A few weeks |
| Beets | 50–70 | Beginning when roots are 1" diameter for baby beets; 2" for mature beets | B, M | Harvest before high heat or hard freeze |
| Bok choy | 40–80 | From 4" tall | B, M | Bolts in hot weather |
| Broccoli | 50–65 | Harvest when green-blue color with tight, full head before flowers open | M | Sometimes offshoots grow after harvest of main head |
| Brussels sprouts | 90–180 | Bright-green, firm, 1"–2" heads | M | Can handle light freezes |
| Cabbage | 60–90 | Heads are firm | M | Bolts in hot weather; can handle light freezes |
| Carrots | 60–80 | ½"+ diameter at shoulder | B, M | Frost tolerant |
| Cauliflower | 55–80 | Head is compact and fairly smooth | M | Bolts in hot weather; frost tolerant |
| Celery | 80–120 | Take what you need starting at 6" tall; 12"+ at maturity | B, M | Tolerates light frost |
| Chives | 30–60 | Starting at 6" tall | B, M | May die back over winter and regrow in spring |
| Cilantro | 45–80 | 6"+ tall | B, M | Frost tolerant; bolts in hot weather |
| Collard greens | 60–80 | 6"+ tall | B, M | Slows production in hot weather |
| Corn | 70–105 | Full, rounded kernels beneath the husk; silks just drying out; milky sap produced when you pop a kernel with your fingernail | M | Produces one usable ear per stalk |

224    American Horticultural Society | *Essential Guide to Organic Vegetable Gardening*

| VEGETABLE/ HERB | DAYS TO MATURITY | HARVEST READINESS | HARVEST STAGES (BABY OR MATURE) | LIFE SPAN |
|---|---|---|---|---|
| Cucumbers | 55–65 | Pickling varieties: 2"–4" long. Slicing: 7"–9" | M | 3+ weeks |
| Dill | 30–55 | 6"+ tall | M | Bolts and produces edible flowers; dies with frost |
| Eggplant | 75–90 | Skin develops a sheen; fruit springs back when squeezed | M | Produces late summer until frost |
| Garlic | 250–270 | ⅓ of leaves turn brown | B, M | New plants will grow if cloves are left unharvested |
| Kale | 50–75 | 4"+ tall | M | Freeze tolerant |
| Kohlrabi | 55–70 | 2"–3" diameter | M | Bolts and turns bitter in hot weather |
| Lavender | 100–110 | When buds form, before they open | M | Produces until frost |
| Leeks | 90–150 | ½"+ diameter | B, M | Freeze tolerant |
| Lemongrass | 95 | Harvest leaves at 12"+; harvest stalk at ½"+ diameter | B, M | Dies with frost |
| Lettuce | 60–80 head; 40–80 leaf | Head lettuce: ready when firm. Leaf lettuce: when 4"+ tall | Head: M. Leaf: B, M | Gets bitter and bolts in hot weather |
| Melons | 65–100 | Cantaloupe: slips off vine when lifted, smells fragrant. Watermelon: underside turns yellowish, tendril on vine dies back, thumping on rind sounds hollow | M | Dies with frost |
| Mint | 70–80 | From 4"+ tall | B, M | Frost tolerant |
| Mustard greens | 45–50 | From 4"+ tall | B, M | Bolts in hot weather |
| Okra | 50–65 | Pods are 2"–3" long; use gloves to harvest or grow spineless varieties | B, M | Dies with frost |
| Onions | 90–120 | Harvest any time; mature when green tops bend and yellow | B, M | Tolerates freezing temperatures |
| Oregano | 80–90 | From 12" tall | B, M | Frost tolerant; best before flowering |
| Parsley | 75 | From 4"+ tall | B, M | Overwinters well |
| Parsnips | 110–130 | Harvest after fall frost, before new spring growth | M | Bolts and turns bitter in hot weather |

# READY TO HARVEST (CONTINUED)

| VEGETABLE/ HERB | DAYS TO MATURITY | HARVEST READINESS | HARVEST STAGES (BABY OR MATURE) | LIFE SPAN |
|---|---|---|---|---|
| Peas | 55–85 | Pods fill with round but tender peas | M | Short spring harvest window |
| Peppers | 60–90 | Fruits are firm and full-sized | B, M | Produces until frost |
| Potatoes | 90–120 | New potatoes ready when flowers bloom; potatoes mature when plant dies | B, M | Harvest before soil temperatures heat up |
| Pumpkins | 85–120 | Color darkens, skin can't be pierced with a fingernail, vine may die back | M | Harvest before frost |
| Radishes | 25–40 | From 1" diameter | B, M | Harvest before the soil gets hot |
| Rhubarb | 410 | Stem is 8"+ long | M | Don't harvest first year; harvest lightly second year; harvest for 8 weeks in following years |
| Rosemary | 80–180 | From 12"+ tall | B, M | May be knocked back by hard freezes |
| Sage | 80–90 | From 12"+ tall | B, M | 3+ years |
| Spinach | 45–60 | 3"+ long | B, M | Bolts in hot weather |
| Summer squash | 50–60 | Fruit firm and skin soft and rubbery | B, M | Dies with frost |
| Swiss chard | 55–65 | From 4"+ tall | B, M | Slows production in hottest weather and comes back in fall |
| Thyme | 90–95 | From 12"+ tall | B, M | 5–6 years |
| Tomatoes | 70–90 | Harvest green at any size; reaches maturity when fully colored and firm | B, M | Indeterminate varieties produce until frost; determinate varieties vary |
| Turnips | 45–70 | From 1" diameter | B, M | Freeze tolerant |
| Winter squash | 85–120 | Color darkens, skin can't be pierced with a fingernail, vine may die back | M | Dies with frost |

# STORAGE

**ONCE YOU BRING** your vegetables indoors, proper care and storage will ensure you get to enjoy them in due time. Not all vegetables should be refrigerated, but for those that should, some want to breathe while others need to be wrapped in plastic. Many vegetables are best eaten straight out of your garden, while some need time to cure. This section will guide you in the best storage method for your harvest.

## TEMPERATURE-BASED STORAGE

For every 10°F deviation from ideal, produce can lose 25 percent of its life span. You will get to know the preferred conditions for various vegetables and herbs.

**Cold temperatures.** Produce bound for cold storage should be kept just above freezing: 32°F to 40°F. In this cold range, some vegetables do best in dry conditions, around 60 percent humidity, and some in moist conditions, at 95 percent humidity. Refrigerators are the most obvious cold-storage option. The main refrigerator area is considered dry. You can create moist conditions using plastic bags and crisper drawers. If your home has a root cellar, this is an ideal cold, moist storage situation.

**Cool temperatures.** In vegetable parlance, "cool" means 50°F to 60°F. This is harder to achieve, but many basements come close. Humidity levels of basements vary, and you can always use a humidifier or dehumidifier to adjust the condition between dry (60 percent humidity) and moist (95 percent humidity). Whether you actually want your basement kept at 95 percent humidity is another story. If you plan to grow a significant amount of produce that needs cool storage, consider a small second refrigerator set to the required levels.

## WASHING BEFORE STORING

One benefit of having a vegetable garden is knowing exactly how your produce was handled before it got to your plate. However, this doesn't preclude the need to wash vegetables and herbs before you eat them. They can still be contaminated by environmental toxins and bacteria. Think about the insects and animals that traverse your garden when you're not watching (and sometimes even when you are!).

All produce can be washed just before you use it, whether eating it fresh or cooking it. Some produce can be washed right after harvesting. The Best Storage Conditions chart on page 229 outlines what should not be washed before storing—these herbs and vegetables should be washed just before using, as they're prone to start decomposing when wet.

Different vegetables are best stored in different ways. Proper storage is essential if you can't enjoy your harvest right away.

Store asparagus in a jar of water in the fridge for the longest shelf life.

Harvesting 227

For the most part, leafy greens can be washed in clean, running water and spun dry before being placed in their storage containers. Knock off soil from your root vegetables while still standing in the garden. You can even use the garden hose to do an initial cleaning to spare your kitchen sink a mud bath. Be sure the roots are dry when you put them into cold storage.

Solid vegetables, such as pumpkins, winter squash, and tomatoes, can be buffed clean with a cloth before being put away.

All vegetables should be rinsed in clean, running water before eating.

Alliums, squash, and potatoes need to be cured before long-term storage to harden their skins or rinds. These squash are sitting in a warm greenhouse for 7 to 10 days prior to being moved into a cool basement for storage.

## CURING

Vegetables designed to store for a long period first have to go through the curing process. Curing sures up the exterior of the vegetable to prevent moisture loss and decay. In the process, it heals minor wounds so, even if blemished, the vegetables will still be usable weeks and months later.

Throughout the curing process, if you find vegetables going bad or having an off smell, discard these. They won't cure properly, and you risk spreading a fungus or bacteria to the rest of the crop.

**Alliums.** For onions and garlic, curing creates their papery skin. When first harvested, the outer layers of these vegetables are still full of moisture. As they cure, the layers dry and give the onions and garlic their protective layers. It is possible to eat onions and garlic without curing; however, they will not have their staying power in storage without it.

Spread onions in a single layer on screens in the shade or in a well-ventilated garage for 1 to 2 weeks, until the tops are completely dry and shriveled. Do not cure them in direct sunlight. When the skins are totally dry, trim the tops to 1 to 2 inches for storage.

Garlic has a similar curing procedure. The bulbs need to be in a warm, dry, well-ventilated space for 3 to 4 weeks. Cut the stems to ½ to 1 inch in length and put them in storage.

**Cucurbits.** For pumpkins and winter squash, the starches in the vegetables are converted to sugars. Eat a butternut squash right after harvest and then eat one after curing, and you can taste the difference in sweetness. Don't cure acorn squash, because this can affect its texture.

Cure pumpkins and winter squash for 7 to 10 days at 80°F to 85°F. Depending on your weather at the time of harvest, this could be in a garden shed, or you might set up a space heater in a small room in your house.

**Potatoes.** Tubers harvested as new potatoes should be eaten relatively soon. Those harvested as mature potatoes can be cured to last for months. Spread out potatoes in a dark, well-ventilated location that's kept between 45°F and 60°F. In 10 to 14 days, they're ready for storage.

# BEST STORAGE CONDITIONS

| COLD, MOIST STORAGE | ROOM-TEMPERATURE STORAGE | COOL, MOIST STORAGE | COOL, DRY STORAGE | COLD, DRY STORAGE | NEEDS CURING | DO NOT WASH BEFORE STORAGE |
|---|---|---|---|---|---|---|
| Artichokes | Basil | Cucumbers | Pumpkins | Garlic | Onions | Artichokes |
| Arugula | | Eggplant | Winter squash | Onions | Potatoes | Asparagus* |
| Asparagus* | | Okra | | | Pumpkins | Basil |
| Beans | | Potatoes | | | Winter squash | Beans |
| Beets | | Summer squash | | | | Broccoli* |
| Bok choy | | Tomatoes | | | | Brussels sprouts |
| Broccoli* | | | | | | Cabbage |
| Brussels sprouts | | | | | | Corn* |
| Cabbage | | | | | | Cucumbers |
| Cantaloupes | | | | | | Dill |
| Carrots | | | | | | Eggplant |
| Cauliflower | | | | | | Garlic |
| Celery | | | | | | Lavender |
| Chives | | | | | | Okra |
| Cilantro | | | | | | Onions |
| Collard greens | | | | | | Oregano |
| Corn* | | | | | | Peas |
| Dill | | | | | | Potatoes |
| Kale | | | | | | Rosemary |
| Kohlrabi | | | | | | Sage |
| Lavender | | | | | | Summer squash |
| Leeks | | | | | | Thyme |
| Lemongrass | | | | | | Tomatoes |
| Lettuce | | | | | | |
| Mint | | | | | | |
| Mustard greens | | | | | | |
| Oregano | | | | | | |
| Parsley | | | | | | |
| Parsnips | | | | | | |
| Peas | | | | | | |
| Peppers | | | | | | |
| Radishes | | | | | | |
| Rhubarb | | | | | | |
| Rosemary | | | | | | |
| Sage | | | | | | |
| Spinach | | | | | | |
| Swiss chard | | | | | | |
| Thyme | | | | | | |
| Turnips | | | | | | |

* Indicates vegetables and herbs that are best used soon after harvest.

## *Special Storage Cases*

While Best Storage Conditions on page 229 covers most crop-storage scenarios, there are a few garden goods with other needs.

### ROOT VEGETABLES WITH GREENS
Store beets, radishes, turnips, and the like with their tops removed. Their greens are delicious and packed with nutrition, and they can and should be eaten. But if the greens are allowed to stay attached, the root will transpire its moisture through the greens and wilt. Separate them to keep each crisp.

### ALLIUMS
Onions and garlic require cold, dry storage. Leeks and chives need cold, moist storage. They're tricky to store alongside other foods, because their pungent flavor and odor are easily transferred to other, more delicate foods. Use airtight containers, when possible, to limit odor transmission.

### POTATOES
New potatoes should be used quickly, spending little time in storage. Cured potatoes are looking for a storage temperature range in between typical cold-storage and cool-storage temperatures. If you can find a place to keep mature, cured potatoes that's 40°F to 45°F with 90 percent humidity, that's where they'll keep best.

### HERBS AS BOUQUETS
While you can wrap most herbs in plastic and store them in the refrigerator crisper drawer, they will also store well standing upright in a jar with a little water in the bottom, a plastic bag draped over top.

Basil is so sensitive to cold that it will turn black in refrigerator temperatures. Leave it in a jar of water at room temperature for its best storage life.

## SAVING FOR LATER

If food preservation is of any interest, storing food properly beforehand makes all the difference in the final product. When you are freezing, dehydrating, pickling, fermenting, or canning your harvest, choose ripe, unblemished, top-quality vegetables and herbs that have been stored properly.

It is likely you will not forget your first garden harvest, whether that's your first bunch of kale for a quiche, a handful of snap peas for a snack, a tomato for a BLT, or leeks for a casserole. By your hundredth harvest, you'll look back and realize how far you—and your garden—have come. With this knowledge about determining the right harvest window, using the proper harvesting method, and keeping your vegetables and herbs until you're ready to use them, this time will come before you know it.

In the next chapter, you'll find profiles of the garden vegetables and herbs you may like to add to your space. The details included there are vital to your planning, planting, and harvesting.

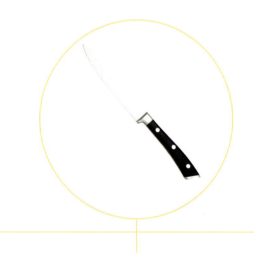

**A SHARP KNIFE,** like scissors, is something you want to have on hand for harvesting. A sharp knife is important for a clean cut. Knives are great for harvesting heads with very thick stems that would be hard to get shears around, such as summer squash, broccoli, and cauliflower.

# HARVEST TOOLS

### SCISSORS
are as simple a harvest tool as you can find. These are great for harvesting herbs with thin stems. While you probably have a pair or two lying around at home, you want one pair of scissors that's dedicated to harvest use. This will ensure they're kept clean and, with luck, you'll always be able to find them when you need them.

### HARVEST SNIPS
differ from scissors in that they have short, straight blades. They're ideal for harvesting herbs and vegetables with thin stems. Snips generally have more oomph than scissors and can do all of the jobs that scissors would.

### GARDEN SHEARS
with a bypass blade—meaning the two blades pass side by side to create a clean cut, as opposed to anvil-style shears that crush the plant material—are best. Shears are more substantial than snips and are meant to cut thicker stems, such as those on okra, pumpkins, and artichokes.

### HARVEST TOTES
come in all shapes and sizes, from wire baskets to flexible plastic tubs. You can even use a large stainless-steel kitchen bowl set aside for this purpose. Wood totes are attractive but hard to clean. Use a tote with a surface that can be sanitized.

### CLEAN GLOVES
are a helpful tool too. You don't have to wear gloves to harvest, but some plants can irritate your skin. Tomatoes, lemongrass, okra, and summer squash are common culprits. Gloves can ward off irritation.

### DISINFECTANT SPRAY
prevents dirty harvesting tools from transmitting issues from plant to plant and causing produce to decline in quality. You can purchase a spray or make your own simple spray of 2 teaspoons bleach per 1 gallon of water. Spray your tools and tote and let the surfaces dry before using the tools again.

CHAPTER 11

# EDIBLE PLANT PROFILES

Buttercrunch types offer a rich flavor and crunchy texture.

# ARTICHOKES

**Botanical name:** *Cynara scolymus* | **Plant family:** *Compositae* (Sunflower) | **Season:** Spring
**Plant parts eaten:** Flower head | **Light:** Full sun | **Life cycle:** Perennial, grown as annual in cool climates

## AN EDIBLE VARIETY OF THISTLE

originally from the Mediterranean, globe artichokes are grown in the vegetable garden for their fleshy immature flower heads surrounded by leaflike bracts. If left to bloom, the plant produces beautiful blue-purple flowers easily recognized as thistle.

## Sow

Plant artichokes from seed or transplants, or propagate from suckers of existing plants. If growing from seed, start 6 weeks before the last frost date in a warm area at least 65°F and transplant when at least four true leaves have appeared and temperatures are consistently in the 60s. If propagating from a mother plant, cut off a sucker 8 to 10 inches tall with the root attached. Replant in a 4-inch hole or pot up to care for indoors over winter before planting outdoors in spring. Depending on the variety, artichoke plants may not flower until the second year.

## Grow

Artichoke plants grow large—3 to 6 feet in height and width. Space plants 3 to 6 feet apart. Prepare the soil with plenty of compost, and fertilize at least once a month. In the heat of summer, plants may go dormant, but they may make new buds in fall. Some gardeners cut back side shoots to encourage a larger central bud, but this reduces the overall harvest. In late fall, cut the plants back to a few inches above the ground and mulch well over the plant crowns to insulate for winter.

The edible portion of an artichoke is the immature flower bud.

## Protect

Space properly to prevent slugs and snails from getting to plants. Water plants deeply at planting time. Otherwise, they are fairly care-free. In colder climates, grow artichokes in large pots and bring indoors through winter.

## Harvest

Starting in early summer, harvest heads when filled out but still closed, cutting 2 inches of stem with the bud. The stem below the bud should feel tender. Once the bud starts opening, both the bud and the stem become tough. Cut the central bud first before cutting any smaller buds or side shoots. Expect to get up to eight or more heads from one plant.

Artichokes are large perennial plants. Give them plenty of room in the garden if you plan to overwinter them.

## Types

Globe artichokes really only have two types: green and purple. 'Green Globe' is a popular variety in warm areas where artichoke is grown as a perennial. In cooler areas, try 'Imperial Star', an early maturing variety known to produce well from seed in the first year.

# ASPARAGUS

Botanical name: *Asparagus officinalis* | Plant family: *Asaparagaceae* | Season: Spring
Plant parts eaten: Spears (shoots) | Light: Full sun | Life cycle: Perennial

**PEOPLE ARE OFTEN SURPRISED** to see how asparagus grows. The spears pop out of the soil whole and intact. If allowed to establish properly in the first few years, your asparagus bed will produce in the same spot for up to 20 years.

## Sow

While it can be grown from seed, most gardeners grow asparagus from crowns (plant roots), ideally 2 to 3 years old. Order asparagus crowns from vegetable seed or plant companies; they will be shipped in early spring for planting. Plant in raised furrows 10 inches deep, 2 to 3 feet apart, draping roots over the mound to help with drainage; asparagus roots can rot in wet soil. Fill in the furrows to cover roots with soil, but don't bury the plant crown.

## Grow

Asparagus prefers slightly more alkaline soil than most vegetables; aim for a pH of 6.5 to 7.5. Amend acidic soil with lime or wood ash. Keep your asparagus bed weed-free to avoid competition. If possible, hand-weeding is best, as hoeing around roots can damage them. After harvesting, leave plants to grow tall, with feathery fernlike fronds. Cut back the plants when they begin to turn brown in fall, and mulch over the bed for winter.

Asparagus harvests require patience but are worth the wait.

## Protect

To help keep weeds down, some gardeners plant a noncompeting cover crop around asparagus plants. Annual winter rye can be sown in late spring; it will die back in summer and enrich the soil. Cowpeas can also be sown around asparagus in early summer to shade soil and add nitrogen. Asparagus beetles may attack plants, eating foliage and damaging stems. Pick off beetles if you see them, and remove the stems in fall so the asparagus beetles can't overwinter in plants.

## Harvest

Don't harvest asparagus the first year after planting, or even the second if you can wait, or if you planted younger crowns. In the second or third year, your plants should be established enough to begin harvesting in spring, or early summer in colder climates. Cut spears with a sharp knife at the base, close to or just below the soil line, when spears are 6 to 8 inches tall and ½ inch thick or less. Stop harvesting after 6 to 8 weeks to allow the plants to recover, ensuring a harvest next season.

Harvest asparagus spears for several weeks in the spring, then allow them to mature to create energy for next year's harvest.

## Types

Asparagus has both male and female plants, and some varieties are all male; male plants are preferable because they don't expend energy making seed. But many beloved heirlooms have both male and female plants, which is fine. 'Martha Washington' is a trusted heirloom variety from the United States with large spears and good flavor. Most varieties are green, but 'Purple Passion' is a purple variety known for its sweetness. In France, asparagus is grown to be white by covering the plants with soil as they grow to exclude light and blanch the stems; this labor-intensive practice is not known to change the flavor much.

# BEANS

**Botanical name:** *Phaseolus vulgaris* | **Plant family:** *Fabaceae* (Pea) | **Season:** Summer to fall
**Plant parts eaten:** Pod, seed | **Light:** Full sun | **Life cycle:** Annual

Dry bean varieties should be allowed to fully mature and dry on the plant before harvest.

Classic green beans (also called snap beans) have long been a favorite crop of home gardeners.

**BEANS ARE ONE** of the easiest vegetables to sow, grow, store, and save. They're nutritious, they provide a good source of vegetable protein, and the plants enrich the soil. This has made them a vital food crop since ancient times and, through human migrations, all across the world. No summer garden is complete without beans!

## Sow
Be patient: Cold, wet weather fosters disease in beans, so wait to sow until it's consistently in the 60s. Plant beans outdoors when soil temp is 60°F, about 1 inch below the soil. Space 2 to 6 inches apart, closer for pole beans and farther apart for bush beans. Rows should be 1 foot apart. Some gardeners will inoculate beans with *Rhizobium* bacteria to boost yields and increase the plant's natural ability to fix nitrogen from the soil; roll seeds in inoculant before planting, or buy pre-inoculated seeds.

## Grow
Beans are easy to grow and prolific. They fix nitrogen in the soil and do not need a lot of fertilizing, but it's a good idea to feed plants as they begin to flower. Pole beans will need a trellis to climb; they can also be planted at the base of tall plants such as sunflowers and corn to climb their sturdy stalks. When vining plants reach the top of their supports, you can pinch off the growing tips to keep them tidy, but it's not necessary.

## Protect
If critters are prone to dig up your bean seeds, cover with a row cover until plants are a few inches tall. Plants are more prone to diseases in cool weather; avoid touching plants when wet, which can transfer bacteria and disease. Planting too closely, where leaves do not get enough airflow to dry out, can lead to powdery mildew.

## Harvest
Snap beans should be harvested when plump but before seeds start to fill out the pods. Ripe beans should snap off the plant easily. Pick snap beans as often as possible to encourage more. For dried beans, allow the pods to dry on the plant. Harvest individually, or you can harvest the whole plant before frost. Cure beans in a dry place for a couple weeks, then thresh beans, removing seeds from the pods, before storing in an airtight container.

## Types
There are hundreds of bean varieties, with many heirlooms from various regions of the country and the world. Bean plants can be bush type, most of which are determinate (producing at the same time), or pole type, vining plants that are indeterminate (producing until killed by frost or other means). Beans can also be categorized by how they're best eaten, either as dried beans (the seeds inside are eaten and the pods are discarded) or as snap beans (the pod is harvested before the seeds mature and is eaten fresh, whole). Lima beans (*Phaseolus limensis*) are grown similarly and can be harvested as either dried beans or fresh.

Edible Plant Profiles   235

# BEETS

**Botanical name:** *Beta vulgaris* | **Plant family:** *Amaranthaceae* (Goosefoot) | **Season:** Cool season, spring, fall
**Plant parts eaten:** Roots, leaves | **Light:** Full sun | **Life cycle:** Annual

**EASY TO GROW** in cool weather, beets are nutritional powerhouses, packed with vitamins and minerals. Though they're grown primarily for the roots, beets are close relatives of Swiss chard and spinach, and beet greens taste just as good.

## Sow

Each beet seed is actually a ball of multiple seeds, called a multigerm. Optionally, soak seeds before planting to boost germination. Sow outdoors a week or two before the last frost date, 2 to 3 inches apart, and lightly cover with soil to ½ inch. Sow again in late summer for a fall harvest. Thin seedlings as each seed will produce multiple plants, or let them grow in place and harvest a few as baby beets. Beets can also be successfully grown in pots.

## Grow

Beets grow best in temps in the 60s. In hot weather, they become tough. Loosen and amend soil with compost before planting, but go easy on the nitrogen while they're growing; beets need a good amount of phosphorus, but too much nitrogen will cause tall greens and small roots. Beets prefer slightly alkaline soil with a pH of 6.0 to 7.0. Beets need average water and evenly moist soil.

Beets are best grown in well-drained soils rich in organic matter.

## Protect

Beets aren't bothered by many insects or diseases. Prevent scab (brown spots on the root) by keeping soil moist and not letting the roots dry out. Bolting can be a problem, particularly in warmer climates. Grow bolt-resistant varieties like 'Red Ace'.

## Harvest

Gently loosen beets and pull from the soil when they reach the desired size. This can be from about the size of a quarter to the size of a tennis ball. They're tough and woody if allowed to get too large. For longer storage in the refrigerator, cut off beet tops and place roots in a plastic bag; they'll last 10 to 14 days before losing quality. Preserve beets by pickling.

Three favorite beet varieties are 'Cylindra', 'Red Ace', and the Italian heirloom 'Chioggia'.

## Types

Beet varieties are distinguished by their shape and color. Most beets are round and globe-shaped, but some more oblong-shaped beets are called cylindra varieties, such as the heirloom 'Formanova'. Most globe beets are dark red-purple, but some are golden orange-yellow, such as 'Touchstone Gold'. In warm climates, choose a variety that matures early (45 to 60 days), such as 'Early Wonder Tall Top'. An heirloom Italian beet called 'Chioggia' is candy-striped red and white and looks beautiful when thinly sliced and eaten fresh on salads.

# 5 Great Greens

We love greens as much as any vegetable, and thankfully, the growing techniques are pretty similar for many of them.

Greens are cool-season plants best grown in spring and fall. Sow outdoors a few weeks before the last frost date, or 4 to 6 weeks before the first frost date. Cover seeds lightly, about ½ inch deep. You can succession-sow greens every few weeks to keep them always in harvest. Greens can handle a little shade.

Quick-growing greens are ready to harvest in 4 to 6 weeks. Most greens grow in a rosette, which means you can harvest leaves from the outside of the plant, and they will continue to produce new growth from the center. Some greens will bolt (flower and go to seed) in hot weather. Biennial greens typically bolt during their second year of growth (but sometimes they bolt during their first year, especially if they are stressed). Most greens will produce flowers that are also edible, but the leaves become bitter with bolting.

Here are some of our favorite greens along with specific advice for each.

**Arugula** (*Eruca sativa*) is also known as rocket, and its flavor is earthy and quite peppery. The serrated, oak-shaped leaves are best picked when young, 2 to 3 inches long.

**Kale** (*Brassica oleracea*) rose to stardom recently when it was declared a superfood. Related to cabbage, it does not form a head but has curly, upright leaves. Kale tastes sweeter after a light frost, and some varieties can grow through a mild winter.

There are so many wonderful—and delicious!—types of greens to grow in the garden.

**Mustard** (*Brassica juncea*) has a pungent mustardy flavor in frilled leaves that are sometimes tinted purple. Look for varieties with deeply lobed, lacy leaves to add to salad mixes. Harvest baby greens when 5 inches tall, or let them grow to full size.

**Spinach** (*Spinacia oleracea*) requires 6 weeks of cool weather to grow and is more cold-tolerant than other greens, making it ideal for a fall crop.

**Swiss chard** (*Beta vulgaris*) is a type of beet that doesn't produce an edible root and instead puts energy into beautiful leaves with colorful, crunchy stems. Chard tolerates heat better than other greens and is less likely to bolt.

# BROCCOLI

**Botanical name:** *Brassica oleracea* var. *italica* | **Plant family:** *Brassicaceae* (Cabbage or Mustard)
**Season:** Cool season, spring, fall | **Plant parts eaten:** Flower buds and stem | **Light:** Full sun | **Life cycle:** Annual

**BROCCOLI ORIGINATED** in Southern Italy. Although it's ubiquitous today, broccoli wasn't well known in the United States until the 1920s, when an Italian company in California began growing broccoli on a trial basis and marketed it to Boston's large Italian population, thanks to the transcontinental railway. It became popular nationwide. Related to cabbage, broccoli is grown for its immature flower buds on thick stems.

### Sow

For a late-spring or early-summer crop, start seeds indoors 6 to 8 weeks before last frost date, or outdoors 2 to 3 weeks before last frost date. For a fall crop, which is best in warm climates, sow outdoors 3 months before the first frost date. Broccoli can also be grown from transplants planted in early spring or midsummer.

### Grow

Add compost to soil before planting; broccoli needs lots of nutrition. Side-dress plants with compost as buds begin forming. Broccoli prefers slightly alkaline soil, which helps prevent clubroot; add lime to soil if pH is below 7.0.

Broccoli is a cool-season crop. Plant it as soon as the soil can be worked in the spring. This gives the plant enough time to mature before hot summer weather arrives.

### Protect

Like all cabbage-family crops, broccoli can be plagued by many insects and diseases, including aphids, cabbage butterflies, cabbage loopers, and harlequin bugs. Cover plants with light row-cover cloth to ward off insects. Clubroot is also a problem with these crops. Amending soil with lime helps, but crop rotation is also vital. Avoid planting cabbage-family crops in the same spot for at least 3 years, preferably more.

### Harvest

Small, compact heads offer the best flavor. Harvest when buds are still tight, before flowers open, and when dark green (or purple for purple varieties). Harvest the central head first, but keep the plant in the garden; many varieties will produce side shoots with smaller clusters of buds that can also be harvested. Broccoli leaves are also delicious and can be used like cabbage leaves. In fall, finish any remaining harvesting before a hard freeze, which will damage plants.

Harvest broccoli while the heads are still compact and before the buds have opened.

### Types

The plant most Americans know as quintessential broccoli is the Italian green heading broccoli; popular varieties include 'Calabrese' and 'De Cicco'. There is also Chinese broccoli with more tender stems, purple sprouting broccoli that is very winter hardy, and broccoli rabe, which produces more open clusters of buds and smaller, more tender leaves. A close cousin of broccoli is Romanesco broccoli (a.k.a. Roman cauliflower), which has a chartreuse-yellow head with spiral-shaped florets; it needs a long cool season, making it hard to grow well in warmer climates.

# CABBAGE

**Botanical name:** *Brassica oleracea* | **Plant family:** *Brassicaceae* (Cabbage or Mustard)
**Season:** Cool season, spring, fall | **Plant parts eaten:** Leafy heads | **Light:** Full sun | **Life cycle:** Biennial

Green and red cabbage varieties both perform well in home gardens.

Harvest cabbage heads while they are still tight.

Give each cabbage plant plenty of room to grow.

**A STALWART CROP,** cabbage was brought to Europe from Asia by the Celts around 600 BCE. Their cold-hardiness and ability to be stored over winter soon made them a favorite crop across Northern Europe. For the same reasons, cabbage was brought to North America by the French in the 1500s. Thomas Jefferson recorded planting eighteen different varieties of cabbage at his garden in Monticello.

## Sow
Direct sow outdoors when daytime temperatures are 65°F to 75°F, or start seeds indoors 4 to 5 weeks before the intended planting date, which should be when temperatures are consistently in the 60s during the day. You can also buy and plant transplants. Plant close together to keep heads small; smaller heads have better flavor.

## Grow
The trick to growing cabbage is cool weather plus plenty of nutrients and water. Prepare the soil with compost before planting, and fertilize after planting. Side-dress with compost every few weeks while growing, and water often, keeping soil consistently moist. Don't water from overhead, which makes heads more likely to rot. In spring, seedlings can take a light frost; in fall, some frost on growing cabbages will actually make them sweeter.

## Protect
Cover with row-cover cloth to prevent cabbage moths and loopers from laying eggs. Rotate along with other cabbage-family crops, not growing in the same spot for at least every 3 years—this will prevent clubroot and other soilborne diseases. A pH above 7.0 will help prevent clubroot disease; add lime to make the soil more alkaline.

## Harvest
Cabbage heads will form in the center of the plant, with surrounding leaves providing protection. For eating fresh, cut the head off the stalk at soil level when the head feels solid and is still green in color (or red-purple if growing red varieties). For storage varieties, pull the entire plant from the ground, remove outer leaves, and cure for a few weeks hanging upside down or wrapped in paper or straw. Store at 32°F to 40°F and 80 to 90 percent humidity for 3 or more months.

## Types
Early varieties are the most tender, but they're prone to split and don't store well. Midseason varieties keep longer in the garden. Late varieties make the largest heads and are best for storing and preserving. Savoy cabbages are an interesting type with pretty crinkled leaves. 'Early Jersey Wakefield' is an old American favorite, first grown in 1840 in New Jersey, with a cone-shaped head up to 15 inches long and 7 inches wide.

# CARROTS

Botanical name: *Daucus carota* | Plant family: *Apiaceae* (Carrot or Parsley) | Season: Cool season, spring, fall
Plant parts eaten: Root, leaves | Light: Full sun | Life cycle: Biennial

Carrots require deep, loose soil to form straight roots.

Try growing purple, yellow, red, and white carrot varieties in addition to the classic orange to add diverse nutrients to your diet.

Carrot seeds are very tiny. It's difficult to space them properly when sowing. Be prepared to thin the seedlings when they are about an inch tall.

**PICTURE A CARROT,** and you likely think long, straight, tapered, and orange. But carrots come in a wide variety of shapes, sizes, and colors. Packed with vitamins (especially beta carotene that becomes vitamin A), minerals, and fiber, they're among the healthiest snack options, and homegrown tastes far better.

## Sow
Sow outdoors 2 to 4 weeks before the last frost date, when soil temps are around 60°F, and 3 to 4 months before the first frost date (midsummer) for a fall crop. Loosen soil before sowing. No need to add compost, which can cause forked roots. Make a ¼-inch furrow, and sow seeds evenly. Cover lightly with soil and water gently. After leaves emerge, thin seedlings to 1 inch apart, and use thinnings like parsley.

## Grow
Fertilize sparingly, once 2 to 3 weeks after germination and again when leaves are about 6 inches tall. Too much nitrogen leads to lush tops but lackluster roots. If garden soil is too heavy or holds water, try growing in containers. Container growing is also ideal for shorter, stubbier varieties. As root tops, called shoulders, pop up above soil, cover lightly with soil to avoid them turning green. Water regularly but don't saturate, which can cause forked or hairy roots.

## Protect
Carrot root fly can damage a crop, tunneling into roots. If they're a problem in your area, cover carrot plants with a light row cover, and grow resistant varieties.

## Harvest
Carrots are ready when 1-inch-wide (or larger) shoulders show above soil. Gently loosen carrots from soil by pulling from the base of the leaf stems, near the carrot shoulders. Watering soil before harvest can help loosen roots. Cut tops off carrots for storage, but don't toss them—mature carrot greens taste like spicy parsley and make for a yummy pesto.

## Types
The modern carrot was bred in Holland and then France, with new types developed in America in the 1800s. Nantes carrots are long (about 7 inches), cylindrical, smooth, blunt-tipped, and juicy because they absorb more water; 'Scarlet Nantes' is the oldest and most famous of this French type. Chantenay carrots have short, cone-shaped roots that can plunge into heavier soils. Danvers carrots started in Massachusetts and have become the quintessential American carrot: 6 to 7 inches long, deep orange, with wide shoulders and a pointed tip. Also American, Imperator carrots are longer, at 10 inches, and need very loose soil to grow well. Carrots are also divided into early season (mature in less than 60 days, or even less if harvested for baby carrots), main crop (60 to 100 days), and storage varieties (good for fall growing and winter storage). Varieties have been bred in a range of colors—white, yellow, orange, red, purple—in all the types.

240 | American Horticultural Society | *Essential Guide to Organic Vegetable Gardening*

# CAULIFLOWER

**Botanical name:** *Brassica oleracea* var. *botrytis* | **Plant family:** *Brassicaceae* (Cabbage or Mustard)
**Season:** Cool season, spring, fall | **Plant parts eaten:** Head of flower buds, stem, leaves | **Light:** Full sun | **Life cycle:** Annual

**A BEAUTIFUL AND UNIQUE** member of the mustard or cabbage family, cauliflower looks and grows like broccoli but has an ivory-white head. It's a marvel of human botanical innovation, introduced to Europe by Arabs and perfected through centuries of breeding. The tight head is actually clusters of flower buds, and each cluster is a floret. The whole head is like a vegetable bouquet. It's not the easiest vegetable to grow, but if you love a challenge—or cauliflower—it's well worth it.

Cauliflower varieties come in purple, orange, yellow, and green, in addition to the classic white.

Harvest cauliflower heads when the curds are fully developed but remain tight.

## Sow

Start seeds indoors 4 to 6 weeks before the last hard-frost date in spring, or indoors in midsummer for a fall crop. Or buy transplants. Cauliflower needs cool weather, so fall is the best time to grow in most areas to prevent bolting. Fall-grown plants are also less susceptible to pests. Space plants 12 to 18 inches apart. Plants grown more closely will form smaller heads.

## Grow

Cauliflower grows best when temperatures are consistently in the 60s during the day and in the 50s at night. Too much heat or stress affects the quality of the head. Keep plants well watered and soil consistently moist. Amend soil with compost at planting and side-dress with compost every few weeks while growing.

## Protect

As heads start forming, tie up several upright leaves loosely over the head, providing a sun shade—called blanching, this will help keep buds tight and the head color white. Rotate crops along with other brassicas, and to avoid potentially spreading disease, don't compost the plants. Cauliflower is the least frost tolerant of the brassicas; cover in the event of frost and light freeze, or harvest beforehand if ready.

## Harvest

Harvest spring-grown cauliflower in midsummer, and a fall-grown crop before first freeze. Cut off the head at the base of the stem using a sharp knife. You can also harvest the leaves, which some cooks say are the most flavorful part of the cauliflower plant.

## Types

Varieties are distinguished largely by color. Most cauliflower varieties are white, but some are purple (such as 'Purple Head') or orange (such as 'Cheddar'). While the colorful florets look lovely raw, they lose much of their color when cooked. Colorful varieties are considered easier to grow, in part because they don't require blanching. Some white varieties, such as 'Snowball', are self-blanching, meaning you don't need to tie up leaves—they wrap around the head themselves.

# CHINESE CABBAGE

**Botanical names:** *Brassica rapa* subsp. *chinensis* and *pekinensis*
**Plant family:** *Brassicaceae* (Cabbage or Mustard) | **Season:** Cool season, spring, fall
**Plant parts eaten:** Greens, ribs (stems) | **Light:** Full sun to partial shade | **Life cycle:** Biennial

**RELATED TO CABBAGE,** this brassica also goes by the names bok choy or pak choi, or Napa cabbage or pe-tsai. Some types (Napa) form a tight conical head, while others (bok choy) have a bulbous base that opens up into a fan of leaves. They're distinguished from other brassicas by their tender ribs that are sweeter and juicier than other cabbages.

## Sow
Start seeds indoors 4 to 6 weeks before your last frost date in spring, or 50 days before your first frost date in fall. Sow ¼ to ½ inch deep. Plant or thin seedlings to at least 6 inches apart. You can also plant from transplants. If planted closely, you can plan to harvest every other bok choy as a baby bok choy.

## Grow
While it does better in sunny conditions, Chinese cabbage can grow in as little as 4 to 5 hours of sun daily. Some shade in hot climates can help prevent bolting. Prepare soil with compost before planting, and keep evenly watered. As a biennial, these plants are meant to bolt in their second year, but a cold snap can trick young plants into thinking they've gone through winter, causing bolting; avoid planting out too early when cold snaps or frost are likely. Hot and dry weather can also cause bolting; in warmer areas, plant Napa cabbage and bok choy in part shade. Also, be sure to mulch around plants to avoid moisture fluctuations. Full-grown Chinese cabbage can withstand a little frost.

The savoyed leaves of Chinese cabbage look beautiful in the garden.

Plant Chinese cabbage transplants as soon as the soil can be worked in the early spring.

## Protect
Like most brassicas, these are prone to several insects. Use a row cover to protect young plants from cabbage moths and loopers, and rotate along with related crops around the garden, not planting in the same spot for at least 3 years.

## Harvest
Bok choy are typically ready to harvest 50 to 60 days after sowing, or when plants are 12 to 15 inches tall. For baby bok choy, harvest when plants are 6 to 8 inches tall. Napa cabbage takes longer to mature (70+ days) and should be harvested when heads feel dense and firm. For either type, cut the base of the stalk with a knife just above the soil line.

## Types
Bulbous bok choy has crunchy, light-colored, mild-flavored stalks and darker green leaves. It's typically cut up for stir-fries, and the juicy rib is the main attraction. Napa cabbage has a compact, cone-shaped head with pale-green crinkled leaves similar to lettuce. Ribs are pronounced but less tender than bok choy. In seed catalogs, you may find Napa cabbage listed under "cabbage," and bok choy may be classified as an "Asian green," but they are both botanically classified as Chinese cabbage.

# CORN

**Botanical name:** *Zea mays* | **Plant family:** *Poaceae* (Grass or Cereal) | **Season:** Summer
**Plant parts eaten:** Fruit (ears) | **Light:** Full sun | **Life cycle:** Annual

**NATIVE TO NORTH AMERICA,** corn is a type of grass. Maize is the original name; the term *corn* historically meant kernel or grain in English and Norse. Native American tribes from the Southwest to the East revered corn as a staple crop, and still do. After soaking up lots of sun and heat, fresh corn is a favorite late-summer treat worthy of holidays and special occasions.

## *Sow*

Plant seeds outdoors in late spring after all danger of frost has passed, 1 inch deep and 8 to 10 inches apart. Plant in rows 2 feet apart with at least five to six rows to create a large block. Planting in blocks allows wind to pass through stalks and spread pollen from the silks atop ears. To plant a traditional Three Sisters garden, plant corn first, and when corn plants are a few inches tall, plant beans at the base of each stalk and a few squash seeds throughout the block.

## *Grow*

Corn plants can reach over 6 feet tall, depending on the variety, so plant at the north end of your garden to avoid corn shading out other plants. Corn needs rich, fertile soil; amend with compost before planting and fertilize plants at least every 2 weeks. Give plants about 2 inches of water per week, more in drier weather as corn is stressed by drought. Increase water when stalks begin to flower. When weeding, try not to disturb corn's shallow roots.

Corn can be a challenge in home gardens simply because many plants are needed to ensure good pollination. If you have the space available, why not give it a try?

## *Protect*

If birds steal your corn seeds, try covering with a row cover until plants are a few inches tall, or start plants indoors and then transplant seedlings. Improper pollination can cause spottily filled cobs; to help ensure pollination, gently shake plants to loosen pollen from tassels onto silks. Water at the roots to prevent fungal diseases from developing on plants.

## *Harvest*

If properly pollinated, corn ears are usually ready to harvest a few weeks after the silks appear. Ears are ready to pick when tassels turn brown, husks start to brown, and cobs feel well-filled. To test, squeeze a kernel; if the liquid is creamy, it's ready. Twist cobs off the plant and dry in the husks or eat fresh.

Corn can be planted in dense groups, in companionship with squash or another vine crop growing beneath.

## *Types*

Corn varieties vary widely, but the two main types are field corn (also called dent or flour corn) and sweet corn. Field varieties are best for making flour and meal, and there are beautiful, diverse Native American varieties, including multicolored 'Painted Mountain' and gold-red 'Roy's Calais'. Sweet corn varieties are sometimes broken down into categories of sweetness, including supersweet varieties bred for the most sugar content. 'Sugar Buns' hybrid is a favorite sweet variety known for easy growing and a long harvest period. There are also ornamental types of corn grown largely for harvest decoration rather than eating, popcorn varieties grown for their snackable dried kernels, and miniature-eared varieties for cooking and eating whole.

# CUCUMBER

**Botanical name:** *Cucumis sativus* | **Plant family:** *Cucurbitaceae* (Gourd or Squash)
**Season:** Warm season, summer | **Plant parts eaten:** Fruit | **Light:** Full sun | **Life cycle:** Annual

There are so many different varieties of cucumbers available for home growing!

Parthenocarpic cucumbers don't require pollination to set fruit. These varieties produce all female flowers and don't require pollination to produce seedless fruits, making them a great fit for greenhouses and polytunnels.

**AFTER TRAVELING WEST** from India to Europe over many centuries, the cucumber was brought to America with Columbus. With a high water content, cucumbers do keep their cool, making them extra refreshing in the heat of summer. A healthy cucumber plant will be so prolific, you'll be picking cool cukes daily.

## Sow
Sow indoors 2 to 3 weeks before last frost date, or outdoors a few weeks after last frost date when temperatures are regularly in the high 60s to 70s. Sow 6 to 8 seeds about 1 inch deep in mounds spaced 3 to 5 feet apart, and thin to 3 to 4 plants per hill; if planting seedlings, plant 3 to 4 per hill. Or space 2 feet apart in rows or blocks.

## Grow
Vines benefit from trellises, such as A-frames, to keep fruit off the ground. Amend soil with compost at planting time, and feed or side-dress with compost every 2 to 3 weeks. Keep soil evenly moist while growing, and water more heavily when plants are fruiting for juicier cukes and to avoid bitter flavor. Cucumber plants are allelopathic, containing growth-inhibiting chemicals that can negatively affect neighbors—but this can be good for weed management. Interplant cucumbers around taller crops like tomatoes, corn, eggplant, and okra.

## Protect
Cucumber plants can be bothered by cucumber beetles. Keeping plants healthy through regular watering and feeding is the best defense. Most plants will also eventually succumb to powdery mildew, especially in humid areas. Keeping plants trellised, with good airflow, will help. Remove affected plants from the garden and don't add them to compost, which can spread the mildew spores.

## Harvest
With cucumbers, bigger is not better. Slicing varieties should be picked when 6 to 8 inches long, pickling varieties at 3 to 5 inches. Pick daily in warm weather—just-right fruit can quickly become yellow, bitter, and too large. Cut from vine leaving 1 inch of stem attached to fruit to prevent water loss. Picking often will encourage more fruiting.

## Types
You'll encounter many classifications of cucumbers when browsing varieties. Greenhouse—sometimes called English or European—cucumber varieties are about 1 foot long, thin, smooth, and tender. These varieties are almost always grown in a greenhouse. Slicing cukes are thick, 6 to 9 inches long, with glossy dark-green skin; 'Marketmore' is the most popular variety in the United States. Pickling types are rounder and smaller with lighter green skin. Bush varieties have shorter vines and may not need trellising. Burpless varieties have less cucurbitacin, a bitter-tasting natural chemical that causes some people to burp when eating cukes. Many Asian varieties have become more widely available in recent years.

# GARLIC

**Botanical name:** *Allium sativum* | **Plant family:** *Alliaceae* (Allium) | **Season:** Cool season, spring, fall
**Plant parts eaten:** Bulb, stalks and young buds (scapes) of hardneck varieties | **Light:** Full sun to light shade
**Life cycle:** Annual or perennial

Garlic is ready to harvest when the foliage has started to yellow, typically in midsummer.

Garlic is planted from individual cloves the autumn before harvest.

**AN ESSENTIAL INGREDIENT** in culinary and medicinal traditions from China to India to the Mediterranean for more than 5,000 years, garlic is a beloved ancient crop that has been so thoroughly cultivated it remains common, even though it does not reproduce sexually or set seeds. The only way to reproduce garlic is to divide the cloves or plant the bulblets produced on the scapes of hardneck types. And since it's planted in the fall for harvest the following summer in most zones, it may be the only thing you grow through the winter.

## *Sow*

Plant garlic cloves in fall, in deep, rich, well-drained soil. Separate individual cloves from the bulb but leave the skin intact. Place cloves root-side down, 6 inches apart, 3 inches below the soil. Cover with 4 inches of mulch; this is vital to protect cloves through winter. Garlic can also be planted in early spring, but cloves will have less time to mature and will be smaller.

## *Grow*

In spring, remove some of the mulch and fertilize new shoots. Garlic does not need a lot of water, and waterlogged soil can cause bulbs to rot. Hardneck varieties will send up a scape, or flowering stalk, around May or June. Cut at the base of the stalk to keep energy going to bulbs. You can then eat the young scapes—they're great sautéed with other veggies.

## *Protect*

In warm climates, garlic sprouts may poke up through mulch before winter, and you'll need to protect tender shoots with additional mulch if expecting a very hard freeze. Garlic isn't prone to insect pests, but it can develop fungal rust on the leaves. Crop rotation of garlic, along with onions and shallots, will help prevent rust.

## *Harvest*

Harvest garlic in midsummer when the bottom 3 to 4 leaves begin to turn brown. Carefully dig or pull up the whole plant. Gently brush some soil off the bulbs without harming the skin; it's fine for bulbs to have some soil still on them when curing. Cure for 2 to 4 weeks in a warm, dry, shaded spot with good air circulation; arrange in a single layer or hang to dry. Once cured, trim roots and leaves, brush off remaining soil, and store dry, papery-skinned bulbs in a cool (55°F), dark place until ready to use. Storage time depends on the variety.

## *Types*

Choose from softneck or hardneck varieties from a reputable "seed garlic" source. Softneck varieties typically have smaller, more pungent cloves, and they store well; they're also better in warmer climates. Hardneck varieties have larger, milder cloves and a stiff central stalk that sends up a scape; they are hardier for colder climates. There are hundreds of heirloom garlic varieties available, many originating from Russia, Germany, and parts of Eastern Europe. 'Music' is a popular German hardneck known for its spicy flavor, and 'Chesnok Red' is a mild-flavored purple-striped hardneck variety from the Republic of Georgia. 'California Early', developed for California garlic farming, is a good all-around softneck choice, adaptable to many conditions, including warm climates.

Edible Plant Profiles

# LETTUCE

**Botanical name:** *Lactuca sativa* | **Plant family:** *Asteraceae* (Aster) | **Season:** Cool season, spring, fall
**Plant parts eaten:** Leaves | **Light:** Full sun or part shade | **Life cycle:** Annual

Lettuce can be grown via direct seeding or by planting transplants out into the garden.

Romaine lettuce types are a delicious addition to the garden.

**RELATED TO DAISIES** and thistles, lettuce originated in the Mediterranean and was grown in Greek and Roman gardens, but it was Louis XIV who popularized the lettuce salad seasoned with herbs in seventeenth-century France. Lettuce is easy to grow in cool weather, great for beginners, and ideal for containers—no vegetable garden should be without it.

## *Sow*

Lettuce grows best around 60°F to 65°F. Tiny lettuce seeds can be sown indoors or outdoors. Depending on the variety, lettuce will germinate in temps as low as the 40s but will have trouble above 70°F. Barely cover seeds will soil; lettuce needs light to germinate. Thin seedlings when they are a couple of inches tall, then replant the thinnings, watering well to help roots reestablish. Sow leaf lettuce every 3 to 4 weeks for a continual harvest.

## *Grow*

Space heading and semi-heading varieties 10 to 12 inches apart. Leaf lettuce can be spaced closer at 6 to 8 inches. Lettuce can be grown as a living mulch under taller plants like peas or peppers; the lettuce shades the soil and the taller plant shades the lettuce. Water at the base of plants and in the morning to prevent moisture on leaves. Lettuce benefits from balanced fertilizer or foliar spray every 2 weeks.

## *Protect*

Heat is the enemy of lettuce. To grow in warmer weather, plant in part shade or use shade cloth to lower the temperature around plants. Also choose more heat-resistant varieties. Aphids can damage lettuce; studies show that companion planting around lettuce with dill, cilantro, and other members of the carrot family—and letting those plants flower—will attract natural predators of aphids and help protect lettuce plants.

## *Harvest*

Full-size heads may take 50 to 60 days before harvest, but leaf lettuce can be harvested in 20 to 30 days. Lettuce becomes more bitter in heat and as it starts to bolt, so harvest in cool weather for the best flavor. The genus name *Lactuca* refers to the bitter, white, latexlike sap that flows from broken leaves and stems, especially on older plants. Cut heads off at the base (stem) when they're firm. You can start picking individual baby leaves off leaf varieties when plants have several leaves that are a few inches tall.

## *Types*

Choose from a wealth of varieties in three types: heading, semi-heading (or cos), and leaf lettuces. Head lettuces include crisphead (iceberg) and butterhead (Boston and bibb). Cos lettuce such as romaine is harvested whole like a head lettuce, but the looser form is more forgiving to grow. Leaf lettuce can be harvested as individual leaves and is great for beginners. All types come in a range of green, reddish, and purple colors.

# MELON

**Botanical names:** *Cucumis melo* and *Citrullus lanatus* | **Plant family:** *Cucurbitaceae* (Gourd or Squash)
**Season:** Warm season, summer | **Plant parts eaten:** Fruit | **Light:** Full sun | **Life cycle:** Annual

**CANTALOUPE, WATERMELON, HONEYDEW**—while they may look drastically different, they are grown in much the same way. Melons were introduced to the Americas with Columbus, and they thrived in warm southern areas. All melons love heat and humidity, and they're a favorite summer treat.

## Sow

Start from seed outdoors after all threat of frost has passed. Melons grow easily from seed and shouldn't need to be started indoors. The exception is if you are in a cool climate with a short summer and want to try melons; you could give seeds a head start indoors 4 weeks before planting, planting outdoors when the weather warms. Space plants 2 to 3 feet apart in rows 5 to 6 feet apart.

## Grow

If you can grow a cucumber, you can grow a melon. All you need is a little patience and a lot of space—or a sturdy trellis. They need rich, fertile, well-drained soil, so work in some compost before sowing or planting. If growing in a smaller space, plan to grow melons on a sturdy trellis, such as one made of steel panels. Melons need a lot of water, but avoid watering from overhead, which promotes powdery mildew on leaves. Feed weekly.

Watermelon vines need a lot of room to ramble. Plant them on the edges of a raised bed and allow the vines to cascade over the side.

## Protect

Proper spacing is essential for avoiding diseases caused by wet conditions and inadequate airflow. Water early in the day to allow leaves to dry out. Cucumber beetles can infect plants with bacterial wilt; using row-cover fabric over plants can help, but it needs to be removed when plants are flowering for pollination. If practicing crop rotation, rotate along with other squash-family crops at least every 3 years. If trellising, you may need to provide a sling for heavy melons so they don't break the vine or your trellis; netting or pantyhose (an old trick) should work.

## Harvest

Knowing when to harvest melons is the stuff of legends. Unlike some fruits and vegetables, melons generally will not continue to ripen off the vine, so it's important to pick them at the right time. Signs of a ripe watermelon include: the spot where the fruit touches the ground turns from white to yellow, the tendril closest to the fruit turns brown and

Cantaloupes and muskmelons can be grown vertically to save space.

dries up, and the fruit has a hollow sound when tapped. A sign of a ripe cantaloupe is that it will easily pull away from the vine—this is called full slip. When a honeydew is ripe, the rind will change color slightly from green to cream-colored, and the fruit will have a sweet smell. If they do not slip off, cut melons from the plant with a couple inches of vine attached.

## Types

Muskmelons and watermelons are the two most common groups of melons. Watermelon seeds are dispersed in the flesh of the fruit, like a cucumber, whereas muskmelon (including cantaloupe and honeydew) seeds are contained in a central cavity, like a pumpkin or winter squash.

Edible Plant Profiles   247

# OKRA

**Botanical name:** *Abelmoschus esculentus* | **Plant family:** *Malvaceae* (Mallow) | **Season:** Warm season, summer
**Plant parts eaten:** Seed pod | **Light:** Full sun | **Life cycle:** Annual

OKRA WAS BROUGHT to the Americas along with slaves from West Africa, and the English word *okra* comes from that region. In other parts of the world where this plant has long been grown, including India, it's referred to as *gumbo,* and the famous Louisiana dish gumbo is named for its key ingredient: okra. Related to hibiscus and cotton, okra is easy to grow in warm, long-season climates and produces beautiful, hibiscuslike flowers that mature into tasty pods.

### Sow
In warm climates, sow seeds after all danger of frost has passed, 4 to 6 inches apart, around the time you sow cucumbers and melons, when soil temperature is above 65°F. In cool climates, start indoors and plant outside when weather warms, or grow in a greenhouse. Soak seeds for several hours before planting to help break down the tough exterior and speed germination. Ideal germination temperature is in the 80s.

### Grow
Add compost to soil before planting. Okra likes fertile, well-drained, even sandy soil. Okra can tolerate heat and drought, but it will grow best if watered deeply once a week. As with tomatoes, if temperatures are consistently above 90°F, pollination may slow down, but it should pick back up when temps dip back into the 80s. Thin seedlings to 1 foot apart. Mulch to control weeds.

Okra is a warm-season crop with an edible seed pod. It requires a long growing season.

### Protect
Okra plants grow to 4 to 5 feet tall with large, hand-shaped leaves. Avoid common fungal diseases by spacing plants properly so they get enough airflow and the large leaves can dry properly. If plants are bothered by whiteflies or aphids, use insecticidal soap, applying according to instructions.

### Harvest
Okra should be ready to harvest 60 to 70 days after planting. When the harvest starts, be ready to pick daily, as pods can quickly grow beyond ideal size. Pick pods when 3 to 4 inches long; they should feel tender and springy and will be bright green (depending on the variety). Wear gloves to protect your hands during harvest. If pods are left to get longer, they will be tough, fibrous, and inedible.

Okra plants grow quite tall. Pods are ready to be cut from the plants when the pods reach 3 to 4 inches in length.

### Types
There are many Southern heirloom varieties of okra, as well as widespread favorites. The all-time favorite 'Clemson Spineless' has smooth green pods. Some okra varieties, such as 'Burgundy', have dark-red pods; these plants also have beautiful red stems with green leaves. To grow in containers, choose a hybrid dwarf variety such as 'Baby Bubba' that's half the size of normal okra plants.

# ONIONS

**Botanical name:** *Allium cepa* | **Plant family:** *Alliaceae* (Allium) | **Season:** Cool season, spring, fall
**Plant parts eaten:** Bulbs, leaves | **Light:** Full sun | **Life cycle:** Biennial

**ONE OF THE OLDEST VEGETABLES** known to humans, onions have been cultivated across the globe for millennia. Fittingly, their name comes from the Latin for *union*, because onions grow a single, united bulb rather than a bulb of many cloves like garlic, onion's close relative. Onions are easy to grow in spring and fall if you choose the right type for your climate.

## Sow

Onions can be started from seeds or sets, or planted from bunches of seedlings purchased from a garden center. Starting from seed takes longer but generally produces larger bulbs that store well. Direct sow outdoors in 2-inch bands as soon as soil is workable in spring (or in midsummer for fall onions). Thin to 2 to 4 inches apart. Growing from sets (small onions) is faster, but onions can be more prone to rotting; sets are more common for growing shallots and perennial onions. Planting onion seedlings is definitely easiest. Just poke a 1-inch hole in the soil with your finger, place the seedling in, and pack soil around to secure it; space 3 to 4 inches apart.

## Grow

Onions have shallow roots and need at least 1 inch of water weekly. Keep the patch well weeded to avoid competition. Onions can be interplanted with other spring and summer crops, including peas, lettuce, tomatoes, and peppers.

Onions are best harvested when the green tops fall over at their base.

## Protect

Avoid crowding onions, which can cause issues with air circulation. If rotating crops is possible in your garden, rotate on a 3-year cycle along with other alliums to avoid soilborne diseases.

## Harvest

Onions reach full size in midsummer if planted in spring, late fall if planted in summer. If onions are planted more closely (2 to 3 inches apart), you can harvest every other onion as a scallion halfway through the season, and allow the rest to grow to full size. Bulbs are ready to harvest when the green tops fall over. The bulbs should pull up easily from the soil. Dry and cure outdoors for a few days, protecting from any rain. When the tops are brown, trim tops to 1 inch from the bulb. To cure further for winter storage, spread out on a wire screen in a dry, warm, well-ventilated spot for up to 2 months, then store for winter.

Cure harvested onions in a warm space for 1 to 2 months. The tops can be removed when they have fully browned.

## Types

Onions are triggered by day length to form bulbs, so it's important to choose a variety suited to the day length in your area. Days lengthen during the growing season the farther you travel north, so grow long-day onions in northern regions of the United States and short-day onions in southern areas. Intermediate-day onions are widely adapted to most areas. You can also choose from white, yellow, and red varieties. Sweet onions don't store as well as pungent varieties, which have chemical compounds that act as preservatives.

# PEAS

Botanical name: *Pisum sativum* | Plant family: *Fabaceae* (Pea and Bean) | Season: Cool season, spring, fall
Plant parts eaten: Pods, fresh seeds (peas), young shoots | Light: Full sun to light shade | Life cycle: Annual

**PEAS ARE A VERY OLD** food crop, cultivated in much of the world since ancient times. They can be savored fresh, or dried for storage, where they will last a very long time, hence their ubiquity. The first spring snap peas rarely make it to the kitchen from the garden, where their juicy crunch can be enjoyed under the sun that helped them grow.

## *Sow*
Direct sow peas outdoors in early spring, 1 inch apart and ½ to 1 inch below soil, when temps are at least in the 40s. Some gardeners presoak seeds to soften the hard seed coat, but it's not necessary. In areas with mild winters, you can sow again in fall about 2 months before the first frost date.

## *Grow*
Dwarf plants won't need trellising if planted closely together or in containers, but more productive climbing peas will need a trellis. Try an A-frame to make peas easier to harvest. Peas don't need a lot of additional nutrients; feed 2 to 3 times per season. Water lightly at first and increase after plants begin flowering. Like all legumes, peas fix nitrogen through their roots. As long as the plants don't exhibit signs of mildew or disease, they can be chopped up after harvest and turned back into the soil to add nutrients.

Shell, sugar snap, and snow peas are all cool-season crops best planted very early in the growing season.

## *Protect*
If you have trouble with birds and other critters stealing your pea seeds at planting time, try starting in trays indoors or outdoors and transplanting young plants, but be careful with the fragile roots. Seedlings are the most susceptible to damage from aphids and other insects. Covering with row-cover cloth until plants are 5 to 6 inches tall will help. Later in the season, plants may get powdery mildew; at this point, they may be ready to pull from the garden. Toss them out instead of composting to avoid spreading the fungus.

## *Harvest*
Pick snap and shelling peas daily when pods are plump and filled out. Harvest snow peas when pods are young and flat and the peas inside are underdeveloped. Snip or snap pods off from the vine rather than pulling on them. Pea shoots, the top 4 to 6 inches of the vine, can also be harvested for stir-fries and salads, but harvesting them will limit plant growth.

Harvest snow peas when the pods are fully formed but before the peas inside swell.

## *Types*
The pods of snap peas and snow peas are eaten whole, while the pods of shelling peas are removed and only the peas inside are eaten. Shelling peas are sometimes called English peas. 'Sugar Snap', a recent variety from the 1970s, has become a household name.

## *Bunching Onions and Leeks*

Related to regular onions, bunching onions and leeks are grown for their succulent shanks that do not bulb. Sow and grow similarly to regular onions, but as the plants mature, hill up soil around the shank to blanch it, keeping it white and tender. Bunching onions typically grow 60 to 65 days before harvest. Leeks require a long growing season of 120 to 150 days.

Bunching onions are another terrific addition to the garden. The stems are eaten, along with the bulbs.

## *Southern Peas*

Also called cowpeas, field peas, crowder peas, or black-eyed peas, Southern peas (*Vigna unguiculate*) were brought to the southeastern United States from West Africa by enslaved Africans. The peas proved easy to grow in the hot climate, needing little water and able to take lots of sun, with the added benefit that the plants, as nitrogen fixers, improved poor soil. Southern pea seeds were passed down primarily in African American families in the Southeast through generations. Popular varieties today include 'Pinkeye Purple Hull' with a maroon eye in the center, 'Zipper Cream' white peas, and 'Piggot' peas that date back to 1850s Louisiana.

Southern pea plant leaves look more like bean leaves, but the plants produce long (6 to 10 inches), green, pealike pods. Harvest the pods when green and plump for fresh peas that are creamy and slightly sweet, or let them dry on the plant to harvest dry peas for storage. The dry peas store very well, another bonus. As a drought-tolerant, heat-tolerant, easy-to-store crop that also enriches the soil and needs no fertilizer, Southern peas deserve consideration from gardeners outside the South.

Southern peas (a.k.a. black-eyed peas) are a staple in many southern gardens. They are both drought tolerant and heat tolerant.

Edible Plant Profiles

# PEPPERS

**Botanical name:** *Capsicum annuum* | **Plant family:** *Solanaceae* (Nightshade) | **Season:** Warm season, summer
**Plant parts eaten:** Fruit | **Light:** Full sun | **Life cycle:** Annual

Peppers, whether hot or sweet, are best planted into warm soil in a full-sun location.

The diversity of peppers available for home growing is amazing!

Get an early start on pepper growing by shielding young transplants with a hoop tunnel covered with greenhouse plastic. When the weather warms, the plastic can be removed.

**THERE ARE SO MANY** pepper varieties, and everyone has a favorite. Today, you can find peppers from all over the world, but peppers originated in Middle America, including Mexico and the Caribbean. They're an essential ingredient in Southwest cuisine and, therefore, Southwest gardens. If peppers have warmth and time, they are fairly easy to grow.

## *Sow*
Start seeds indoors about 8 weeks before planting outdoors; plan to transplant after all danger of frost has passed and soil temperatures are in the 80s. Temperature for germination should be in the 80s, and in the 70s for growing seedlings. Thin to 1 plant per 4-inch pot. Space plants 12 to 18 inches apart and water well at planting.

## *Grow*
Close spacing is preferred for plant support and leaf cover. It also creates a microclimate that may improve fruit set. Stake pepper plants to support fruit-laden limbs; tying off the main stem to a simple wooden stake is usually sufficient. Peppers need rich, well-drained soil, but avoid giving plants too much nitrogen, which will give lush leaves but prevent fruit from setting. Many peppers, especially hot varieties, are drought tolerant, but plants benefit from regular water.

## *Protect*
In cooler climates, use a row cover to warm soil and plants, but remove when plants are flowering and when temperatures are in the 80s to avoid blossom drop. If you have problems with specific diseases in your area, choose resistant varieties. Like tomatoes, peppers may get blossom-end rot; providing consistent moisture helps. Fruiting may slow down in the heat of summer, but if you wait, plants will bounce back in late summer as temperatures start to cool down.

## *Harvest*
Pick peppers when they reach full size and color for the variety. All peppers start out green, but some ripen to another color: yellow, orange, red, purple, or even almost black. Simply snip peppers off the plant to harvest.

## *Types*
Peppers are typically divided into sweet varieties and hot, though there are some crossovers. Subtypes of hot peppers include cayenne, habanero, jalapeño, poblano, and serrano. Bell peppers are some of the largest sweet peppers, while snacking peppers are bite-sized. 'Shishito' is an Asian variety that's grown in popularity recently; these bright light-green peppers are great grilled or stir-fried, and while most are sweet, one in several can have a touch of heat.

# POTATOES

**Botanical name:** *Solanum tuberosum* | **Plant family:** *Solanaceae* (Nightshade) | **Season:** Warm season in North, cool season in South and West | **Plant parts eaten:** Tuber | **Light:** Full sun | **Life cycle:** Annual

**NATIVE TO THE ANDEAN MOUNTAINS** in South America, potatoes are related to tomatoes, peppers, and eggplant. In a roundabout journey, the potato was introduced to Europe first before being introduced to North America in the early 1700s. Potatoes are underground tubers. They're propagated by budding rather than seeds.

## Sow

Buy certified disease-free seed potatoes, which are potato tubers meant for propagation. Many regional seed companies sell seed potatoes that will ship when the time is right for planting in your area. Potatoes have "eyes" that are small buds. Plant small seed potatoes whole, but cut larger ones into pieces, each with an eye. Allow the cut side to heal and harden for a day or two before planting.

## Grow

Potatoes are planted 4 to 6 weeks before the last frost date in spring, or 90 to 120 days before the first frost date for a fall crop. Potatoes need temps in the 60s to germinate and grow. Some gardeners use St. Patrick's Day (March 17) as a marker for planting potatoes. Before planting, work compost into soil. Plant seed potatoes eyes up, 3 to 4 inches below soil, spacing 1 foot apart. As shoots emerge and get 6 to 8 inches tall, begin to "hill" soil around plants, always leaving a few inches of green plant exposed. Continue hilling every few weeks as plants grow. This prevents light from reaching the tubers. Potatoes also grow well in permeable bags or containers; in that case, as the plant grows, just add soil to the bag or container to cover more of the plant.

Potatoes are grown from "seed potatoes," which are not seeds but rather tubers saved from the previous season.

## Protect

Cover plants if an unexpected late frost happens after planting. Damp, humid, warm weather encourages the many diseases to which potatoes are susceptible. Make sure your plants get full sun and are spaced adequately so the foliage can dry out. Also be sure to rotate potatoes along with other nightshades. If potatoes get blight or another disease, do not add them to your compost pile.

## Harvest

Potato plants produce flowers that look very similar to eggplant flowers. (Fun fact: The flower color almost always reflects the tuber color, so lavender flowers for purple potatoes.) After the flowers bloom, you can begin looking for small, or "new," potatoes underground. Gently dig around the base of the plant to find them, being careful not to puncture the potatoes. For full-size potatoes, wait until the whole plant begins to die back before digging them up or pulling the whole plant, tubers and all. Be sure to check the surrounding soil for stragglers. Let potatoes cure until the skin is dry, brush off the soil, then store out of the light in a humid place around 40°F. Light causes potatoes to turn green and develop solanine, which is toxic and will make you sick.

Digging potatoes is a lot like hunting for treasure.

## Types

There are potatoes of many colors (white, yellow, pink, red, purple) and shapes (round, oblong, oval, fingerling) to choose from. When looking at varieties, it may be best to look at the days to harvest; potatoes are classified as early season (60 to 80 days), mid-season (80 to 95 days), and late season (95 to 130 days). They are planted at the same time but harvested at different times. Try growing varieties that aren't readily available at stores, like 'French Fingerling' (pink and yellow, mid to late) and 'Adirondack Blue' (purple, early to mid).

Edible Plant Profiles 253

# PUMPKINS

Botanical name: *Cucurbita pepo* | Plant family: *Cucurbitaceae* (Gourd or Squash)
Season: Warm season, summer to fall | Plant parts eaten: Fruit | Light: Full sun | Life cycle: Annual

**NATIVE TO THE AMERICAS,** pumpkins were grown by Indigenous people well before Europeans arrived. Their large leaves on long, vigorous vines proved beneficial as a living mulch growing beneath corn and beans—this traditional trio is called the Three Sisters. Pumpkins are known for gracing front porches in fall and being pureed into pies, but Native Americans also dried the nutrient-rich fruits and ground them into a type of flour. Given lots of space, they're easy to grow.

## *Sow*

Sow outdoors in late spring, after the frost date and when soil temp is in the mid-60s or above. Spacing varies widely by variety, from 12 to 72 inches, depending on the size of the vine and fruit; consult spacing recommendations for the variety you're growing. In cooler climates, get a head start indoors 3 weeks before transplanting outdoors.

## *Grow*

Pumpkins need sun, space, and time, but fertile soil helps too. Work compost into soil before planting. Mulch the pumpkin patch to help soil retain moisture. Water regularly, but don't water overhead, which can promote fungal disease.

Pumpkins are a fun crop for home gardeners to grow. Just be sure to give them plenty of room.

Smaller pumpkin varieties can easily be grown up trellises and obelisks to save space.

## *Protect*

With their large leaves and the long time these plants stay in the garden, powdery mildew is nearly inevitable on pumpkins. But you can delay or even prevent the effects in a few ways. Grow resistant varieties. Choosing varieties that mature early also helps. And space plants properly, making sure there is enough airflow through the leaves. If you do see mildew on plants, use an organic fungicide like neem oil according to package instructions.

## *Harvest*

Pumpkins should be harvested before heavy frost. When the pumpkin reaches the mature size and color of the variety, cut the stem, leaving 2 or more inches on the pumpkin. Avoid carrying the fruit by the stem. Cure for 7 to 10 days in a warm, dry location, ideally in the 80s with good ventilation. Store in the 50s with at least 50 percent relative humidity.

## *Types*

Pumpkin varieties are often categorized by their modern use: either for pie or for decoration. Pie pumpkins have been selected for flavor, texture, and lots of flesh. Decorative pumpkins are known for shape, size, and durability; while they're edible, they don't usually taste great. 'New England Pie' is a classic for desserts—4 to 6 pounds with orange skin and flesh and a creamy texture. 'Racer' is a favorite for carving jack-o'-lanterns—12 to 16 pounds, with a blocky shape. White pumpkins are also fun for decorating. The large pumpkins grown for competitions are often complex hybrids involving a genetic combination of squashes and pumpkins.

# RADISH

**Botanical name:** *Raphanus raphanistrum* subsp. *sativus* | **Plant family:** *Brassicaceae* (Cabbage or Mustard)
**Season:** Cool season, spring, fall | **Plant parts eaten:** Roots, leaves | **Light:** Full sun | **Life cycle:** Annual

There are a surprising number of radish varieties available to gardeners. From left to right: 'Cherry Belle', 'French Breakfast', and 'Icicle'.

Sow a row of radish seeds every few weeks from very early spring through late spring for a continual harvest. Start sowing them again in late summer for a fall harvest.

Harvest radish frequently to keep the roots from splitting or getting pithy.

**CULTIVATED SINCE** the beginning of civilization, radish was one of the first crops brought to America by Europeans. The name comes from the Latin for *root*, and homegrown radish roots are anything but bland. Colors dazzle like jewels in white, pink, purple, red, and black. Some pack a delightfully peppery punch.

## Sow

Radishes are easy to grow in cool weather. Sow directly outdoors in early spring, 4 to 6 weeks before last frost date, and in late summer, at least 4 to 6 weeks before first frost. Succession-sow every few weeks for a continual harvest rather than a glut. Thin seedlings to at least 1 inch apart.

## Grow

Keep soil evenly moist to avoid woody roots. Radishes, especially small round types, grow well in containers, but watch soil moisture as containers tend to dry out more quickly. Too much heat and dry soil can stress plants, leading to tough roots.

## Protect

Plants are susceptible to flea beetle damage. Flea beetles like radishes so much that in companion planting, radish is sometimes used as a trap crop to protect summer veggies like tomatoes and eggplant. Row covers protect radish plants from flea beetles. Slugs and cabbage root maggots can also nibble at radish roots.

## Harvest

Radishes grow quickly, and smaller types can be ready to harvest in as little as 3 to 4 weeks. Gently loosen soil to pull up radishes. They're crispiest when fresh, but soaking radishes in ice water can perk up roots a day or two after harvest. Leaves are also edible.

## Types

Radish varieties generally come in two types: round and long. Many flavorful Asian varieties have become more widely available. Try 'French Breakfast' in spring: Harvest long red roots at about 2 inches and eat fresh with just butter and salt. Popular watermelon radish from China is whitish green outside, vibrant pink inside; sow in late summer and harvest when 2 to 3 inches for a spicy-sweet, colorful snack. Long, tapered daikon radishes are another delicious option. They're great for pickling.

Edible Plant Profiles 255

# SUMMER SQUASH

**Botanical name:** *Cucurbita pepo* | **Plant family:** *Cucurbitaceae* (Gourd or Squash)
**Season:** Warm season, summer to fall | **Plant parts eaten:** Fruit | **Light:** Full sun | **Life cycle:** Annual

**SUMMER SQUASH** adds a splash of bright color to the summer table and garden. The soft-skinned fruits have small edible seeds, making them easy to prepare. Provided insects don't get to them, they're also easy to grow.

## Sow

Direct sow as soon as all danger of frost has passed, or start indoors 3 to 4 weeks before planting if in a cooler climate. Ideal soil temp for germination is 85°F. Summer squash are large, bushy, semi-vining plants with big leaves. Space plants 18 to 24 inches apart. Some gardeners will succession plant squash every 3 weeks to get a continuous supply all summer rather than too much squash all at once.

## Grow

Give plants full sun, compost-enriched soil, and plenty of water, especially when fruiting. Squash (and all cucurbits) have separate male and female flowers, and pollen needs to be transferred from male to female for plants to bear fruit. If bees aren't present, pollination can be done by hand; use a small paintbrush to transfer pollen. You can distinguish female flowers from male because females have thicker stems and a small round ovary at the base that grows into fruit when pollinated.

Summer squash is among the most productive crops a gardener can grow.

Harvest summer squash before the fruits reach "baseball bat" size for the best flavor and texture.

## Protect

Covering plants with row-cover cloth can be helpful for a few reasons. It can help warm soil in cooler climates, stave off cucumber beetles, and prevent squash vine borers from laying eggs. Just be sure to uncover when plants are flowering to ensure pollination. Sowing a second succession planting of summer squash a few weeks after your initial planting can mean reduced damage from squash vine borers. Summer squash can get powdery mildew; be sure to space plants properly and avoid watering from above.

## Harvest

Once plants start producing, check a few times a week to harvest. Cut fruits off when they reach the desired size, which varies by type and variety. Some gardeners also like to harvest squash blossoms to eat—harvest in the morning when closed or partially open. To ensure you also get a crop of fruit, only harvest male flowers, and leave some males for pollination.

## Types

Summer squash types include zucchini, yellow summer squash, and pattypan squash that is shaped a bit like a flying saucer. Zucchini are usually harvested at 6 to 8 inches, yellow squash at 4 to 6 inches, and pattypan at 2 to 3 inches.

# TOMATO

**Botanical name:** *Solanum lycopersicum* | **Plant family:** *Solanaceae* (Nightshade)
**Season:** Warm season, summer | **Plant parts eaten:** Fruit (all other parts are poisonous)
**Light:** Full sun | **Life cycle:** Annual

**ORIGINALLY FROM SOUTH AMERICA,** tomatoes are one of the most popular vegetables for home gardeners. With thousands of varieties of every color, shape, and size, you can grow new varieties every summer. Tomatoes thrive in warm weather with lots of sunlight: 8 or more hours of sunlight daily, with temps in the 70s and 80s. In colder, short-season climates (Zones 5 and below), tomatoes may be best grown in a greenhouse or using methods to increase soil temperature.

## Sow
Start seeds indoors 6 weeks before the last frost date. In the warmest regions (Zones 9 to 10), tomatoes can be sown and planted later to grow as a fall crop. Or, skip seed starting and buy transplants, picking from a wide selection at garden centers in late spring.

## Grow
Plant tomatoes outside when soil temps are at least 60°F, or 2 to 4 weeks after the last frost date. Compact varieties can be grown in large containers. A favorite planting tip: Dig a deep hole, pinch off lower leaves, and plant so half the main stem is below the soil. This can lead to stronger roots and stronger plants. Tomatoes need rich, fertile soil, and plants benefit from a weekly dose of organic fertilizer such as fish emulsion. Water deeply to encourage strong roots. Provide support to keep leaves and fruit off the ground; options include stakes, cages, and string or wire trellises.

Tomatoes are available in a rainbow of colors and a variety of plant and fruit sizes.

## Protect
Tomatoes are prone to pests and diseases that differ by region. Many varieties have been bred for resistance. Blossom-end rot (see page 163) is common, caused by issues with calcium uptake; try to keep soil evenly watered. Plants may not set fruit when temperatures are below 50°F or above 90°F, but they generally bounce back when the temperatures return to ideal. Keep tomato foliage dry when watering and provide ample space between plants to help reduce fungal diseases.

## Harvest
Let tomatoes ripen on the plant as long as possible. Pick when almost fully red (or the intended color of the variety). Snip the stem just above the fruit. If birds or rodents threaten, or if the weather calls for heavy rain (which could cause splitting), harvest before fully ripe and allow to ripen indoors. Store on the counter, not in the refrigerator, which can damage texture and flavor.

Proper spacing and support is essential for tomato plant health.

## Types
Tomato plants generally fit into two types: determinate (which grow to a certain height and set fruit all together) and indeterminate (which will grow until killed by frost, continually setting fruit). Tomato fruits generally come in three types: large round fruit for slicing, plum-shaped for preserving and making sauce, and small cherry fruit for snacking and salads.

There are hundreds of hybrid and heirloom tomato varieties in combinations of plant and fruit types (hybrid determinate slicer, heirloom indeterminate cherry, etc.), many adapted to specific conditions. For example, early-season varieties such as 'Early Girl' ripen quicker, ideal for a short growing season, while heat-tolerant varieties like 'Heatmaster' can withstand higher temperatures. Many heirlooms also share interesting stories, some uniquely American. 'Cherokee Purple' originated from Cherokees in East Tennessee.

# WINTER SQUASH

Botanical name: *Cucurbita* spp. | Plant family: *Cucurbitaceae* (Gourd or Squash)
Season: Warm season, summer to fall | Plant parts eaten: Fruit | Light: Full sun | Life cycle: Annual

**THEIR NAME IS** a bit of a misnomer, since winter squash do not grow through winter. Instead they're planted in late spring, grow through summer, are harvested in fall, and can be stored through winter. Some of the sweetest spoils from the vegetable garden, winter squash are packed with nutrition and flavor. If you can devote space to them in your garden, you won't be sorry.

## Sow
Plant seeds outdoors after frost date and when soil temp is in the mid-60s or above. Or start indoors 3 to 4 weeks before transplanting. Some varieties are shorter bush types and some are longer vines, so spacing varies.

## Grow
Patience is key with winter squash. Fruit develops for months before it's ready to harvest in late summer to early fall. As with pumpkins, fertile, well-drained soil is best; work compost in before planting. Vines can be trained to grow on arch trellises, but developing fruit may need extra support.

If you have limited space in your garden, opt for bush varieties of winter squash. They do not produce long vines and are more compact than regular types.

## Protect
Avoid powdery mildew by spacing plants according to recommendations for the variety, and don't water overhead. Some winter squash varieties, including butternut, are more resistant to insects (such as squash vine borers) than summer varieties, but plants can still benefit from covering with row-cover cloth in the early stages of growth.

## Harvest
Fruits can handle a light frost or two but should be harvested before a hard frost. Size and color depend on the variety. You'll know they're ready when the skin is hard and can't be easily dented with a fingernail. Another indicator of ripeness: the color of the spot where the fruit touches the ground changes from yellow to golden or orange. Cut fruit from the vine, leaving an inch of stem. Cure for 7 to 10 days in a dry location that ideally gets sun. Store in a warm, dark location for up to several months.

Butternut is among the most popular winter squash types.

## Types
The name winter squash encompasses a few species, including *C. moschata*, *C. maxima*, and *C. pepo*. They are very closely related to pumpkins, and some varieties will be classified as both depending on the source. A few popular types are globe-shaped acorn, hourglass-shaped butternut, thin-skinned delicata, orange-red kuri or kabocha, and spaghetti squash, with its stringy edible inside that resembles pasta.

## Funky Vegetables to Try

Beyond the tried-and-true veggies, consider these less common selections. They're fun additions or alternatives, depending on your climate.

**Cucamelon** (*Melothria scabra*), also called Mexican sour gherkin, produces fruits that look like tiny 1-inch watermelons but taste like cucumbers. They need similar climate and care as cucumber plants, but the vine is longer (10 feet), needs a trellis, and can become aggressive if not pruned.

**Dandelion** (*Taraxacum officinale*) is often considered a weed in lawns, but it's been harvested as a food and medicine plant since ancient times. The bitter leaves have diuretic properties; use them to spice up salads. Grow on purpose, or harvest ones that pop up in your garden, as long as they haven't been sprayed with any chemicals.

**Ground cherries** (*Physalis pruinose*), also called husk cherries, are sweet little golden berries growing within paper husks, similar to tomatillos, their relative. Also related to tomatoes, they require similar conditions but are more resilient, tolerating drought, stress, heat, and cold.

**Jerusalem artichoke** (*Helianthus tuberosus*) originates from North America, grown from and for the nutty tubers that taste a bit like artichokes. They produce beautiful flowers in summer, are cut back in fall, and are harvested by digging up as needed in winter. This perennial can spread quickly and aggressively if not regularly harvested.

**Kohlrabi** (*Brassica oleracea* var. *gongylodes*) prefers mild, cool weather, similar to other members of the cabbage family. It produces a bulb-shaped root similar to a turnip but grows above ground, with Sputnik-like protrusions of leaves. Harvest both the bulb and leaves.

**New Zealand spinach** (*Tetragonia tetragonoides*) offers an alternative to gardeners in warmer climates who have trouble growing regular spinach, or anyone who wants spinach in summer. Leaves are larger than regular spinach, and the plant grows like a groundcover.

**Peanuts** (*Arachis hypogaea*) grow best in warmer climates, as they require 130 days to mature. The flowers of this annual legume send stalks down to the ground, where the seeds form in pods under the soil. That's why peanuts are also called ground nuts. Try an heirloom variety such as 'Carolina African Runner', believed to be the first peanut brought to America by enslaved Africans.

**Purple sprouting broccoli** (*Brassica oleracea* var. *italica*) planted in fall will grow slowly through winter in temperate areas and produce florets in early spring. It's a good option for keeping something growing through winter. Plants are larger than regular broccoli and should be spaced farther apart, 18 to 24 inches.

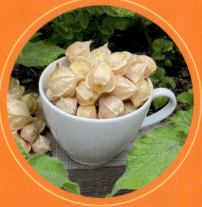

From left: cucamelon, ground cherries, purple sprouting broccoli

Edible Plant Profiles

# Herbs

## BASIL

Botanical name: *Ocimum basilicum*
Plant family: *Lamiaceae* (Mint)
Season: Warm season, summer
Light: Full sun
Life cycle: Annual

Basil originated in India, but for some, its flavor is synonymous with Italian food. It's often considered a good companion to tomatoes both in the garden and on the plate. Studies have shown that interplanting basil with tomatoes deters thrips, a tiny insect that transmits spotted wilt virus, and it could also help with tomato relatives like eggplant, peppers, and potatoes.

Sow basil outdoors after all danger of frost, ¼ inch deep or just lightly covered with soil. You can also start indoors 3 to 6 weeks before planting. Space plants 1 foot apart, or interplant with tomatoes and other summer crops. Basil likes hot weather and lots of sun.

As plants branch out and leaves develop, harvest leaves often. Rather than picking individual leaves, cut stems 6 inches below the growing tips, then remove leaves to use in the kitchen. This pruning will keep the plants bushy and produce more leaves. Pinching flower buds will also keep plants producing leaves, but the flowers also attract beneficial insects and are pretty additions to bouquets.

'Sweet Basil' is the classic Italian green basil, but there are many varieties to choose from, including ones with purple and bronzy leaves ('Dark Opal'), tiny leaves ('Spicy Globe'), and scented leaves ('Cinnamon'). Asian varieties such as Thai basil have a more licoricelike flavor. Columnar basil varieties (such as 'Greek Columnar') have an upright growth habit that makes them ideal for container designs.

Sweet basil

## CHIVES

Botanical name: *Allium schoenoprasum*
Plant family: *Alliaceae* (Allium)
Season: Warm season, spring, summer
Light: Full sun to light shade
Life cycle: Perennial

Related to onions and garlic, chives grow in grasslike clumps of thin leaves to about 6 to 8 inches tall. In spring, they produce pretty, cloverlike purple blooms that are also edible. They're grown for the leaves instead of the bulbs like other onion plants. Use chives fresh or dried.

Chives are very easy to grow. They can be grown from seed; sow around the last frost date and thin to a few inches apart. Or start from divided plants—you likely have a friend or neighbor who will give you some chives, as the plants spread and need to be divided every 3 years or so. Plant transplants 6 inches apart.

This is a cut-and-come-again plant, so you can cut back chives to use, and they will regrow quickly. Harvest when leaves are 6 inches tall, and cut back to 2 inches above the roots. Chives have very few problems, such as pest or disease issues. Common chives are the most popular, but you can also grow garlic chives, which are also known as Chinese leeks and have broader leaves and onion-garlic flavor.

## CILANTRO

Botanical name: *Coriandrum sativum*
Plant family: *Apiaceae* (Parsley or Carrot)
Season: Cool season, spring, fall
Light: Full sun to partial shade
Life cycle: Biennial

The seeds of the cilantro plant are the spice called coriander, and some people also call the fresh plant "coriander." Cilantro is popular in Indian, Mediterranean, and Mexican cuisine, but some people don't like the taste. If you do like it, consider it for your garden as it's easy to grow as long as the weather is cool.

Sow outdoors in early spring. Cilantro bolts quickly in the heat, making it a good candidate for succession planting (and for growing in partial shade). Sow every 1 to 2 weeks for a continuous supply. Thin plants to 6 to 8 inches apart. Harvest the leaves often, cutting back to where a side stem branches off the main stem. Use fresh, as cilantro leaves don't preserve well by drying.

If your cilantro is bolting, you might let it stay in the garden if you have space, as the flowers can attract beneficial insects and are edible too. When the flowers dry on the plant, the coriander seeds will be apparent. Harvest them for your spice cabinet, storing in an airtight glass container such as a recycled spice jar, or save them as seeds for next year.

## DILL

Botanical name: *Anethum graveolens*
Plant family: *Apiaceae* (Parsley or Carrot)
Season: Warm season, spring to summer
Light: Full sun
Life cycle: Biennial

Fresh dill (sometimes called dill weed) brightens dishes with unmistakable flavor, and the fresh or dried seeds are a key ingredient in pickling. While common dill is often grown, there are also special varieties including 'Fernleaf' (known for its compact form and resistance to bolting) and 'Bouquet' (which flowers early with large blooms, making it a preferred variety for pickling).

Like its relatives carrots and parsnips, dill has a long taproot, which makes it difficult to transplant. Instead, sow directly outdoors around the last frost date in spring. Lightly cover seeds with soil to ¼ inch. Thin plants to 8 to 12 inches apart. Dill can grow to 3 or 4 feet tall, so plant in a spot sheltered from the wind, such as tucked around taller summer plants like tomatoes. Dill will cross-pollinate with leaf fennel, so if you're saving seed and don't want your plants to intermingle, separate them in the garden.

Umbel-shaped dill flowers attract beneficial insects such as parasitic wasps that will benefit vegetables in your garden by feeding on other insects such as aphids. If allowed to go to seed, dill will self-sow in the garden, coming back every year. You can also harvest the dill seed for use in the spice cabinet. Whole dill flowers also make a beautiful addition to pickle jars.

Cilantro

## LAVENDER

Botanical name: *Lavendula angustifolia*
Plant family: *Lamiaceae* (Mint)
Season: Warm season, summer
Light: Full sun
Life cycle: Perennial

Hardy to light frosts and freezes in Zones 5 to 8, lavender is grown as a foundational planting in warmer areas. Plant it on the ends of garden beds to help attract pollinators and beneficial insects to the vegetable garden. Its perfumy flowers can also be used in body care and in baking and cooking.

Lavender is rarely grown from seed because it has such a long germination time; instead, grow from cuttings. To propagate, take 2- to 3-inch cuttings from side shoots of established plants, and place in moist, sandy soil where they will get plenty of sun and be protected from frost. After a year, you can plant them out in the garden. Or buy a transplant or two and plant them at least 2 feet apart.

Lavender does not need a lot of water and can be prone to fungal diseases caused by too much moisture. It can be planted near rocks, such as by a retaining wall, to help with drainage. Lavender prefers slightly basic soil, so you can add lime to raise the pH if needed. Wait until the second year to prune or harvest from the plant. To harvest flowers, pick when in blossom but before full bloom, typically in midsummer.

Choose from several lavender varieties known for their country of origin (or popularity). English lavenders such as 'Hidcote' are the hardiest and best for northern areas. French lavender is more tender, with a camphor scent like rosemary; plant it in containers and bring indoors for winter. Also tender, Spanish lavender is known for its toothed leaves and distinctive flower heads with top petals resembling purple flags.

## LEMONGRASS

Botanical name: *Cymbopogon citratus*
Plant family: *Poaceae* (Grass)
Season: Warm season, summer
Light: Full sun
Life cycle: Tropical perennial

A favorite herb in Asia, where it grows wild, lemongrass is a perennial tropical plant that thrives on heat but can be grown in containers in other climates. Plants can become large, so it's advisable to grow them in pots in any climate if your garden is on the smaller side.

Lemongrass is rarely started from seed. Grow from transplants, or try growing your own plant from a stalk. In spring or summer, trim the base of a fresh stalk of lemongrass and place in water on a sunny windowsill. It will grow roots; when roots are 1 inch long, place the stalk in a 6-inch pot with potting soil. Bring indoors in winter and place back outside in summer.

After the lemongrass leaves have become at least 1 foot tall, you can harvest stalks. Look for stalks that are ⅓ inch thick but preferably larger. Cut the stalk just below ground level. The white-to-light-green swollen base and about 1 inch above are the most tender parts; trim off the leaves above that.

Lemongrass

## MINT

Botanical name: *Mentha* spp.
Plant family: *Lamiaceae* (Mint)
Season: Spring to fall
Light: Full sun to partial shade
Life cycle: Perennial

Mint is beloved all over the world. It was valued as a wild herb by Native Americans before Europeans brought their own varieties to also grow here. There are hundreds of varieties, each known for its particular scent and taste, many of which resemble other flavors and aromas (like chocolate, apple, and pineapple). Peppermint and spearmint are two tried-and-true types. Use peppermint medicinally, in teas or just by chewing on leaves, to aid digestion and soothe stomachaches.

The most important thing to know about mint is that it runs wild. More literally, it spreads through runners, stems (also called stolons) that grow horizontally underground and give rise to roots and vertical stems at points called nodes. Mint will take over your garden if you're not careful. To keep it in check, grow it in containers. You will even need to watch it in containers, as stolons will creep through drainage holes in pots if left directly on soil.

Otherwise, mint is a delight! Plant from transplants or cuttings or a neighbor's runners they're trying to get rid of. Its beautiful green leaves reappear early in spring and shine all summer. Plant peppermint or spearmint near outdoor living areas and in your garden to keep some insects away (such as mosquitoes) while attracting others—bees, wasps, and other pollinators love mint flowers, which bloom in midsummer.

## OREGANO

Botanical name: *Origanum vulgare*
Plant family: *Lamiaceae* (Mint)
Season: Warm season
Light: Full sun
Life cycle: Perennial

Related to mint and grown similarly, oregano originates from the Mediterranean and has a pungent, slightly spicy, slightly camphorous flavor. Greek oregano is typically used for both Greek and Italian cooking. Its small white flowers attract beneficial insects. Marjoram is related to oregano and grown the same; marjoram's only difference is a slightly milder, earthier flavor than oregano.

Plant oregano from transplants or cuttings. In a small garden, you will only need 1 to 2 plants, as oregano spreads. Space 1 foot apart, or closer if you're trying to create a mat of oregano. Underplant midsize and taller crops such as cabbage, broccoli, peppers, and tomatoes with oregano. However, like other Mediterranean herbs, oregano doesn't like wet soil, so be mindful not to soak soil when placing near crops that need more water. If you have clay soil, amend with sand to improve drainage before planting oregano, or plant in terra cotta pots, which dry out quickly so roots don't sit in wet soil.

Start harvesting oregano as soon as stems have several sets of leaves. Cut off a section and then strip leaves from the stems to use. Prune often to keep the plants to a bushy habit. Oregano doesn't require fertilizer or much care, and it doesn't have many problems with insects or diseases.

## PARSLEY

Botanical name: *Petroselinum crispum*
Plant family: *Apiaceae* (Parsley or Carrot)
Season: Cool season
Light: Full sun to partial shade
Life cycle: Biennial

Native to the Mediterranean, parsley is a must-have for the herb garden, but it's also beneficial in the vegetable garden, especially if left to flower in its second year. Similar to the umbel-shaped flowers of its cousins dill and fennel, parsley's blooms attract beneficial insects to the organic vegetable garden.

Most people recognize the two main types of parsley: flat-leaf (also known as French parsley) and curly leaf. They taste similar, but the leaf shape differs. Flat-leaf parsley can be mistaken for cilantro, they look so similar. Curly parsley is unmistakable.

Start parsley plants from seed indoors, or sow directly outdoors in early spring. It's slow to germinate, but it should show up in 3 to 6 weeks, depending on the weather. (It will be faster if it is warm.) Or you can start from transplants. Parsley prefers cool weather; plants benefit from shade in summer, and they will grow through winter in a sunny, sheltered spot. To harvest, simply cut leafy stems at the base. Harvest from the outside of the plant, which will keep producing more stems and leaves from the inside. Parsley is vitamin-rich and full of fresh flavor.

## ROSEMARY

Botanical name: *Rosmarinus officinalis*
Plant family: *Lamiaceae* (Mint)
Season: Warm season
Light: Full sun
Life cycle: Tender perennial

Rosemary's piney scent and flavor make it an old favorite. It's known to be good for the brain, which may be why it's traditionally been used to invoke memory: "Rosemary for remembrance." In the vegetable garden, place it at the ends of beds as anchor plants, or grow in large containers, which is ideal for many reasons. Common rosemary has an upright habit and can grow to 6 feet tall. Creeping rosemary grows to only 1 foot tall.

Grow from cuttings or transplants rather than from seed. Rosemary seeds take a long time to germinate and aren't very reliable. Space plants at least 12 to 24 inches apart; plants can grow much larger, but pruning will keep them in check. Plant where they'll get full sun and very good drainage as rosemary can't stand wet soil. Growing in terra cotta pots helps provide good conditions as the clay dries out quickly. Rosemary tolerates a wide range of soil pH, though 6 to 7 is ideal.

Rosemary can't withstand hard freezes. North of Zone 8, it's best to grow in containers and bring them in during winter. If you're on the line, you can also try growing against a south-facing brick wall or other surface that captures and retains heat. To harvest, simply cut a length of stem, then strip needlelike leaves from the stem. Pick rosemary year-round.

Curled parsley

Sage

## SAGE
Botanical name: *Salvia officinalis*
Plant family: *Lamiaceae* (Mint)
Season: Warm season
Light: Full sun
Life cycle: Perennial

Sage leaves are known for antibacterial and antiviral properties. The plants are also thought to deter cabbage moths, so you can try planting your cabbage-family crops near sage. Seeds don't germinate well or quickly, so grow from cuttings, transplants, or divided plants. Plant in well-drained soil, 18 to 20 inches apart.

While sage grows best in warm weather, it stays alive through the cold. One of the hardiest herbs, sage can withstand temperatures well below zero. For a particularly cold spell, cover with straw mulch for protection. You may want to replace plants every few years as they become woodier and less productive.

Common sage, also known as garden sage, has gray-green leaves and pale-blue flowers. Many other sages can be grown in your garden. The purple 'Purpurea' variety sports purple-red foliage and can be used just like common sage. The golden selection 'Aurea' has leaves edged with chartreuse yellow and has a more compact habit. Sage is a beautiful plant to work into an edible landscape or ornamental-edible container scheme.

To harvest leaves, cut back top growth up to 6 inches. Ideally, cut in the morning but after plants have had a chance to dry out. If you're planning on growing as a perennial and keeping plants through winter, cut sparingly during the first year of growth.

## THYME
Botanical name: *Thymus vulgaris*
Plant family: *Lamiaceae* (Mint)
Season: Warm (for growth)
Light: Full sun
Life cycle: Perennial

Vital in French cooking, thyme also can serve a crucial role in the vegetable garden as a living mulch. Some low-growing, creeping types even make a mat that's good for paths. Thyme is thought to benefit many vegetables, including cabbage-family plants, tomatoes, and potatoes. However you grow thyme, you're sure to love its soft flavor reminiscent of its relatives: rosemary, lavender, mint, and sage.

Start plants from cuttings or buy transplants. Space plants 8 to 12 inches apart. Harvest stems of thyme up to 6 inches as needed or cut back the entire plant that amount, and it will regrow. Leaves become less available in midsummer as the plants begin to bloom, but the blossoms beckon bees to the garden.

Thyme is hardy to light frost and freezes above Zone 5 but needs to be mulched to survive severe winters. Like sage, it becomes woody and scraggly after a few years, when you may want to replace plants.

Grow common thyme or try other varieties; you can mix and match in your garden. French thyme is a little sweeter, with pink flowers instead of white. Lemon thyme has a strong lemon scent but is not as hardy. Sprawling silver thyme makes a good edging plant; it has pale-blue blooms and pretty white edging on green leaves.

# JOIN THE AHS

**TO JOIN THE AMERICAN HORTICULTURAL SOCIETY** and enjoy all the benefits membership has to offer, please visit our website at ahsgardening.org/join or scan the QR code below for our membership information page.

All members receive an exciting lineup of benefits that share the joy of gardening and strengthen your skills and knowledge.
- Receive our award-winning magazine, *The American Gardener*.
- Get free admission and privileges at more than 360 public gardens and arboreta throughout North America through the AHS Garden Network.
- Enjoy discounts on educational programs, garden shows, seeds, books, and more.
- Discover opportunities to explore the world's finest gardens on trips with fellow plant lovers.
- Access members-only gardening resources on our website.
- And much more.

# ACKNOWLEDGMENTS

**THE AHS EXTENDS GRATITUDE** to its Horticultural Advisory Council members who contributed their expertise during this book's review process:

Dr. James Folsom
Dr. Mary Hockenberry Meyer
William McNamara
Claire Sawyers

The AHS staff and supporting consultants involved in the review process for this book were Suzanne Laporte, David Ellis, Courtney Allen, Mary Yee, Susan Friedman, and Dan Adler.

The AHS expresses thanks to the book's acquiring editor, Jessica Walliser, and to the team at Cool Springs Press.

# PHOTO CREDITS

Alamy: Pages 14 (left & right), 16 (top), 112, 126 (top), 127 (top), 147, 154, 187 (top left), 239 (left)

American Horticultural Society: Page 3

Cathy Wilkinson Barash: Pages 18, 20 (top left & bottom left), 22 (top left & top right), 23 (top & bottom), 27 (bottom left), 37, 55 (bottom left), 82, 83, 86 (top & bottom), 90, 122 (top), 201, 236

Charlie Nardozzi: Pages 81, 167, 173

Christy Wilhelmi: Pages 42, 170, 211 (bottom)

Collections of The Henry Ford: Page 16 (bottom)

Heritage Image Partnership, LTD/Alamy: Page 12 (top & bottom)

Howard F. Schwartz, Colorado State University, Bugwood.org: Pages 204, 210 (middle)

Janet Davis: Pages 20 (bottom right), 21 (bottom right, top left & bottom left), 22 (bottom), 88, 92, 103 (right), 158

Jennifer McGuinness: Pages 40 (right), 55 (top), 56 (top right), 126 (middle), 188

JLY Gardens: Pages 4, 13 (top), 17, 21 (top right), 28, 38, 40 (left), 56 (bottom middle & bottom right), 58, 59 (bottom), 61, 62, 65 (bottom), 66, 68, 70 (bottom), 71, 76, 77, 78, 84 (right), 97 (top), 102 (left), 103 (left), 104, 105, 114, 116, 121, 125, 134 (bottom), 137 (bottom), 139 (right), 140, 141 (bottom), 148, 156 (top), 161 (top), 162 (right), 163, 168 (middle), 177, 180, 181, 182, 190, 191 (left & right), 192, 194, 196 (bottom), 197, 199 (right), 202, 203 (top), 206 (top), 207 (bottom), 210 (left & right), 212 (right), 214 (top right & bottom right), 215 (top right & bottom right), 218, 221 (bottom), 232, 234 (right), 235 (right), 238, 239 (middle & right), 240 (right), 245 (middle & right), 246 (left), 247, 250 (bottom), 251 (left & middle), 253 (right), 254 (left), 255 (right), 256, 257 (left), 258 (left), 259, 260, 263

Johnny's Selected Seeds: Page 186 (bottom right)

Kathy Jentz: Pages 45 (right), 107, 127 (middle), 168 (right), 183 (top), 195

Kelly Coultas/Alamy: Page 26 (bottom left)

Leon Werdinger/Alamy: Page 26 (top right)

Nativestock.com/Marilyn Angel Wynn/Alamy: Page 11

Niki Jabbour: Pages 20 (top right), 24 (top right & top left), 26 (top left), 34 (right), 35, 44, 56 (bottom left & top middle), 60, 84 (left), 85, 122 (bottom), 137 (top), 142 (bottom), 152, 164, 179 (top), 211 (top), 212 (left), 214 (sidebar), 219, 220 (middle & bottom), 227 (top), 243, 252 (right), 255 (left), 258 (middle)

Noelle Johnson: Pages 6, 56 (top left)

Shutterstock: Pages 13 (bottom), 15, 24 (top middle), 25 (top right, top left, bottom right, bottom left), 26 (bottom right), 27 (top), 32, 34 (left), 45 (left), 48, 54, 55 (middle), 64, 65 (top), 67, 89, 91, 96, 97 (bottom), 101, 102 (right), 108, 110, 111, 113, 117 (top), 119, 128, 129, 130, 134 (top), 135, 136 (left, middle & right), 139 (left), 141 (top), 142 (top), 144, 146, 150-151, 156 (bottom), 157, 161 (bottom), 162 (left), 166, 171, 174-176, 179 (bottom), 184-185, 186 (top & bottom left), 187 (bottom & top right), 191 (middle), 193 (left, middle & right), 196 (top), 198, 207 (top), 209, 213 (top & bottom), 215 (top left, top middle, bottom left & bottom middle), 230-231, 233 (right), 234 (left), 235 (left), 237, 241, 242 (right), 244, 245 (left), 246 (right), 249, 250 (top), 251 (right), 253 (left), 254 (middle and right), 257 (right), 258 (right), 261, 264

Susan Mulvihill: Pages 7, 9, 24 (bottom left & bottom right), 59 (top), 63, 70 (top), 80, 87, 117 (bottom), 159 (bottom), 168 (left), 199 (left), 206 (bottom), 220 (top), 221 (top), 228 (bottom), 242 (left), 248 (left), 252 (left)

Tracy Walsh Photography: Pages 10, 27 (bottom right), 39, 50, 55 (bottom right), 74, 94, 126 (bottom), 127 (bottom), 132, 159 (top), 169, 172, 178, 183 (bottom), 216, 227 (bottom), 228 (top), 233 (left), 240 (left), 248 (right)

United States Department of Agriculture: Page 31

William M. Brown Jr., Bugwood.org: Page 203 (bottom)

# INDEX

## A

*Alliaceae* (onion) family, 52
annuals, 52–53
aphids, 44
*Apiaceae* (carrot/parsley) family, 52
artichokes, 233
arugula, 237
*Asparagaceae* (asparagus) family, 52
asparagus, 234
*Asteraceae* (aster) family, 52

## B

basil, 260
beans, 11, 235
beets, 236
beneficial insects, 44, 71, 99, 196–197
biennials, 53
biodiversity, 71, 85
biofungicides, 209–210
blossom-end rot, 163, 165
bolting, 59
*Brassicaceae* (cabbage/mustard) family, 52
broadforking, 154
broccoli, 238
bunching onions, 251

## C

cabbage, 239
calico test, 111
cantaloupe, 247
carrots, 240
cauliflower, 241
chaos gardening, 92–93
*Chenopodiaceae* (goosefoot) family, 52
Chinese cabbage, 242
chives, 260
cilantro, 261
climate change, 36, 54
community gardens, 41
compost
    animal manure and, 125
    benefits of, 103–104
    guidelines for, 105
    management of, 107
    materials for, 106
    planning and, 45
    purchasing, 104

three-bin systems, 107
    troubleshooting issues with, 108–109
container gardening, 24
cool-season crops, 56–57
Cooperative Extension program (USDA), 15, 33, 116
copper products, 210
corn, 11–12, 243
cover crops, 173–175
crop rotation, 84, 205–206
cucamelon, 259
cucumbers, 89, 244
*Cucurbitaceae* (Gourd) family, 51, 53, 60, 70

## D

dandelion, 259
diatomaceous earth (DE), 199
dill, 261
diseases
    bacterial infections, 203
    biofungicides, 209–210
    common, 208
    copper products, 210
    crop rotation and, 205–206
    disease-resistant crops and, 205
    disease triangle, 205
    fungal infections, 204
    horticultural oils and, 210
    identifying types of, 203–204
    intensive planting and, 83, 207
    moisture and, 207
    neem oil and, 210
    organic disease controls, 209–210
    plant spacing and, 207
    plant trimming and, 207
    removal of infected foliage, 209
    sulfur products and, 210
    tool sterilization and, 207, 209
    viruses, 203
    weeds and, 206
drainage, 112, 118

## E

edible landscaping, 90–91
environmental movement, 16

# F

*Fabaceae* (pea/bean) family, 53
fertilizers, 164, 166–167
flowers, 70–73
food forests, 91–92
food preservation, 15
frost/freeze dates, 32–33, 35

# G

garden beds
    animal manure and, 125
    bermed beds, 123
    in-ground vs. raised, 122–123
    soil amendments, 123–124
    *See also* raised beds
garden history, 11–16
garden maintenance
    applying fertilizers, 166–167
    chop-and-drop garden cover, 173
    cover crops, 173–175
    early-season tasks, 178–179
    late-season tasks, 182–183
    mid-season tasks, 180–181
    mulching, 159–160
    off-season tasks, 184–185
    organic fertilizer types, 167
    plant effects from nutrient deficiencies, 165
    preparation for winter, 172
    pre-season tasks, 176–177
    support for vertical growing plants, 168
    troubleshooting water stress, 171
    watering, 169–170
    watering options, 170
    weeding, 158
    *See also* soil maintenance
garden maps, 46–47
garden styles
    container planting, 24
    hügelkultur, 26
    indoor growing, 25
    in-ground beds, 22
    intensive planting, 26
    lasagna gardening, 27
    permaculture planting, 25
    potager gardens, 23
    raised beds, 20–21
    square-foot gardening, 26
    straw-bale gardening, 26
garlic, 245
greenhouses, 34, 214
ground cherries, 259
gypsum, 156

# H

harvesting
    days-to-maturity calculations, 217–218
    fruiting plants, 219
    harvest styles, 220–223
    leafy greens/herbs, 219
    pod plants, 219
    readiness charts by plant, 224–226
    root vegetables, 218–219
    signals of readiness, 218
    tips for, 223
    tools for, 230–231
heirloom seeds, 17
herbicides, organic, 120–121
herbs, 260–265
honeydew melon, 247
horticultural oils, 210
hügelkultur, 26

# I

Indigenous gardening, 11–12
indoor gardening, 25
in-ground beds, 22
insecticidal soaps, 198–199
intensive planting, 26, 82–83
interplanting, 85–86, 89

# J

Jerusalem artichokes, 259

# K

kale, 237
kohlrabi, 259

# L

ladybugs, 44
*Lamiaceae* (mint) family, 53
lasagna gardening, 27
lavender, 262
layered planting, 86, 88–89
leeks, 251
lemongrass, 262
lettuce, 246
living mulch, 89

# M

*Malvaceae* (mallow) family, 53
mason jar test, 101
melons, 247
microclimates, 30, 36–37, 40
mint, 263
Munsell color scale (for soil), 110
mustard greens, 237

# N

National Organic Program (NOP), 8
neem oil, 198, 210
New Zealand spinach, 259
nitrogen, 162–163
NOAA, 35–36

# O

okra, 248
onions, 249
oregano, 263
Organic Foods Production Act (1990), 16
organic gardening tenets, 8

# P

parsley, 264
peanuts, 259
peas, 250
peppers, 252
perc tests, 112
perennials, 25, 52–54
permaculture planting, 25
pests
    aphids, 191
    *Bacillus thuringiensis* (Bt) and, 199, 201
    beneficial insects and, 44, 71, 99, 196–197
    biological controls for, 196–197
    cabbage looper, 191
    carrot rust fly, 191
    climate change and, 194
    critter control, 201–202
    cucumber beetles, 192
    diatomaceous earth (DE) and, 199
    flea beetle, 192
    insecticidal soaps and, 198–199
    Mexican bean beetle, 193
    neem oil and, 198
    organic controls, 198–201
    pest traps, 195
    row covers, 195
    signs of, 190
    slugs, 192

spinosad and, 201
squash bugs, 193
squash vine borers, 193
types of, 191–193
wireworm, 192
phosphorus, 163–164
pH tests, 113
planning
    compact varieties, 61
    cool-seasons crops, 56–57, 62–63
    design principles, 41–45
    frost and freeze dates, 32–33
    garden maps, 46–47
    garden placement, 39–41
    growing season and, 33–34
    long-season vs. short season, 58–59
    precipitation amounts, 35
    seasonal observation and, 30
    selecting favorite foods, 62–63
    space-saving garden design, 60
    Sunset Climate Zones, 32
    tools for, 48–49
    USDA Plant Hardiness Zones, 30–31
    warm-season crops, 56–57, 62–63
    water use and, 38
plant families, 51–53
planting
    bulbs, 139
    choosing seeds and, 134
    crowns, 139
    cuttings, 139
    direct sowing seeds, 137–139
    seed starting, 135–136, 141–145
    seeds vs. starts, 132–133
    sets, 139
    space, 43
    tall plants/trellises, 43
    thinning seedlings, 138
    tomatoes, 147
    tools for, 150–151
    transplanting starts, 146–149
    troubleshooting seedling issues, 138
    winter sowing, 140
planting style
    block planting, 78–79
    chaos gardening, 92–93
    considerations for, 75–76
    container planting, 80–81
    edible landscaping, 90–91
    food forests, 91–92
    intensive planting and, 82–83
    interplanting and, 85–86
    layered planting, 86–88

quick reference guide, 93
row planting, 77–78
square-foot gardening, 79
succession planting and, 84
vertical planting, 86–88

plants
block planting and, 79
compact varieties, 61
cool season vs. warm-season, 56–57
flowers, 72–73
herbs, 260–265
for interplanting, 86
for layering, 89
for living mulch, 89
long-season vs. short-season, 58–59
plant effects from nutrient deficiencies, 165
seed starting time by plant, 149
for succession planting, 84
transplanting time for, 149
transplant time by plant, 149
weather protection and, 211–213
*See also* diseases; *individual profiles*; pests

*Poaceae* (grass) family, 53
pollination, 44, 70
*Polygonaceae* (buckwheat) family, 53
potager gardens, 23
potassium, 164
potatoes, 12, 230, 253
potting mix recipe, 135
precipitation, 35–36
pumpkins, 254
purple sprouting broccoli, 259

# R

radishes, 255
raised beds, 20–21, 125–128
reverse-season climates, 35
ribbon test, 101
rosemary, 264
row covers, 34

# S

sage, 265
school gardens, 14–15
seed catalogs, 13, 134
seed commons, 67
seeds
choosing, 134
cucumbers and, 89
direct sowing, 137–139
genetically modified (GM) seeds, 66
heirloom seeds, 17, 66

hybrid seeds, 65
open-pollinated seeds, 65
organic gardens and, 66
perennial volunteers and, 55
regional/ancestral, 67
winter sowing, 140

seed saving, 12, 68–69

seed starting
containers for, 141
light and, 142–143
potting mix for, 135
repotting, 144
soil blocks, 142
soil for, 135–136
thinning, 143
tools for, 150–151
transplanting, 146
troubleshooting, 145
warmth and, 136, 144
water and, 136

site preparation
composting in place/sheet mulching, 120
drainage and, 118
garden style and, 117
herbicides for weed removal, 120–121
leveling site, 117–118
sod removal, 122
solarizing, 119–120
tilling vs. no-tilling methods, 119, 122, 153
tools for, 129
water access and, 118

soil
assessing biological activity, 111
assessing color, 110
assessing drainage, 112
clay soil, 155–156
compaction of, 114
contamination of, 116
defining, 96
living organisms in, 96–99
loam, 157
nitrogen and, 162–163
overall quality assessment, 115
pH of, 113, 157
phosphorus, 163–164
plant effects from nutrient deficiencies, 165
planting styles and, 76
potassium, 164
salinity of, 114, 157
sandy soil, 156
structure, 102
testing nutrients in, 161–162
texture determination, 100–101

Index **271**

tools for working with, 129
soil contamination, 116
soil maintenance
    adding organic material, 155
    adjusting salinity, 157
    breaking up clay, 155–156
    broadforking, 154
    loam, 157
    no-till benefits, 153
    plant effects from nutrient deficiencies, 165
    sandy soil, 156
    soil amendment vs. fertilizer, 164
    stabilizing pH, 157
    testing nutrients in, 161–162
soil organisms, 98–99
*Solanaceae* (nightshade) family, 53
Southern peas (cowpeas), 251
spinach, 237
square-foot gardening, 26, 79
storage
    alliums, 230
    curing, 228
    herbs and, 230
    potatoes and, 230
    root vegetables with greens, 230
    storage guidelines by plant, 229
    temperature-based, 227
    washing before, 227–228
straw-bale gardening, 26
succession planting, 13, 59, 84
sulfur products, 210
summer squash, 256
Sunset Climate Zones, 32
Swiss chard, 237

# T

thyme, 265
tomatoes, 12, 61, 147, 257
tools
    cleaning/sharpening, 185
    for garden care, 154, 186–187
    for garden planning, 48–49
    for harvesting, 223, 230–231
    for planting, 150–151
    for plant protection, 214–215
    for soil maintenance, 129
    sterilizing, 207, 209, 223
transplants, types of, 67

# U

United States Department of Agriculture (USDA), Cooperative Extensions, 15, 33
urban gardens, 14–15
USDA Plant Hardiness Zones, 30–31

# V

vertical gardening, 60, 86–88
victory gardens, 15–17
volunteer plants, 55

# W

warm-season crops, 56–57
water
    assessing how length for, 169–170
    collecting rainwater, 38
    garden placement and, 38, 40
    intensive planting and, 83
    options for providing, 170
    seed starting and, 136, 144
    site preparation and, 118
    troubleshooting water stress, 171
watermelon, 247
weather protection, 211–213
weeds, 120–121, 158, 206
wildlife, excluding, 45
winter squash, 258